ABOUT THE AUTHOR

VICTOR DAVIS HANSON was educated at the University of California, Santa Cruz, and the American School of Classical Studies at Athens, and received his Ph.D. in Classics from Stanford University. He farmed full time for five years before returning to academia in 1984 to initiate a Classics program at California State University, Fresno. Currently, he is Professor of Classics there and Coordinator of the Classical Studies Program.

Hanson has written articles, editorials, and reviews for *The New York Times, The Wall Street Journal, The Daily Telegraph, International Herald Tribune, American Heritage, City Journal, The American Spectator, National Review, Policy Review, The Wilson Quarterly, The Weekly Standard,* and *The Washington Times,* and has been interviewed on numerous occasions on National Public Radio and the BBC, and appeared with David Gergen on *The NewsHour with Jim Lehrer.* He writes a biweekly column about contemporary culture and military history for *National Review Online.*

He is also the author of some eighty scholarly articles, book reviews, and newspaper editorials on Greek, agrarian, and military history, and contemporary culture. He has written or edited fourteen books, including *The Western Way of War, The Soul of Battle,* and *Carnage and Culture.* He is a Senior Fellow of the Hoover Institute, Stanford University.

He lives and works with his wife and three children on their forty-acre tree and vine farm near Selma, California, where he was born in 1953.

BETWEEN
WAR AND PEACE

BETWEEN WAR AND PEACE

Lessons from Afghanistan to Iraq

VICTOR DAVIS HANSON

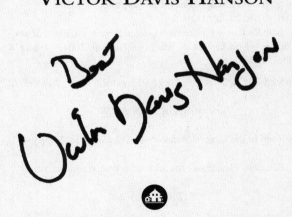

RANDOM HOUSE TRADE PAPERBACKS
NEW YORK

Some of the essays in this work have been previously
published in *City Journal, Commentary,* and *National Review Online.*

Library of Congress Cataloging-in-Publication Data

Hanson, Victor Davis.
　Between war and peace: lessons from Afghanistan to Iraq /
by Victor Davis Hanson.
　　p. cm.
　Contents: The war against terror—The dilemma of the
Middle East—Supporting Israel?—Anti-Americanism—Europe—
The three-week war—A new foreign policy?
　ISBN 0-8129-7273-2
　1. Middle East—Relations—United States. 2. United States—
Relations—Middle East. 3. War on Terrorism, 2001– 4. Iraq War,
2003. I. Title.
DS63.2.U5H36 2004　　　973.931—dc22　　　2003066727

Text design by Mary A. Wirth

Printed in the United States of America on acid-free paper

Random House website address: www.atrandom.com

9 8 7 6 5 4 3 2 1

First Edition

FOR CARA AND PAULI

Contents

Introduction

The present volume is a sequel of sorts to *An Autumn of War,* a collection of essays I wrote about the war against terror, arranged in chronological order from the al Qaeda attacks on September 11 to the defeat of the Taliban in Afghanistan and subsequent events until January 2002. *Between War and Peace* takes up the narrative in January 2002 and ends in early July 2003, chronicling the evolving war against al Qaeda, the ongoing conflict in the Middle East, rising anti-Americanism abroad, our growing rift with Europe, the war with Iraq and its troubled aftermath—and how study of the past offers us some hope of making sense of all these seemingly insolvable crises that seem to have erupted on September 11, 2001.

Once more I have left the articles and editorials in the form in which they appeared in the past two years, except for a few small corrections of typographical, grammatical, or spelling errors. Again, the book is in part a diary of actions recorded as they unfolded, and thus I think has some value in allowing the reader to assess the validity of arguments made at the time in light of what we now know from the actual events that later transpired.

However, in this volume I have also arranged the articles both topically and chronologically to provide greater thematic unity and coherence. Indeed, the war against terror that once seemed relatively straightforward in our efforts to destroy the al Qaeda bases in Afghanistan rippled out in unforeseen ways during the subsequent eighteen months to involve a full-fledged invasion of Iraq, a diplomatic showdown with the United Nations and our European allies, an escalation of conflict in Israel and on the West Bank—and then a sudden effort at rapprochement, and a renewed debate here in the United States about the nature, morality, and intent of American foreign policy, leading to protests in intensity not seen since the turmoil of Vietnam.

I had thought that the pessimism that presaged defeat in Afghanistan—the mountains, remember, were too high, the weather too cold, the religious calendar too foreboding, the factions too numerous, the Taliban too ferocious, and the country itself the graveyard of the British and Russian armies—might have been dispelled by the miraculous victory over the Taliban in a matter of six weeks at a cost of a handful of American lives. But it was not to be, as the renewed display of gloom during 2002–3 would prove.

Voices that had warned of quagmire in Afghanistan sought to reclaim legitimacy by forecasting millions of refugees and thousands of American dead in Iraq, with the Arab street exploding, the Middle East erupting, and our shores being attacked by a variety of revenge-minded terrorists from the Middle East. And yet when that war was won in three weeks at a cost of a few hundred American lives, as 180,000 allied soldiers subdued a country of twenty-six million, rather than being contrite about a continual misreading of events, prominent critics of both engagements, and indeed much of the mainstream media, focused on the difficult problems of reconstruction in the two countries—almost as if the acknowledged costly (over 200 Americans were killed in

Afghanistan and Iraq once formal hostilities ceased) challenges to implant democracy in aftermath of the two worst regimes in the Middle East redeemed their initial predictions of military paralysis.

Just as *An Autumn of War* ended after the amazing victory in Afghanistan amid the pundits' predictions of disaster to come in Iraq, so too the victory in less than half the time over Saddam Hussein seemed to prompt cries of Vietnam redux in Baghdad.

As I write on July 4, 2003, we are again told—after one of the most remarkable military victories in American history—that we are in perpetual crisis: no firm evidence of weapons of mass destruction in Iraq as yet uncovered; no word about the ultimate fate of Saddam Hussein; and constant sniping and assassination of American troops in postwar Iraq with deaths now reaching well over one hundred. Yet we forget that occupation is never easy— consider the mess of restoring order to territories of the former Japanese empire in 1946—and our task is made more difficult both by the sheer rapidity of a victory designed to shock rather than kill a large number of Baathist troops and the unlikely task of implanting consensual government in a region where democracy has no history.

Yet I remain optimistic that American efforts during postbellum occupation—based as they are on formidable military strength coupled with a humanitarian message of liberal reform and aimed at eradicating rogue regimes that facilitate terrorism and destruction—will eventually be as successful as were our remarkable military victories in Afghanistan and Iraq.

The themes of *Between War and Peace* differ somewhat from those essays of *An Autumn of War.* Whereas before I had thought that the inability of many prominent Americans to assess the advantage of Western militaries over their opponents, and indeed to appreciate the resiliency and enormous power of liberal democracies in general, was a result of either naïveté or ignorance about the nature of war, I sensed that as the aftershocks of September 11 continued, there was something far deeper and more profound that explained our endemic cultural pessimism. A theme, then, that underlies all these sometimes wide-ranging essays is my own search for answers for how and why so many educated and bright Americans seem to embrace a reductive worldview about the role and nature of their own country—almost as if the more America proved itself powerful and moral in its efforts to eradicate medieval fascists and implant democracies in their places, the more many of our own experts sought to demonstrate that we either could or should not.

Much of my own sense of things, of course, grew out of life-long residency on a small farm in the San Joaquin Valley of California and my own training as a classicist and military historian who teaches Latin and Greek to mostly minority students at California State University, Fresno. The two worlds are not as antithetical as they might seem. The Greeks, after all, were a rural people, and the literature of a Homer or Thucydides often reveals a tragic view of the human condition often shared by contemporary agrarians who through the daily experience of battling nature to obtain a living—and now so often failing—agree that there are certain constraints on us all across time and space, given that the physical world remains unforgiving and the nature of man himself stays constant.

By "tragic," of course, I mean the acceptance of certain givens in the human experience of any age: that culture and civilization are a thin veneer that protect us all from the innate savagery of our natural selves, that the world does not provide us with the reality of utopian perfection but rather with more mundane practical choices between something better and something probably worse, and that there are certain discernable, certain absolute criteria that exist to permit us to make necessary moral judgments even amid the relativist chaff of the times.

For the academic year 2002–3 I was, however, also the visiting Shifrin Professor of Military History at the United States Naval Academy at Annapolis. As part of the responsibilities of that professorship, I gave a number of lectures at various military installations and talked with hundreds of officers and civilian consultants throughout the year, especially during the March and April fighting with Iraq. The result was that I took a keen interest, as some of these essays will demonstrate, in the contrast between civilian and military life, and why the armed forces, of all places, seemed to have found practical solutions to a variety of stubborn social and cultural problems—achieving racial harmony and integration, inculcating a sense of purpose and mission in a purportedly bored lost generation of youth, and marrying abstract knowledge with common sense and muscular strength—in areas where our more vaunted universities and other government agencies have simply failed.

I must thank once more Kathryn Lopez of *National Review*, as well as Neal Kozodoy of *Commentary*, and Myron Magnet of *City Journal* for both help in editing these essays and permission to have them here collected in one place. In addition, columns are drawn from *The New Criterion*, *The Wall Street Journal*, and *The New Atlantis*, and I thank the editors of those journals as well to republish essays here. My wife, Cara, and daughter, Pauli, helped to arrange and select the articles, and I relied on their good sense in ways more numerous than I can cite. My literary agents, Glen Hartley and Lynn Chu, as has been true the past thirteen years, gave invaluable advice in preparing the collection for publication. Professor of Classics Bruce Thornton, a colleague at CSU Fresno, read many of the essays in their first draft, and provided a variety of suggestions that improved them. Robert Loomis, my editor at Random House, and Casey A. Reivich saw the book through production, and helped each step of the way.

VDH
July 4, 2003
Selma, California

I

THE WAR
AGAINST TERROR

As the catastrophe of September 11 faded somewhat in the collective memory of many citizens, the war on terror transmogrified into a variety of new theaters. Increasingly the suicide bombings against Israel—so similar in method and intent to the al Qaeda attacks against Washington and New York—brought Americans closer to the Middle East.

Meanwhile terrorists, here at home, whether snipers in Maryland and Virginia or failed cells on the West Coast, seemed to be almost daily arrested. In response to this ongoing challenge I thought three themes should be paramount in our national dialogue: terrorism is neither new nor immune from remedies; it does not necessarily arise out of poverty, much less are its adherents typically poor or illiterate; and it rarely exists for long as an independent entity apart from state support and sanctuary.

Thus, proven counterinsurgency and resolute military force, and isolation of rogue regimes, coupled with a political agenda that promotes political reform, can usually debilitate the practitioners of terror within a few years. In the case of the Middle East, such a strategy entailed not just hunting down al Qaedists but also removing the two worst governments, in Afghanistan and Iraq; tough talk with abettors such as Iran and Syria; and a renewed skepticism about once-close relationships with the autocracies in Saudi Arabia, Egypt, and Jordan.

Finally, we must remember that terror is a method, not an enemy per se. We fought Nazis, not Tiger tanks; Soviet expansionism, not KGB assassins. There is no "Republic of Terror" or soldiers with "Terror" emblazoned on their uniforms. States, rogue governments, Islamo-fascist cadres, and complacent populations either actively or complicitly promote terror as part of a larger struggle against the United States.

1

---•===◎===•---

The Wages of September 11

THERE IS NO GOING BACK

September 11 changed our world. Those who deny such a watershed event take a superficially short-term view and seem to think all is as before simply because the sun still rises and sets.

This is a colossal misjudgment. The collapse of the towers, the crashing into the Pentagon, and the murder of three thousand Americans—all seen live in real time by millions the world over—tore off a scab and exposed deep wounds, which, if and when they heal, will leave ugly scars for decades. The killers dealt in icons—the choice of 9/11 as the date of death, targeting the manifest symbols of global capitalism and American military power, and centering their destruction on the largest Jewish city in the world. Yes, they got their symbols in spades, but they have no idea that their killing has instead become emblematic of changes that they could scarcely imagine.

Islamic fundamentalism has proved not ascendant but static, morally repugnant—and the worst plague upon the Arab world since the Crusades. By lurking in the shadows and killing incrementally through stealth, the vampirish terrorists garnered bribes and subsidies through threats and bombs; but, pale and wrinkled in the daylight after 9/11, they prove only ghoulish, not fearsome.

The more the world knows of al Qaeda and bin Laden, the more it has found them both vile and yet banal—and so is confident and eager to eradicate them and all they stand for. It is one thing to kill innocents, quite another to take on the armed might of an aroused United States. Easily dodging a solo cruise missile in the vastness of Afghanistan may make good theater and bring about braggadocio; dealing with grim American and British commandos who have come seven thousand miles for your head prompts abject flight and an occasional cheap infomercial on the run. And the ultimate consequence of the attacks of September 11 will not merely be the destruction of al Qaeda but also the complete repudiation of the Taliban, the Iranian mullocracy, the plague of the Pakistani madrasahs, and any other would-be fundamentalist paradise on earth.

Foreign relations will not be the same in our generation. Our coalition with Europe, we learn, was not a partnership but more mere alphabetic nomenclature and the mutual back-scratching of Euro-American globe-trotters—a paper alliance without a mission nearly fifteen years after the end of the Cold War. The truth is that Europe, out of noble purposes, for a decade has insidiously eroded its collective national sovereignty in order to craft an antidemocratic EU, an 80,000-person fuzzy bureaucracy whose executive power is as militarily weak as it is morally ambiguous in its reliance on often dubious international accords. This sad realization September 11 brutally exposed, and we all should cry for the beloved continent that has for the moment completely lost its moral bearings. Indeed, as the months progressed, the problems inherent in "the European way" became all too apparent: pretentious utopian manifestos in lieu of military resoluteness, abstract moralizing to excuse dereliction of concrete ethical responsibility, and constant

American ankle-biting even as Europe lives in a make-believe Shire while we keep back the forces of Mordor from its picturesque borders, with only a few brave Frodos and Bilbos tagging along. Nothing has proved more sobering to Americans than the skepticism of these blinkered European hobbits after September 11.

America learned that "moderate" Arab countries are as dangerous as hostile Islamic nations. After September 11, being a Saudi, Egyptian, or Kuwaiti means nothing special to an American—at least not proof of being any more friendly or hostile than having Libyan, Syrian, or Lebanese citizenship. Indeed, our entire postwar policy of propping up autocracies on the triad of their anticommunism, oil, and arms purchases—like NATO—belongs to a pre-9/11 age of Soviet aggrandizement and petroleum monopolies. Now we learn that broadcasting state-sponsored hatred of Israel and the United States is just as deadly to our interests as Scud missiles—and as likely to come from friends as enemies. Worst-case scenarios like Iran and Afghanistan offer more long-term hope than "stable regimes" like the Saudis; governments that hate us have populations that like us, and vice versa; the Saudi royal family, whom ten thousand American troops protect, and the Mubarak autocracy, which has snagged billions of American dollars, are as afraid of democratic reformers as they are Islamic fundamentalists. And with good reason: Islamic governments in Iran and under the Taliban were as hated by the masses as Arab secular reformers in exile in the West are praised and championed.

The post-9/11 domestic calculus is just as confusing. Generals and the military brass call civilians who seek the liberation of Iraq "chicken hawks" and worse. Yet such traditional Vietnam-era invective I think rings hollow after September 11, and sounds more like McClellan's shrillness against his civilian overseers who precipitously wanted an odious slavery ended than resonant of Patton's audacity in charging after murderous Nazis. More Americans were destroyed at work in a single day than all those soldiers killed in enemy action since the evacuation of Vietnam nearly thirty years ago. Indeed, most troops who went through the ghastly inferno of Vietnam are now in or nearing retirement; and, thank God, there is no generation of Americans in the present military—other than a few thousand brave veterans of the Gulf, Mogadishu, and Panama—who have been in sustained and deadly shooting with heavy casualties. Because American soldiers and their equipment are as impressive as our own domestic security is lax, in this gruesome war it may well be more perilous to work high up in lower Manhattan, fly regularly on a jumbo jet, or handle mail at the Pentagon or CIA than be at sea on a sub or destroyer.

Real concern for the sanctity of life may hinge on employing, rather than rejecting, force, inasmuch as our troops are as deadly and protected abroad as our women, children, aged, and civilians are impotent and vulnerable at home. It seems to me a more moral gamble to send hundreds of pilots into harm's way than allow a madman to further his plots to blow up or infect thousands in high-rises.

Politics have been turned upside down. In the old days, cynical conservatives were forced to hold their noses and to practice a sometimes repellent Realpolitik. In the age of Russian expansionism, they were loathe to champion democracy when it might usher in a socialist Trojan horse whose belly harbored totalitarians disguised as parliamentarians. Thus they were so often at loggerheads with naïve and idealist leftists.

No longer. The end of the specter of a deadly and aggressive Soviet communism has revived democratic ideology as a force in diplomacy. Champions of freedom no longer sigh and back opportunistic rightist thugs who promise open economics, loot their treasuries, and keep out the Russians. Instead, even reactionaries are now more likely to push for democratic governments in the Middle East than are dour and skeptical leftists. The latter, if multiculturalists, often believe that democracy is a value-neutral Western construct, not necessarily a universal good; if pacifists, they claim nonintervention, not justice, as their first priority. The right, not the left, now is the greater proponent of global freedom, liberation, and idealism—with obvious domestic ramifications for any

Republican president astute enough to tap that rich vein of popular support.

All this and more are the wages of the disaster of September
11 and the subsequent terrible year—and yet it is likely that, for
good or evil, we will see things even more incredible in the twelve
months ahead.

Written on September 9 and published in
NATIONAL REVIEW ONLINE *on September 11, 2002.*

2

Al Qaedism

FROM CRIMINALITY TO POLITICS
IN THE BLINK OF AN EYE

A disturbed teen crashes a light plane into an office building in Florida and leaves a suicide note, apparently praising the work of bin Laden. Relieved that hundreds were not killed, officials properly assure us that his desperate act is a sign of mental illness or family despair, and not connected to global terrorism. At the Los Angeles airport a supposedly unhinged Egyptian émigré murders innocents at the El Al Airline counter; we are reminded by pundits and diplomats that the anti-Semite once again acted alone and thus was not a part of an al Qaeda cell.

Snipers in Maryland and Virginia blast apart civilians at random. Thereafter we are advised that although one was an angry Black Muslim and the two previously had expressed approval of the September 11 attacks and had very disturbing appurtenances in their car, both were not in any formal sense a part of al Qaeda. Arrests of various conspirators on both the East and West Coasts, who either visited Afghanistan or helped to organize Islamic "charities" as fronts for terrorists raise more controversy than relief—as anguished relatives swear that the indictment of such American patriots is proof of anti-Islamic prejudice rather than proper homeland security. We still do not know the exact circumstances of the anthrax letters; yet we are lectured that earlier reports that one of the September 11 murderers may have had a cutaneous form of the rare disease and that letters connecting the bacilli with terrorist fury were probably bogus.

This caution is perhaps fine and proper, as it should be, since there is not always legal proof implicating any of these events with a worldwide al Qaeda network. But in some sense, it doesn't matter.

The violent terrorist acts share an ostensible theme of either reflecting the aims of al Qaeda or professing some sympathy with radical Islamic fundamentalism. They are as dangerous as the work of terror cells because they presage a sporadic, spontaneous, and nearly unpredictable outbreak of violence that is also decentralized and untraceable. In short, rather than being al Qaeda shock troops, these killers and criminals are al Qaedistic—or perhaps show symptoms of a malady we should call "al Qaedism."

One did not need to be a formal follower of Hitler to be fascistic, or a member of Stalin's party to be communistic. In fact, the Greek suffix "-istic" ("like" or "pertaining to") can mean simulation of, or empathy with, the real thing. What are the symptoms of such a pathology like al Qaedism? How does it spread? And how can it be eradicated?

Thousands of Americans are wicked or mentally troubled, often with records of criminal activity or signs of such intent. Most murder, maim, rob banks, or commit other such mayhem, and leave it at that, seeking no claim of higher political import for their odious crimes. But not all—and not after 9/11.

On the campus in the 1970s, both petty criminals and megalomaniac thugs sought to mask their selfish and narcissistic agendas under the more cosmic cloak of the antiwar movement, national liberation, or utopian egalitarianism. So the felons of the Black Panther Party, the grim killers and bank robbers of the Symbionese

Liberation Army, and many of the mad bombers of the Weather-
men were encouraged by the rhetoric of the nebulous resistance
movement to act out their violent propensities—in hopes that allegiance to some half-baked philosophy would make them revolu-
tionaries rather than the felons they were.

So it was with criminals like the would-be mass murderer
Richard Reid and the two snipers, who all had either a prior rap
sheet or displayed signs of real instability, but perhaps wished to
evolve from two-bit losers into momentary warriors—on the idea
that their crimes might at last find transcendence in some sort of
ad hoc jihad. In that sense, the cheap rhetoric of al Qaeda—a godless and oppressive United States wars unjustly against poor Muslims and the dispossessed of the globe; Jews conspire everywhere;
decadent Western society must cede to a puritanical Islam—can
energize an otherwise pedestrian cruelty and thereby salvage a
cause from a personal sense of failure and inadequacy.

Rather than confront the reality of past character flaws, mental
instability, failed marriages, or the bleak future of no money, dead-
end jobs, or social ostracism, the al Qaedist—whether an erstwhile
Black Muslim, a Middle Eastern immigrant with a criminal past,
or a mixed-up, pampered suburbanite who dabbles in fundamentalism—seeks notoriety for his crimes, and therein perhaps at last a
sense of importance.

Unfortunately to the sniper's innocent targets in Virginia and
Maryland—or any others who will die by unhinged al Qaeda
wannabes—it makes no difference whether they were the victims
of terror or terroristic behavior. Law-enforcement officials, of
course, are growing worried about such trends—as if the ideology
of al Qaeda quite independently across time and space can infect
crazy, mean people and prompt them to act out their dreams in
violently anti-American fashion. Al Qaedism, after all, can serve as
a sort of receptacle for extreme lunatics of the anti-Americanism
brand who seek purer and more violent avenues of expression.

In the 1930s there were literally thousands of unbalanced
Westerners outside Germany who paraded around in black shirts

and aped Hitler. No doubt had the Third Reich not been demolished the more deranged would have continued to dress up their criminality with Nazi slogans, violent anti-Semitism, and terrorist acts. But by 1945 few would-be National Socialists were prominent. Violent fellow travelers were common in the 1930s and 1940s; indeed, the archives of arrested Stalinists often reveal those who tried to find some higher plane to act out their innate criminal propensities, alleviate deep personal maladies, or simply assuage their own failure by displaying anger toward Western society. Yet we see few such dangerous misfits after the fall of the Berlin Wall.

To rid us of al Qaedists, then, we must first not merely destroy al Qaeda, but do so in such comprehensive and humiliating fashion that the easy emulation of the radical Islamicist agenda not only draws opposition from friends and family but utter ridicule. And at home, Americans must not be afraid to address extremism when they see it, refute it—and do so in such a way that its perpetrators incur shame and odium on themselves rather than inspire the criminal, hateful, or mentally ill to equate their anger and failure with a virulent anti-Americanism.

I suppose it was entirely legal last Halloween for the New Black Panther Party and its Islamic fundamentalist allies—firebrands like Imam Abdul Alim Musa, Imam Muhammad Asi, Imam Abdel Razzag Al Raggad, and others—to voice empathy for the Taliban, express publicly racist and anti-Semitic hatred, and convey sympathy for those who murdered three thousand Americans. But it was not a very moral act for C-Span to broadcast that repulsive propaganda live from the National Press Club at a time of war.

Watching protesters in the recent antiwar march in Washington on public television no doubt gives balance to the debate, but again broadcasting shots of posters that declared I LOVE IRAQ, BOMB TEXAS or photos of the president of the United States with a Hitlerian mustache and Nazi salute crosses the line of good taste.

By the same token, it is very American for zealots to shout displeasure at their government, but their slurs that the president of the United States, the vice president, and the secretary of defense are the "true axis of evil" rather than Stalinist North Korea, fascistic Iraq, or theocratic Iran have consequences in the future that we cannot predict in the present. And we should be concerned that an apparent Iraqi national, recently returned with permission from Saddam Hussein's regime, leads Americans in chants about their amoral war. We should cringe, too, when the former attorney general, Ramsey Clark, compares an American administration to Heinrich Himmler, the architect of the Gestapo. There are ripples from such hate and we are seeing how insidiously they can lap into crazy minds.

In other words, we have a moral responsibility to oppose such extremism and, yes, subversion. Such hateful anti-American language can lend a sense of legitimacy and encouragement to a John Muhammad, a mixed-up teenage John Lee Malvo, or an angry anti-Semite Hesham Mohamed Modayet at the Los Angeles airport, and so elevate their pathologies into something apparently "meaningful," or perhaps even enrage them to at last act.

Of course, the real task of preventing isolated but often violent and deadly terroristic acts requires the defeat and degradation of al Qaeda abroad. But stopping al Qaedism here at home is as much a social and cultural as a legal or military challenge. We cannot censor those who carry signs that advocate bombing Texas, but we should surely censure them—and hope that another loser like John Williams, John Walker Lindh, Jose Padilla, or Richard Reid is not watching them on C-Span, ready to attack Americans as a creepy jihadist John Muhammad, Abdul Hamid, Abdullah al-Muhajir, or Abdel Rahim.

Written on October 30 and published in
NATIONAL REVIEW ONLINE *on November 1, 2002.*

3

It's Not the Money, Stupid!

WAR APPARENTLY MUST BE ANYTHING
OTHER THAN GOOD VS. EVIL

It has only been a little more than a year since September 11 and already therapeutic voices are back, suggesting that we are somehow culpable for our own calamity because we did not give away enough money to the Middle East. Not long ago the well-meaning and sincere Senator Murray of Washington contrasted the purported civic philanthropy of Osama bin Laden with the supposed failure of the United States to help those impoverished in the Middle East. She was apparently perplexed over why so many Islamic countries hate us—and perhaps thinks that instead of warring with Iraq we should spend the projected billions in war costs on more foreign aid to convince the Arab masses to like us rather than him.

Would that the senator's trust in human nature be true! Then, armed with her logic of the Enlightenment and Christian notions of peace and goodwill, we might abandon deterrence, write big checks, and so make the world anew on more utopian and moral principles.

But unfortunately Senator Murray's musings are not merely infantile but quite dangerous, and for a variety of reasons—besides her very wrong inference that a few million dollars of bin Laden's cynical largesse can be compared to the multibillions of past United States aid and private American philanthropy.

First of all, all dictators and thugs—compare Hitler's autobahns, Mussolini's trains, or Mao's anti-opium campaigns—invest in public works as useful social capital to be weighed against their more-nefarious acts. In the graveyard of post-Taliban Afghanistan, skeletons of Soviet dams, highways, tunnels, and schools loom everywhere, the legacy of manipulative Communists who sought to extend the carrot of material improvement even as they brandished the stick of tyrannical killing.

Like all cynical mass murderers, bin Laden did not run his public works by a Senate oversight committee. Instead he calculated his rent for terrorist camps and outlaw sanctuary with the vouchers of a few roads and madrasahs.

Senator Murray also assumes that a hostile people's anger is either logical or justified. But just as frequently as genuine grievances over poverty, wars break out over perceived hurts. In the mind-set of a Patty Murray, Hitler's Germans or Tojo's Japanese might have gone to war because Britain and the United States were stingy with their aid or praise, not because we appeared both affluent and weak, without will or power to stop initial aggression. The specter of the humiliation and defeat of supposed "decadent" democracies—if done on the cheap—is a powerful narcotic that offers thugs the conceit of status and a sense of national accomplishment.

True, the so-called masses of the Middle East have grounds for redress—who wouldn't without elections, free speech, sexual equality, religious tolerance, or the rule of law? But their want arises largely from self-created failures and runs the gamut of tribalism, corruption, fanaticism, and frequent apartheid of women and non-Muslims—not a lack of dollars and euros. The depressing ruins that are now a large part of Kabul, Beirut, and Cairo, or the moral black holes of Teheran, Riyadh, Damascus, and Baghdad were the dividends of indigenous Middle Eastern genius, not of outside Western machinations. Promoting democracy, not handing out food, practicing appeasement, or tolerating suicide bombing, will do far more for the disenfranchised on the West Bank.

Instead in the therapeutic thinking of Senator Murray war arises only from material need. Thus, lend a helping hand and offer a few billion, and—presto!—logically millions should love us. Stalin's ruined postwar Russia, however, did not appreciate American forbearance in Eastern Europe or offers of billions of dollars in Marshall Plan money. Just as likely, it saw such conciliatory outreach as either stupidity or weakness—if not the laxity of a Western power overly worried about its own sense of morality.

Tragically, evil states and cabals always exist; and they sometimes have only contempt for more moral peoples who choose not to use their superior power that might entail messy wars. Had we offered still more charity, the Arab street might have appreciated such generosity about as much as the Jordanians and Egyptians now show gratitude for billions in American debt relief, grain, and military assets—or our past salvation of Islamic Afghans, Kuwaitis, Somalis, Kosovars, and Bosnians.

In war, clarity of purpose—which is not a relative construct—counts for everything, being liked by one's enemies very little at all. When one examines the moral universe of bin Laden and the vast majority of Arab governments—whether Iraq, Libya, Saudi Arabia, Syria, Yemen, or Lebanon—then why wouldn't they dislike the United States?

And in a war fought over fundamental differences, enemy displeasure is not always discernable—and when it is, rarely regrettable. We do not know precisely what the Iranian, Syrian, or Iraqi people think of the United States because any who voice their heartfelt views would be either jailed or killed. But at least we are finally learning that dictatorships that claim our alliance (various kings, sheiks, and "presidents") foster anti-Americanism; while overt enemies (for example, the mullahs, Taliban, and Saddam

Hussein) prompt either popular indifference or goodwill toward
the United States. Personally, I would be pleased that the Taliban,
Saddam Hussein, most of the mobs cheering Pakistani assassins,
and others writing anti–Semitic editorials did not like America—
and would be shocked and ashamed if they did.

Humans are also fickle. By nature they are prone to gravitate
toward conventional rather than real wisdom. Most feel comfortable with consensus and victory, and become dejected in shame
and defeat. Read of the contrasting opinions that Germans held
about the United States between 1941 and 1947: we remained the
same; they changed. Millions of pro–Hitler Germans did not dis-
appear in 1945, but they professed to us that their ideas had. They
liked us far better after they were poor and beaten than when they
were rich and unconquered.

Why the change? Because the wages of their pride and cynical
calculation led to the ruin of the Third Reich and a realization
that Nazism was as impotent as its values were bankrupt. So if the
United States wins in Iraq, and if it establishes with justice and
humility a consensual government under international auspices,
most Middle Easterners will either grow mute or once more, as in
1991, a few will start naming their children after an American
president. Indeed, I imagine right now in Kuwait there are a few
families with teenage George Bushes changing the diapers of their
toddler sibling bin Ladens—while an embryonic George W. Bush
awaits birth.

The suburban soccer fields of Seattle are not quite the same
types of places as the wilds of Yemen, the palaces of Riyadh, or
the barracks of the Republican Guard. Senator Murray in her own
life talks as though she has never bumped into anybody quite like
Osama bin Laden. But our terrorist nemesis thinks he has seen
quite a few Senator Murrays in the last two decades of impotent
American responses to his campaign of terror—guilt-ridden,
naïve, and ultimately either too "moral" or too worried to crush
him. And so far, Mr. bin Laden has proved the more astute, since
he really would understand a Patty Murray far better than she him.

Sadly, prosperous Westerners never seem to learn of the folly of honoring appeasement and naïveté—the awarding of Nobel Peace Prizes to the likes of a Le Duc Tho and Yasser Arafat, as if global praise might make them statesmen rather than murderers, to a Kim Dae Jung, as if his demonstrable kindness would pacify rather than embolden North Korea, or to ex-president Carter, as if his well-meaning parleys with tyrants could bring peace. As chief executive emeritus, his saintliness now plays well; but we forget in the rough and tumble of his presidency that Mr. Carter's brag that he had no "inordinate fear of communism" was followed by the brutal Russian invasion of Afghanistan, that sending Ramsey Clark to apologize to the Iranians did not win the release of the American hostages in 1980, and that UN ambassador Andrew Young's praise of Cuban troops in Africa and his clenched-fist, Black Power salutes to African leaders did not stop Communist intervention and bloodletting abroad.

The United States cannot lose the struggle on the battlefield, as we did not lose the Vietnam conflict in the strict military sense either. But we most surely can fail in this war if our citizens and leaders reach for their checkbooks as the fundamentalists reach for their guns—or convince themselves that our enemies fight because of something we, rather than they, did.

Written on January 1 and published in
NATIONAL REVIEW ONLINE *on January 3, 2003.*

II

◆═◆◇◆═◆

THE DILEMMA OF THE
MIDDLE EAST

After September 11—as suicide bombing spread in Israel, was commonplace in Chechnya, and took hundreds of lives from Bali to North Africa—a great debate arose in the United States concerning its relationship with the Middle East and the culture that seemed, at least in an indirect way, to foster terrorism and a number of rogue states. To what degree were American policies of Realpolitik that grew out of the Cold War, the heritage of European colonialism, and the cynical recycling of petrodollars for sophisticated weaponry responsible for the current mess of rising populations that increasingly were poorly fed, housed, and educated, and subject to horrific government oppression in places like Iraq, Libya, and Syria?

Or was the problem, at least in part, self-induced? Did endemic problems such as a lack of religious tolerance and diversity, a prevailing gender apartheid, absence of consensual government, and a disastrous experiment with Soviet-imported state socialism imposed on a traditional tribal society explain why the Middle East had not evolved in the postwar period to the same degree as a Korea, China, South America, or Eastern Europe? And were autocracies like those in Jordan, Saudi Arabia, and Egypt bastions of moderation in a sea of fundamentalism and state-inspired terrorism, or, in fact, deadly triangulators that accepted American aid or troops even as they sought support for their illegitimacy by winking at or in fact subsidizing stealthy terrorists? Did a new reconstituted Iraq pose more danger than Saddam Hussein to the royal family of Saudi Arabia, given its own autocracy and fear of modernization and liberalization?

And could (or should) we advocate, ignore, or in fact implant democratic society in a region where it had no history, either as an idealistic enterprise or a no-nonsense matter of our own national security? In these essays I argued that Arab problems grew largely out of their own failures and the acceptance of such an exegesis should be a critical element in our policy-making. Not only could admissions of Western culpability not entirely or even in large part explain past Arab pathology, but the embrace of guilt would lead either to unquestioned aid or unwise concessions and thus send exactly the wrong message to the contemporary Middle East—that outsiders alone should or could correct problems that were in fact endemic and cried out first for indigenous reform.

Some of the measures advocated—withdrawal of troops from Saudi Arabia, the isolation of Yasser Arafat, and armed action against Saddam Hussein (see Chapters 29 through 38)—in fact, were embraced by the United States, and, as argued in some of these essays, I think they will have an overall salutary effect on both the region and our own relationship with the Arab world in the tumultuous years to come.

4

⊷══◉══⊶

Postmodern Palestine

THE NEW AMORALITY IN THE MIDDLE EAST

There is a postmodern amorality afloat—the dividend of years of an American educational system in which historical ignorance, cultural relativism, and well-intentioned theory, in place of cold facts, has reigned. We see the sad results everywhere in the current discussions of the Middle East and our own war on terror.

Palestinians appeal to the American public on grounds that three or four times as many of their own citizens have died as Israelis. The crazy logic is that in war the side that suffers the most casualties is either in the right or at least should be the winner. Some Americans nursed on the popular ideology of equivalence find this attractive. But if so, they should then sympathize with Hitler, Tojo, Kim Il Sung, and Ho Chi Minh, who all lost more soldiers—and civilians—in their wars against us than we did.

Perhaps a million Chinese were casualties in Korea, ten times the number of Americans killed, wounded, and missing. Are we, then, to forget that the Communists crossed the Yalu River to implement totalitarianism in the south—and instead agree that their catastrophic wartime sacrifices were proof of American culpability? Palestinians suffer more casualties than Israelis not because they wish to, or because they are somehow more moral—but because they are not as adept in fighting real soldiers in the full-fledged war that is growing out of their own intifada.

We are told that Palestinian civilians who are killed by the Israeli Defense Forces are the moral equivalent of slaughtering Israeli civilians at schools, restaurants, and on buses. That should be a hard sell for Americans after September 11, who are currently bombing in Afghanistan to ensure that there are not more suicide murderers on our shores. This premise hinges upon the acceptance that the suicide bombers' deliberate butchering of civilians is the same as the collateral damage that occurs when soldiers retaliate against other armed combatants.

In fact, the tragic civilian deaths on the West Bank make a less-compelling argument for amorality than the one revisionists often use in condemning the Dresden, Hamburg, and Tokyo bombings. Then British and American planes knowingly incinerated civilians in their quests to shut down the war-making potential of the Third Reich and Imperial Japan. Unlike what the B-17s and B-29s did to stop fascist murdering on a global scale, the Israelis are not carpet-bombing indiscriminately. Rather they are doing precisely what we ourselves were forced to do in Mogadishu: fighting a dirty urban war against combatants who have no uniforms, shoot from houses, and are deliberately mixed in with civilians. So far the Israelis have probably killed fewer civilians in a year of fighting on the West Bank than our trapped soldiers did in two days of similar gun battles in Somalia.

An ignorance of historical context is also critical for such post-modern revisionism. If the conflict is due to the Israeli occupation of the West Bank, then the first three wars for the survival of Israel itself must be conveniently ignored. If there is a push for the exchange of land for peace, then we must overlook that some in the Arab world who have suggested just that bromide in the past three decades were either assassinated or executed. And if we accept that both sides are equally culpable for the current killing, we must forget that less than two years ago the Palestinians rejected an Israeli offer to return 97 percent of the West Bank, along with other major concessions, assuming that unleashing the present intifada could get them still more.

Facts mean nothing. The dispute is purportedly over the principle of occupation—but next door, Syria holds far more Lebanese land than Israel does of the West Bank. The dispute is supposedly over ethnic intolerance and gratuitous humiliation—but Kuwait, quite unlike Israel, ethnically cleansed their entire country of Palestinians after the Gulf War. The dispute is said to be about treating the "other" fairly—but Syria and Iraq summarily expelled over seven thousand Jews after the 1967 war, stole their property, and bragged that they had rid their country of them. The upcoming Arab summit could spend weeks just investigating the Arab murder and persecution of its own people and Jews.

Multicultural distortion also appears in a variety of strange ways. Palestinian spokesmen harangue Americans about their tilt toward Israel. Yet they also speak in grandiose terms of an "Arab summit" and a global Islamic brotherhood. Apparently, fellow Muslims, Arabs—and kindred autocracies—are supposed to support Palestinians unquestioningly because of religious, cultural, and political affinities. Yet we multicultural Americans are not entitled to exhibit similar sympathy for Israel, which, like us, and unlike Mr. Arafat's regime, is a Western, democratic, open, and free society.

Why do such bankrupt arguments find resonance? I think the causes have now permeated well beyond a few coffeehouse theorists blabbering away in Cambridge or Palo Alto. Rather, it is because we live in a society in which playground fights in our schools are now often adjudicated by concepts such as "zero tolerance" and "equal culpability." Rather than exercising moral judgment—and investing time and energy in such investigation—our school principals simply expel any student caught fighting, as if the bully and his victim occupy the same moral ground.

Our schoolbooks devote more space to Hiroshima than to the far, far greater casualties on Okinawa. Students are not told that the two tragedies are connected—as if the American bombing to prevent an enormous bloodbath on the Japanese mainland is somehow not a direct result of the Japanese imperial military's efforts a few weeks earlier to unleash thousands of kamikazes, and through suicide attacks and banzai charges kill every American (and tens of thousands of civilians) on the island rather than surrender.

Rather than do the hard work of learning about the historical relationships, conflicts, and similarities between Islamic and Christian culture, East and West, and Europe and Asia, our teachers simply avoid the trouble. They claim that all cultures are just "different," and thereby hope to avoid the hard and unpleasant questions that might prompt hurt feelings and eventual enlightenment, rather than jeopardize their own immediate raises and promotions. No wonder I have had college students who affirm that British imperialism in India was no different from Hitler's attempt at dominance in Europe—as if there were gas chambers in New Delhi, as if the Nazi "super-race" might have sought to eradicate the caste system, or as if Gandhi's civil disobedience would have worked against Himmler.

I do not think there is some grand postmodern scheme afloat to undermine the legacy of empiricism, history, and logic. Rather, the spread of such amorality is simply a result of our own sloth and timidity—and perhaps ultimately the dangerous dividend of an increasingly affluent and cynical society. Teachers, professors, and reporters embrace such dubious notions because they bring either rewards or at least the satisfaction of being liked and in the majority.

It is also less demanding to watch television than read, safer to blame or praise both than investigate the culpability of one, neater to create rather than recall facts, and better to feel good about oneself by adopting platitudes of eternal peace and universal tolerance than to talk honestly of evil, war, and the tragic nature of man. When you combine such American laziness and lack of intellectual rigor with worries over oil and anti-Semitism, then our baffling nonchalance about the current war against Israel begins to make sense.

Moral equivalence, conflict-resolution theory, utopian paci-fism, and multiculturalism are, of course, antirational and often silly. But we should also have the courage to confess that they bring on, rather than avoid, conflict and killing, and breed rather than eradicate ignorance. In short, they are not ethical ideas at all but amoral in every sense of the word.

Written on March 27 and published in
NATIONAL REVIEW ONLINE *on March 29, 2002.*

5

History Isn't on the Palestinians' Side

Arafat's Strategy Is Suicidal in More Ways Than One

For all the efforts of our contemporary theorists to harness and sometimes refashion history, the facts of the past belong to no one—and won't go away. Those who conjure it up often discover to their dismay that they themselves are subject to its brutal laws of truth. The Palestinians are fast learning of history's ironies and unintended reminders, as they seek to invoke the past to convince Americans of the righteousness of their present plight.

Take the idea of the occupation of Arab lands since 1967, which the Palestinians now cite as a singular historical grievance that needs immediate rectification through intervention of the United States. But, sadly, occupation and partition are the bastard children of war; and history, rightly or wrongly, is not kind to states that repeatedly attack their neighbors—and lose.

Ask the millions of poor Germans who had their ancestral lands confiscated by Poland and France—and their country subsequently partitioned for a half century. Why do the Russians still occupy portions of the old Japanese homeland decades after the surrender? How is it that the British won't give up Gibraltar long after their successful battles against the Spanish fleet? And why must the world give far more attention to Palestine than it does to Tibetans, Irish, and Chechens?

The situation on the West Bank is not only commonplace in history's harsh calculus, but prevalent even throughout the Arab world today. Right next door in Lebanon, Syria controls far more Arab land than does Israel. And if Palestinians suffer second-class citizenship under Israeli occupation, they are worse off in occupied Lebanon, where, as helots, they are denied basic rights to employment, health care, and government services.

Kuwait ethnically cleansed itself of all Palestinians—perhaps a third of a million—just a decade ago. Well after the 1967 Six Day War, the Jordanians themselves slaughtered thousands. Before the intifada, more Palestinians sought work in a hated Israel than in a beloved Egypt. History suggests that there is more going on in Palestine than the morality of occupation.

The Palestinians have turned to suicide bombers—terrorists boasting of a new and frightening tactic that cannot be stopped. But they should recall the kamikazes off Okinawa that brought death, terror, and damage to the American fleet—before prompting horrific responses that put an end to them for good, and a lot more besides. In general, the record of terrorist bombers—whether Irish, Basque, or Palestinian—who seek to reclaim "occupied" lands is not impressive in winning either material concessions or the hearts and minds of the world.

Palestinian spokesmen decry asymmetrical casualty figures, as if history has ever accorded moral capital to any belligerents that suffered the greater losses in war. Again, ask Imperial Japan or Nazi Germany whether the ghosts of millions of their dead today carry such moral weight, inasmuch as their governments once sought war against their neighbors.

Deliberately trying to blow apart civilians will never be seen as the moral equivalent of noncombatants dying as a result of the street fighting in the West Bank. Afghans accidentally killed by errant bombing in Kandahar are different from those deliberately incinerated on September 11. Somalis killed in Mogadishu by American peacekeepers—many more civilians dying there in two days than in two years on the West Bank—are not the same as those murdered by thugs in jeeps trying to steal food from the starving.

Americans learned in Vietnam and Mogadishu that it is hard to distinguish civilians from soldiers when gunmen do not always wear uniforms and take potshots from the windows of homes: they are real killers when alive, but somehow count as "civilians" when dead. The problem is not that the Palestinians are losing more than the Israelis due to their greater victimhood or morality but rather that they find themselves losing very badly to a military far more adept at fighting.

Nor do the Palestinians' cries for justice exist in a historical vacuum. True, the current Arab-Israeli war—at least the fourth since 1948—is fought over the West Bank; but that is only because the theater of operations has changed somewhat since the Arab world lost in its first three attempts to destroy Israel proper. Less than two years ago, Yasser Arafat was offered almost all of the West Bank and would now be the unquestioned strongman of his own tribal fiefdom had he taken such a generous Israeli offer. His own scheming and the intifada—not Israeli extremism—brought back to him his old nemesis, Ariel Sharon. Again, the problem for the Palestinians is not that Americans are ignorant of the historical complexities of the Middle East, but that we know them only too well.

Palestinian spokesmen give us moralistic lectures about remaining disinterested as "honest brokers"—even as they appeal to Arab anti-Semitism and racial solidarity on grounds of national, religious, and ethnic empathy. That double standard puzzles America, because by any such measure we also find affinity in shared values, and have almost none with the Palestinians, who, like the entire Arab world, do not embrace real democracy, free speech, open media, or religious diversity.

Nor is it good public relations for illegitimate dictatorships of the Arab League to shake fingers at democracies in America and Israel on issues of equality and fairness. The problem is not that the Palestinians object to the idea of displaying preferences per se, but that their own biases and prejudices have so little appeal to Americans. We are told that the Palestinians have a long memory of, and reverence for, the past—especially the injustice of fifty years of lost homelands. But Americans are not ahistorical. We remember September 11—and the Palestinians who cheered our dead before being admonished by a terrified Arafat.

For the past three decades Palestinian terrorists and their sponsoring brotherhoods have murdered Americans abroad. Palestinians embraced Saddam Hussein's cause and clapped as Scuds plunged into Tel Aviv and blew apart American soldiers in Saudi Arabia. An entrapped Arafat now calls for American succor, but a few months ago scoffed that the United States was irrelevant as far as he was concerned. The problem, again, is not that Americans have forgotten Palestinian acts, but that we remember them all too well.

The Arab world warns of its martial prowess and deadly anger—as American flags burn, threats to kill us are issued, and "the street" shakes its collective fist. But we Americans remember 1967, when we gave almost no weapons to the Israelis—but the Russians supplied lots of sophisticated arms to the Arabs. In the Six Day War, the state radio networks of Syria, Egypt, and Jordan boasted to the world that their triumphant militaries were nearing Tel Aviv even as their frightened elites pondered abandoning Damascus, Cairo, and Amman. And we recall the vaunted Egyptian air force in 1967, the invincible Syrian jets over Lebanon, the Mother of All Battles—and the Republican Guard that proved about as fearsome as Xerxes' Immortals at Thermopylae.

A beleaguered Arafat now wildly works his Rolodex for support for his autocracy. But history answers cruelly that strongmen in their bunkers are as impotent as they are loquacious—and as likely to receive disdain as pity. Muammar Qaddafi was a different man after the American air strike proved his military worthless and his person no longer sacrosanct. The rhetoric of the Taliban in September promised death; in October they and their minions went silent. In wars against bombers and terrorists, the past teaches us that peace comes first through their defeat—not out of negotiations among supposedly well-meaning equals.

We all would prefer, and should strive for, peaceful relations with the Egyptians, the Jordanians, the Syrians—and all the other twenty-some dictatorships, theocracies, and monarchies of the Middle East—as well as a state for the Palestinians. But the day is growing late; our patience is now exhausted; and, sadly, an hour of reckoning is nearing for us all. The problem is, you see, that we know their history far better than they do.

Written on March 30 and published in
NATIONAL REVIEW ONLINE *on April 2, 2002.*

6

---❂❖❂---

Occidentalism

THE FALSE WEST

A merican professors have long lectured to our students about
purported Western biases and cruel misconceptions toward
the "Other." According to Edward Said and other postcolonial
critics, much of our dim view of Arabs is a product of an "Orientalism" that was constructed by European intellectuals of the
nineteenth-century West—blinkered folk actively engaged as colo-
nialists overseas and conditioned by an earlier pedigree of prejudice toward the East dating from Herodotus and Aeschylus.
According to such supposedly biased and unsophisticated views,
Asians and Arabs were considered tribal, emotional, less-sophisti-
cated peoples, prone to violence, fundamentalism, and irrational
thinking, simply because they did not understand, or chose not to
follow, Europe's rather brutal notions of capitalism, nationalism,
rationalism, and Christianity.

Few any longer accept such a simplistic, black-and-white por-
trait—especially when a number of erudite Europeans made great

efforts not only to live among and understand the Islamic world but also to criticize their own culture's interactions with it. Indeed, "Orientalism" is a superficial charge that does no justice to a wide range of liberal nineteenth-century thinking and the present array of modern Middle East Studies programs throughout America and Europe.

What really is startling, however, is not how the West in an earlier age—before easy communications and cheap travel—misunderstood the Arab and Islamic worlds, but rather how today—Internet, jets, student visas, television, and all—the *East* continues to stereotype the West, with not a clue about its intrinsic nature.

We should call this bias "Westernism"—or, perhaps, "Occidentalism." In general we can describe it as the mentality of desperately wanting something that one either cannot understand or that one, in fact, blindly and in ignorance loathes. Millions of Arabs have now come in contact with the dividends of Western capitalism and industrial production, most clearly in their easy acceptance of everything from cell phones and televisions to antibiotics and chemotherapy—everything that makes life a little easier materially, and occasionally somewhat longer. Sheiks from Saudi Arabia go to London or New York for bypass surgery, not to Cairo or Amman; they buy their Viagra from the States, not from apothecaries in Yemen. The Arab street purchase appliances that are made in China or Japan on Western blueprints, rather than producing them en masse in Damascus or improving on their designs at Baghdad University.

The Israelis produce among the best tanks in the world, and export everything from drip-irrigation technology to computer software; their enemies whine that America does not give them more and better weapons. Not even Saddam Hussein could establish a modern aircraft factory, nor could the formidable Assad dynasty produce a single destroyer. All the arms in all the Arab countries are either imported from Europe, Japan, or America, or licensed and built from Western designs in China and Korea.

We see such a very thin facing of material prosperity in almost every picture that is broadcast from the Middle East—thousands of consumer goods, movies, videos, and processed food that would be impossible without the West. Bin Laden himself, after calling for a medieval caliphate, bought a cell phone, a video camera, and sophisticated weapons—products that his own antirationalist madrasahs and mosques could not produce. The Taliban liked SUVs, but the government and school system they established ensured that not a single Afghan would ever acquire the knowledge to produce such pricey appurtenances. The killers in Palestine must bring in everything, from their rifles to their bombs—and the expertise to use them. Those few who do possess indigenous knowledge of sophisticated destruction either are foreign-educated or got the requisite information off the Internet.

The lust for the West is not only a matter of material addiction; there is a yearning for its freedom, modernity, and liberality as well. On American university campuses, Arab students often are the most vociferous questioners at lectures, and bask in the Western idea of completely unrestricted free speech. At rallies and on call-in radio stations, Islamic visitors on visas keenly exercise their rights of sharp critique—by openly condemning our own Mideast policy, our president, and indeed our country itself. Non-Westerners metamorphose into hyper-Westerners when they come here to study.

Diplomats from the Middle East are a funny sort. They are at home in Western ties and suits, and with cocktails and limos, and adept at the free-for-all of commercial television—adroit, too, in the subtle nuances of our politics, and aware of the possible nexus between the cause of the Palestinians and a vast labyrinth of American victimology. They grow silent only when caught in an obvious untruth, abject anti-Semitism, or incontrovertible evidence of state-sponsored terrorism—occasions when their newly found Western candor would earn them a bullet or prison billet upon landing on the tarmac at home. Likewise, al-Jazeera has the entire fluff of the Western news media down pat—the jazzed-up background music, the computer-simulated graphics, the photogenic airhead newsreaders—everything except true free speech, criticism of government, and doubts about religious orthodoxy.

So this entire familiarity with Western goods and practices ultimately is superficial. The Arab world is suffering from a deep-seated schizophrenia as it slowly sorts out its ambiguous feelings toward the hated West. Do you despise a country that gives you oil-drilling equipment, Ford SUVs, and contact lenses, along with Spider-Man and McDonald's, as being crass, godless, and decadent? And if so, do you express such loathing between Big Macs as you park your air-conditioned Wagoneer, board a 767, or put in eyedrops for your glaucoma? Are America's unveiled, auto-driving, and sometimes belly-baring women sluts, or worse?—or do they accomplish far more than exciting the baser passions, such as doubling the workforce and bringing critical brain power to the very pinnacles of society? Should you even shake hands with a Western woman, pay her to join your harem, lecture her about chastity—or hire her to economize your bureaucracy, control your aircraft traffic, design your power grid, sort our your legal codes?

And what exactly is this mysterious Western paradigm—the right to speak freely when visiting America but not when you return to Egypt? If you are an envoy from the Sudan, Palestine, or Saudi Arabia, do you condemn America on *Crossfire* and *Fox News,* but then curb such criticism when it concerns Arafat and the royal princes at home? Quite simply, very few in the Arab world realize that the reason we produce CAT-scanners and F-16s and Apaches and they do not—or the reason they come here to be schooled and we, as a rule, do not go there—is that our universities are free, our governments elected and tolerant, our people welcome to choose any religion or none, and our schools secular and meritocratic rather than fundamentalist and tribal.

Occidentalism—this counterfeit affinity with, and superficial knowledge of, the West—is most apparent in politics, where America's support for Israel is wrongly attributed to Zionist conspiracies and Jewish influence rather than the sharing of America's liberal values with the Middle East's only true democracy. When we see Israeli women in uniform, we think of our own—not those veiled in Pakistan. When we see the fiery debates in the Knesset, we recall our own Congress—not Syria's faux parliament. When we witness in the last few years Rabin, Netanyahu, Barak, and Sharon, we think of Reagan, Bush, Clinton, Bush II—not of the uninterrupted tenure of an Arafat, Mubarak, or Hussein.

In short, Occidentalism is a simulacrum of the West, and it is an insidious and often tragic phenomenon. One uses the Internet, a handy device that one's own society could not create or repair, to spread fundamentalism. One has a parliament and a president—even a staged election or two, on occasion—but no free press, real opposition, or unbridled speech. A writer likes Western acclaim, the genre of the novel, and literary prizes based on merit, not obsequiousness—but finds stone-throwers in the courtyard when one's narrative dares to question the hold of Islam. One travels abroad to become a vociferous Western student—but upon graduation goes from a vocal lion on an American campus to a timid mouse in the Gulf.

At day's end, the Arab world will have to sort out these paradoxes and contradictions and decide how traditional, how fundamentalist, or how autocratic and closed its societies should be in rejecting some, all, or none of the West's material and ideological dynamism. But we here in America have our own choices to make—and it is high time that we confront Occidentalism squarely and without pretense.

Politically, our officials must at last realize that Israelis tell the truth more often than Palestinians do—not because of genes or superior morality, but because their system of a free press, informed citizenry, and vocal opposition requires them to. We must not take too seriously Arab hatred that is predicated on real grievance, but realize that most antipathy is the result of this unhealthy stew of envy, anger, and desire for the West, a concoction that can so often be as humiliating to them as it is dangerous to us—as we saw with the Westernized murderers on September 11.

As a people and a government, we must realize that our West is not Westernism; that all the suits, jet planes, and televisions in the Gulf do not add up to gender equity, free speech, or religious tolerance—and that the latter are precisely what ensures the life that is good, and humane, and uniquely our own. We must accept that the most parochial and ridiculed American—selling real estate in Des Moines or hammering nails in Provo—in fact knows far better who and what he is, what his own culture is and is not about, and what the Arab world stands and does not stand for, than does the wealthiest, most sophisticated, and most glib Westernized intellectuals and professors of the Middle East. We wish all this were not so, but it is—and we should get used to it, fast.

Written on April 8 and published in
National Review Online *on April 10, 2002.*

7

A Ray of Arab Candor

The just-released Arab Human Development Report, commissioned by the United Nations and drafted by a group of Middle Eastern intellectuals, utterly confirms the deep pathology gripping the Arab world that Western analysts have long noted. Yet what was truly astounding about the account was less its findings than the honest acknowledgment that Arab problems are largely self-created.

Khalaf Hunaidi, who oversaw the economic portion of the analysis, remarked, "It's not outsiders looking at Arab countries. It's Arabs deciding for themselves." And what they decided is, sadly, ample proof of Arab decline. Per capita income is dropping in the Arab world, even as it rises almost everywhere else. Productivity is stagnant; research and development are almost absent. Science and technology remain backward. Politics is infantile. And culture, in thrall to Islamic fundamentalism and closed to the ideas that quicken the intellectual life of the rest of the world, is "lagging behind" advanced nations, Hunaidi says.

Yet this novel panel of Arab intellectuals, remarkably, didn't attribute the dismal condition of Middle Eastern society to the usual causes that Western intellectuals and academics have made so popular: racism and colonialism, multinational exploitation, Western political dominance, and all the other -isms and -ologies that we've grown accustomed to hear about from the Arabists on American university campuses.

Instead, the investigators cited the subjugation of women that robs Arab society of millions of brilliant minds. Political autocracy—either in the service of or in opposition to Islamic fundamentalism—ensures censorship, stifles creativity, and promotes corruption. Talented scientists and intellectuals are likely to emigrate and then stay put in the West, since there is neither a cultural nor an economic outlet for their talents back home but sure danger if they prove either honest or candid. The Internet remains hardly used. Greece, a country thirty times smaller than the Arab world, translates five times the number of books yearly.

The report didn't give precise reasons for the growing Arab hostility toward the United States, but its findings lend credence to almost everything brave scholars like Bernard Lewis and Daniel Pipes have been saying for years. With exploding populations, and offering little hope for either material security or personal freedom, unelected governments in the Gulf, Egypt, and northern Africa have allowed their press the single "freedom" of venting popular frustration against a very successful Israel and the United States.

Instead of discussing elections in Egypt, debating the Sudanese government's budget, or advocating academic freedom in Syria, state-run newspapers and television stations spin countless conspiracy theories about September 11. They dub the Jews subhuman and worse, promise eternal jihad against the West, and churn out elaborate explanations for why a tiny country like Israel is responsible for everything from train wrecks in Cairo to lawlessness in Lebanon.

What can Americans learn from this newly honest Arab self-appraisal? We should put no more credence in the preposterous "postcolonial" theories that ad nauseam argue that Westerners are still to be blamed a half-century after the last Europeans vacated the Middle East. Post-Marxist analyses that claim international conglomerates stifle the Arab world are just as silly. Nor must we believe that the Israeli-Palestinian conflict or our own support for Israel is the problem. Instead, the simple fact is that hundreds of millions of people are going backward in time in an age when global communications hourly remind them of their dismal futures. Frustration, pride, anger, envy, humiliation, spiritual helplessness—all the classical exegeses for war and conflict—far better explain the Arab world's hostility toward a prosperous, confident, and free West.

But our own academic left isn't alone in misjudging the Middle East. The Realpolitik of our own government that allies us with Saudi Arabia, Egypt, Jordan, and other "moderate" Arab states offers little long-term hope for an improved relationship with the people of the Middle East. It is no accident that America is more popular in countries whose awful governments hate us— Iraq and Iran, for example—than among the public of our so-called allies. Saudis, Kuwaitis, Pakistanis, and Egyptians, after all, have been murdering Americans far more frequently than have Iranians, Iraqis, and Syrians.

We have replaced our old legitimate fears of godless Marxism in the Middle East with new understandable worries over fanatical Islamic fundamentalism to justify our own continued support for corrupt dictatorships. Yet the old excuse that there is no middle class in the Arab world, no heritage of politics, and few secular moderates will no longer do. It should be our job to find true democrats, both in and outside of the existing governments, and then promote their interests at the expense of both the fundamentalists and the tribal grandees. Chaos, uncertainty, risk, and unpredictability may ensue, but all that is better than the murderous status quo of the current mess.

The contemporary Arab world is like the old Communist domain of Eastern Europe and the Soviet Union, with its political and intellectual tyranny. We should accept that, and then adopt the same unyielding resolve to oppose governments that lie, oppress, and murder—until they totter and fall from their very own corrupt weight. There was a silent majority yearning to be free behind the Iron Curtain, and so we must believe that there is also one now, just as captive, in an unfree Middle East.

Written in June and published in
CITY JOURNAL *on July 3, 2002.*

8

Our Enemies, the Saudis

Even if we were not attempting to prosecute a war against terror, the time would have long since arrived to reconsider our relations with Saudi Arabia. That the Saudis, of all people, should now be regarded as a virtual ally in this conflict only underscores the need at last to settle matters between us. Although the catalogue of disagreements on our agenda is long, and many of the items are by now familiar, it is helpful to review the list.

By any modern standard of civilization, the Kingdom of Saudi Arabia is a bizarre place. In an age of spreading consensual government, the House of Saud resembles an Ottoman sultanate staffed by some 7,000 privileged royal cousins. The more favored are ensconced in plush multimillion-dollar palaces and maintain luxury estates abroad in Paris, Geneva, Marbella, and Aspen. All 7,000 haggle over the key military and political offices of the kingdom—normally distributed not on the appeal of proven merit but more often through a mixture of blood ties, intrigue, and bribes.

Polygamy is legal, and practiced, among the Saudi elite. Everywhere in the kingdom, women are veiled, secluded, and subject to the harsh protocols of a sexual apartheid. A few female Saudi professionals who in 1991 drove cars as a sign of protest mostly ended up arrested and jailed. Women who have traveled to the West remain under the constant surveillance of the Committee for the Advancement of Virtue and Elimination of Sin, a Taliban-like government watchdog group of clerics and whip-bearing fanatics.

There is no religious tolerance in Saudi Arabia for creeds other than Islam; in our State Department's own muted nomenclature, "Freedom of religion does not exist" there. The Wahhabi strain of fundamentalist Islam—over thirty thousand mosques and growing—is prone to occasionally violent spasms. The Saudi constitution is defined officially by governmental decree as the Koran, and the legal system is the domain of clerics who adjudicate by an array of medieval codes and punishments. Presently the UN Committee Against Torture is asking the Saudis to curtail flogging and amputations; so far, the Saudis have answered that such punishments have been an integral part of Islamic law "for 1,400 years" and so simply "cannot be changed."

Although Westernized Saudis in suits and ties, often personable, with impeccable English and an array of American friends, are ubiquitous on our airwaves, they are mere darting phantoms of a free press. Dozens of state-run papers and private but publicly subsidized media vent the most virulent anti-Semitic hatred in the Arab world—fundamentalist screeds or "poetry" equating Jews with monkeys and calling for their extermination. Editors are free only in the sense that they can draw on their own creativity in expressing real dislike for the United States and Israel, perhaps to be rebuked on the rare occasions when such venom is made known to the very deferential American media elite who interview the royals on our evening television shows. The Saudi Press Agency is as careful in monitoring news accounts as informers are in observing classrooms, or as clerics in scrutinizing cultural events for the presence of women.

Criticism of the royal family, Saudi government, and religious leaders is legally forbidden and strictly monitored. The few dissident writers in the kingdom are jailed, blacklisted, and sometimes have their books banned and driven off the Arab-language market. The names of the censoring ministries—Supreme Information Council, Press Information Council, Ministry of Information, Directorate of Publications—come right out of Orwell's *1984*.

After September 11, the world is slowly learning how the Saudi princes have pulled off their grafting of a high-tech cultivar onto medieval roots. It has been accomplished through bribes to clerics, cash to terrorists, welfare to the commons, and largesse to prominent Americans: money in some form to any and all who find the House of Saud either too modern or too backward. Such inducements have been indispensable because the vast wealth that Western petroleum companies developed for the royal family, plus the tourist treasures of Mecca and Medina, brought neither a stable economy nor general prosperity. The kingdom's accidental boon was not invested broadly in viable industries, secular education, or political reform, but instead lavished on ill-conceived projects and a royal elite who squander too much of it on luxury cars, houses, clothes, jewels, gambling, and trips abroad—sins against both Islam and Western laws of economic development. Impressive architecture and a vast educational system belie the fact that many of the elite's new buildings do not contribute to the economy and that the madrasahs do more harm than good.

But now the Saudis are $200 billion in debt. The population is soaring. The imams are worried more about unrest than about their stipends. Thirty percent of Saudis remain unschooled, and nearly as many are barely literate, their resentment against a coddled elite mitigated only by carefully measured doses of anti-Western Wahhabism and the satisfaction that at least the millions of guest Asian and Arab helots, imported to perform much of the society's wage labor, are more unfree than they. Efforts at creating viable irrigated agriculture and petrochemical industries have had but mixed success—and then only thanks to massive infusions of oil-dollar subsidies.

It is not just human capital that is bought from abroad. Almost every item deemed important to the modernization of the kingdom—from drilling bits and heavy machinery to the phone system and power grid—is shipped in. The expertise to use, repair, and improve such critical appurtenances rests either with foreigners or with the few thousand Saudis trained abroad.

The Saudi royals are thus these days an increasingly troubled bunch. They are quite understandably exasperated that they have failed to earn needed capital by developing nonpetroleum industries, and that their citizenry lacks either the practical skills to create thriving commercial enterprises or the individual drive and initiative to build businesses from the ground up. They are even more irked that their imported gadgets have brought with them hostile ideas, critical lectures, and unwelcome advice, as if air conditioners and neurosurgeons should come without consequences and as freely as oil out of the desert. And they are still more dyspeptic that some people persist in thinking there is something unhealthy in the fact that fifteen of the nineteen hijackers on September 11 were Saudi nationals.

It is common to hear that Osama bin Laden, a naturalized Saudi Arabian whose family still has close ties to the inner circles of the monarchy, deliberately chose Saudi nationals for the September 11 murders in order to poison the otherwise amicable relations between the kingdom and the United States. Maybe so—but the gambit, if that is what it was, was certainly made easier by the thousands of Saudis who willingly traveled to Afghanistan over the last few years to train in bin Laden's terrorist camps. Royal denials notwithstanding, Saudi government money has for years been funneled into madrasahs to encourage radical anti-Americanism as well as to fund the al Qaeda terrorists. Allegedly the purpose has been as much to provide insurance against subversive activity directed at the kingdom itself as to subsidize attacks on the United States. And there may be, after all, a sick genius in a system that can shift the hatreds of an illiterate Saudi youth away from the jet-setting sheiks who have diverted his nation's treasure and onto the anonymous Americans who created that wealth, who ship the kingdom its consumer goods, and who defend it from the neighborhood's carnivores.

But that anomaly raises the key question: Why *have* close relations with the Saudis been a cornerstone of American foreign policy for decades, as brought to our attention most recently in a series of slick Saudi-financed ads showing American presidents from Franklin Roosevelt to George W. Bush in warm embraces with a variety of sheiks? The answer is banal: oil, and nothing more. Otherwise, Saudi Arabia's small population of 22 million would earn it less clout than Egypt. Otherwise, the kingdom is no more strategically located than nearby Yemen. Otherwise, its sponsorship of terrorism would ensure it a place on the State Department's list of rogue states such as Syria and Iran. In fact, a more sinister status: Saudi terrorists have now killed more Americans than all those murdered by Iranians, Syrians, Libyans, and Iraqis put together.

The actual Saudi percentage of the world's crude oil and gas reserves is a matter of dispute. On the one hand, there are still unexplored vastnesses in the kingdom itself; on the other, there is an indeterminable amount of oil lying beneath Russia, West Africa, the Arctic, and the seas. But it is reasonable to suppose that Saudi Arabia holds 25 percent or more of the remaining petroleum now known to exist. Thus, for at least the next two decades, the kingdom's oil is thought to be critical to the world economy, in particular to the prosperity of Japan, Europe, and the United States.

In the past, our devil's bargain with the kingdom was as utilitarian as it was unapologetic. They kept pumping the oil—either to us directly or as untraceable currents into the huge world pool— and we promised to ignore both the primeval nature of their domestic society and their virulent hatred of Israel. In the Cold War, the geopolitics of containing an expansionist Soviet Union made this mutually beneficial concordat easier to stomach. There was also a certain familiarity bred by the growing multitude of

Americans who traveled to Saudi Arabia to construct the civilized veneer of the kingdom and of Saudis who came here to obtain the expertise that would presumably ensure some kind of future autonomy. Perhaps the idealistic among us once thought that their intimate and sustained exposure to Americans might eventually lead to liberalization.

Even after the Cold War, however, "stability," rather than autonomy or liberalization, was the operative word when it came to our interest in Saudi Arabia. In theory, we did not press the royal family for democratic reform on their assurances that something far worse and far more radical—à la Algeria or Iran—might come to power in the chaos of elections. This seemed fair enough; who wanted another Khomeini or Mullah Omar atop a quarter of the world's oil supply? Or, worse, a Hitler-like thug who would hold one election and one alone? So we shrugged as the Saudis more recently permitted our troops to defend them, our experts to train them, and our merchants to profit from their oil while they, for their part, managed to hold their noses at our liberated women, prominent Jews, and crass dissemination of videos, fast food, raucous music, and general cultural wantonness.

Marshall Wyllie, a former chargé at the U.S. embassy in Saudi Arabia, once summed up the American policy best: "We need their oil, and they need our protection." Armed to the teeth with American weaponry that for the most part they are unable to maintain or operate competently, bolstered by a frontline trip wire of uniformed American soldiers, and static in their resistance to change, the Saudis preened that they were the reliable deliverymen of inexpensive and plentiful oil in a way that the lunocracies in Iraq, Iran, or Libya were not. And, admittedly, there was something to that claim, at least enough to enable us to think that our policy toward them was neither illogical nor even inherently amoral.

Saudi princes did tend to choose predetermined successors when the ruling sheik of the day passed on, without the gunplay typically seen in succession fights elsewhere in the Arab world.

Unlike the Iraqis, they never torched the oil fields; unlike the Iranians, they never stormed our embassy for hostages; unlike the Libyans, they never bombed our airliners. But as if in imitation of their own perspective on reality, our approach to *them* has also been static and equally blinkered, and in particular has taken no account of the huge alterations in the post–Cold War world.

These changes were already in play well before September 11. The international oil matrix is far more complex than during the Gulf War even a decade ago. Russia is now rapidly becoming the world's most important producer, and the demise of the Soviet bloc has meant that the entire world is now under active exploration. Whereas most other nations are no longer overly worried about the politics of oil exportation, and are positively indifferent to the old Marxist rhetoric about Western capitalist exploitation, the petroleum policy of Saudi Arabia—which has threatened or implemented at least three embargoes in past decades—remains both entirely self-interested and never far from the radical interests in the Middle East.

The sheiks, however, are being led by events that are rapidly careering out of their control. If Saudi Arabia pumps less oil, there will be shocks and disruptions, but also, eager new producing countries will soon fill the void; if the Saudis export more, then the price may well collapse altogether. And because new, nonpetroleum-based technologies are on the horizon, both to produce electricity and to power transportation, not to mention the increased efficiency promised in the near future by hybrid engines, most exporting countries now worry about getting what oil they have out of the ground rather than watch it sit untapped and decline in value in the latter half of the century.

In sum, a Saudi Arabia with a sizable debt and no real nonpetroleum economy needs consumers as much as, or more than, consumers need Middle Eastern producers. Saudi Arabia is ever so slowly losing its vaunted place as the world's price-fixer, and its past history and present machinations reveal it to be no more or less a friend of the United States than any other Islamic exporting country. If the Saudis declared another embargo, it might fare about as well as Saddam Hussein's recent ban of exports to the United States—and cause a surge in pumping and exploration in Russia and South America.

There is, then, no real need for us to be frightened by the loss of the kingdom's oil friendship. But we should be concerned by the evidence of its strategic enmity. It may be true that the Saudis are neither Iraqis nor Iranians nor Libyans; but it is quite dangerous enough that they are Saudis.

The PLO archives made public by the Israeli army in the wake of its recent operations on the West Bank have confirmed that the kingdom actively gives cash to a variety of terrorist organizations and showers with money (or free trips to Mecca) the families of suicide bombers. This bounty can no longer be seen as mere post-mortem charity, but rather as premeditated financial incentives for murder. What that means is that the kingdom's suicide killers of September 11 who butchered our civilians were not so at odds with basic Saudi approaches to the conflict after all.

The much-vaunted Saudi "peace plan" for the Middle East does not alter this troubling picture. What was striking (stunning, really) about the proposals was not the grudging willingness after a half-century to recognize the existence of the State of Israel but the complete absence in them of any gesture—planned state visits to Tel Aviv, direct talks with Jerusalem, cessation of state propaganda, curtailment of terrorist subsidies—that might suggest more than a public-relations ploy to deflect growing American furor after September 11. Current Saudi peace feelers are mostly explicable as salve for wounds the Saudis themselves have inflicted, and which they are suddenly worried have become infected in a very aggrieved host.

Then there is radical Islam. Despite suicide bombings in Lebanon, the first World Trade Center attack, the 1996 assaults against the Khobar Towers complex in Saudi Arabia, the 1998 bombings at the embassies in Kenya and Tanzania, and the hole blasted in the USS *Cole* distracted Americans used to believing that such vicious wasps deserved little more than an occasional swat. But after the murder of three thousand Americans, and the various anthrax, dirty-bomb, and suicide-attack scares, Americans are finally seeing militant Islam not merely as a different religion, or even as a radical Jim Jones–like cult, but as a threat to our very existence.

Saudi Arabia is the placenta of this frightening phenomenon. Its money has financed it; its native terrorists promote it; and its own unhappy citizenry is either amused by or indifferent to its effects upon the world. Surely it has occurred to more than a few Americans that without a petroleum-rich Wahhabism, the support for such international killers and the considerable degree of ongoing aid to those who would destroy the West would radically diminish.

Finally, Saudi Arabia has shown an increasingly disturbing tendency to interfere in the domestic affairs of the United States, both in religious and political matters. Whereas our female soldiers, who are in the Arabian desert to preserve the power of the sheiks, cannot walk about unveiled, their hosts show no such cultural inhibitions when here in America. Right after September 11, the FBI was asked by the monarchy to help whisk away members of the bin Laden family from the Boston area to find sanctuary back home. Any government that can request—and promptly receive—federal help for the family of a terrorist, whose operatives, 75 percent of them Saudis, had hours earlier vaporized three thousand American civilians, has too much confidence in its clout with the United States government.

Saudi television commercials seeking to influence American public opinion are now nightly fare. Thousands of Saudi students are politically active on American campuses. Local imams reflect the extreme and often anti-American views of senior Muslim clerics who channel the biggest subsidies from the Middle East. Saudi Arabia's cash infusions to Muslim communities in America ensure that Wahhabi fundamentalism takes hold among Arab guests living in the United States. As Daniel Pipes has tirelessly documented in these pages, the danger to us now is not just without but within, and its ultimate address is, more often than not, Riyadh.

To sum up, all the old reasons that prevented us from breaking away from Saudi Arabia are no longer compelling. More and more, the royals' oil policy is neither pro-Western nor so crucial as it once was in determining world pricing. The present government has been an active abettor of terror, and perhaps the most virulent anti-Israeli Arab country in the region. Al Qaeda and other terrorists have received bribe money from the Saudis, without which they could not operate so effectively. That the monarchy has not been forthcoming in tracking those with ties to the September 11 murderers reflects its real worry about where such investigations might lead. And Saudi cash has been a force for radicalism right here in the United States, casting into doubt the legitimacy and purpose of almost every Islamic charity now operating within our borders. Nor should we forget that no country in the world is more hostile to the American ideas of religious tolerance, free speech, constitutional government, and sexual equality.

Can the United States, then, revamp its policy toward Saudi Arabia, perhaps to conform with our stance toward similarly belligerent regimes like Libya or Syria? The beginning of wisdom is to acknowledge that such an about-face would hardly be easy—if for no other reason than that many of the royal family are close friends of powerful Americans in the oil and defense industries, on university campuses, and within government. Their pedigree stretches back to the likes of Clark Clifford, Spiro Agnew, and Richard Helms in the days when ARAMCO used to lobby to prevent American TV networks from broadcasting such delicacies as the 1979 film *Death of a Princess* (a surreal chronicle of the public execution of a royal Saudi princess and the beheading of her lover on charges of fornication).

Moreover, most elite Saudis here in America are longtime residents, generous hosts, and superficially friendly. They tend to be adept at American-style public relations, whether emerging in coats and ties for interviews, receptions, and political galas or time-traveling back to the ancient netherworld of flowing robes and headdress when negotiations toughen. The few American journalists who bring up the sordid side of Saudi behavior usually appear gratuitously rude to guests who come across as sensitive, hurt, and in full denial.

But the point of any attempt to change our relationship is not so much to punish the Saudis for past hostility and duplicity as to create a landscape for real revolution in the Middle East—a reordering that might in its turn prevent a future clash of civilizations. Such an attempt must be made with no illusions that we have any real control over distant events, and with full recognition of the impracticability of growing democracy in a culture without the soil of tolerance or a middle class. *Are* there Saudi dissidents who are committed to democracy and can stand up to Wahhabi madness? Our task is to find them, or help to create them, and then to aid them all.

This will sound like a mission impossible, but consider: American businessmen may find the royal family hospitable (over $300 billion in arms sales since the 1991 Gulf War), but most foreign workers in the kingdom mistrust their employers; most Arabs elsewhere resent the abject corruption and conspicuous consumption of the House of Saud; and most Saudis themselves would be happy to see the pampered princes go—some, admittedly, in exchange for Islamist clerics, but others for any consensual government that could end the present kleptocracy. Besides, while we are pursuing this long-term goal, there are steps that could and should be taken in the meantime.

One of them is to recalibrate our oil policy, encouraging— with loans, joint pipeline ventures, and long-term contracts— exploration in Russia and elsewhere in the former Soviet Union. Not only would such suppliers increase the pool of the world's oil and gas, and thereby lessen Saudi influence, but at least in the case of Russia we would be buying from a struggling democracy rather than from a small elite already as rich as many of its own silenced people are poor. And, speaking of energy, there are things to be done on the home front as well: conservatives might withhold their opposition to government-mandated efficiency standards for new cars and trucks, liberals their opposition to Arctic oil drilling.

Another interim but absolutely crucial step is the seemingly peripheral matter of dealing with Iraq. In a world where our enemies are perfectly prepared to blow up our buildings and murder our civilians at work, we can no longer tolerate the continuance of a mad regime with interest in poison gas and potential nukes. Iraq is significant, moreover, not just for the evil that it is today but for the good that it might represent tomorrow. Once freed from Saddam Hussein, its rather prosperous and secular people could help change the moral balance of the Middle East, immediately posing a challenge to Saudi Arabia, Kuwait, and the other Gulf states. Not only would a liberated Iraq become a friendly oil producer, but its very existence would raise a host of fruitfully embarrassing questions about such matters as why there need be American troops in Saudi Arabia at all, and against whom those troops are defending the sheiks if not their own people.

What the United States should strive for in the Middle East is *not* tired normality—the sclerosis that led to September 11, the Palestinian quagmire, and an Iraq full of weapons of mass destruction. Insisting on adherence to the same old relationship is akin to supporting a tottering Soviet Gorbachev instead of an emerging Russian Yeltsin, or lamenting the bold new world ushered in by the fall of the Berlin Wall—a radical upheaval that critics once said was too abrupt and perilous given the decades of dehumanizing Soviet tyranny, the inexperience of East European dissidents, and the absence of a Westernized middle class. Wiser observers have long argued that where governments hate us most, the people tend to like us more, sensing that we at least oppose those who bring them misery.

Only by seeking to spark disequilibrium, if not outright chaos, do we stand a chance of ridding the world of the likes of bin Laden, Arafat, and Saddam Hussein. Just as a reconstituted Afghanistan eliminated the satanic Taliban and turned the region's worst regime into a government with real potential, so, too, a new Iraq might start the fall of dominoes in the Gulf that could wipe away the entire foul nest behind September 11.

Even should fundamental changes go wrong in Saudi Arabia, the worst that could happen would not be much worse than what we have now—thousands of our citizens dead, a crater in New York, millions put out of work, Israelis blown up weekly, and almost a half-billion people in the Arab world unfree, hungry, illiterate, and informed by the perpetrators of evil that America and Israel are at fault. As a student said to me shortly after September 11, "What are we afraid of? Are they going to blow up the World Trade Center with thousands in it?"

Written in July and published in
the July 2002 issue of COMMENTARY *magazine.*

9

Middle East Tragedies

PRESSING AHEAD IS OUR ONLY CHOICE

The images are jarring, the hypocrisies appalling, the rhetoric repulsive. Only in the Arab Middle East—and the Islamic world in general—are suicide-murderers operating and indeed canonized, even blessed with cash bonuses. An inveterate liar like the Iraqi information minister Mohammed Saeed al-Sahaf is lauded for his defense of a mass killer like Saddam Hussein—and at last lampooned *not* on moral grounds, but because his yarns about thousands of dead Marines are finally exposed by the sound of American tanks rumbling his way. The last gassings in the modern world—Nasser's in Yemen and Saddam's in Kurdistan and Iran—were all Mideastern; so are promises of virgins in exchange for bombing women and children.

Pick up any newspaper and the day's bombings, killings, and terror are most likely to have occurred somewhere in the Islamic world. The big, silly lie—Jews caused 9/11, the United States used atomic weapons against Iraq, Americans bombed mosques—has been a staple of Middle East popular culture. The hatred of Jews is open, unapologetic, and mostly unrivaled on the world stage since the Third Reich.

I think the American street—and as we have learned in the case of anger toward the French, there surely is such a thing—has finally thrown up its hands with Arab ingratitude. Egyptian, Jordanian, and Palestinian recipients of billions of dollars in American aid routinely reply by trashing the United States, whether in the street, through government publications, or via public declarations in Arab and European capitals.

In embarrassed response, we are tossed the old bone by their corrupt leaders—"Ignore what we say publicly and look instead privately at what we do." Arab apologists claim that if we Americans back off from the only democracy in the region we would win back good graces in the Middle East; but we know that such perfidy toward Israel would only win us contempt, as we would be shown to be not merely opportunistic but weak and scared into the bargain as well.

Shiites, once murdered en masse by Saddam Hussein, now turn on the American and British liberators who alone in the world could do what they could not. Iraqis, freed by us from their own homegrown murderers, in thanks now blame us for not stopping them from robbing themselves. Our citizens are routinely blown to pieces in Saudi Arabia or shot down in Jordan, even as we are told that Americans, after losing three thousand of their citizens to Islamist killers, are not being nice to Arab students and visitors because we require security checks on them and occasionally tail those with suspicious backgrounds who overstayed their visas. Egyptians march and shout threats to America and the West—and then whine that thousands in Cairo and Luxor are out of work because most over here take them seriously and choose to pass on having such unhinged people escort them around the pyramids and the Valley of the Kings. Have all these people gone mad?

The world is watching all this, and it is not pretty. After talking to a variety of foreigners who do not necessarily share the

American point of view, I conclude that South Americans, Europeans, Asians, and Africans don't much like what they see in the Middle East—and blame those over there, not us, for the old mess.

The general causes of these Middle Eastern pathologies have been well diagnosed since September 11 ad nauseam. The Arab world has no real consensual governments; statism and tribalism hamper market economics and ensure stagnation. Sexual apartheid, Islamic fundamentalism, the absence of an independent judiciary, and a censored press all do their part to ensure endemic poverty, rampant corruption, and rising resentment among an exploding population. Siesta for millions is a time not for napping between office hours, but for weaving conspiracies over backgammon.

Class, family, money, and connections—rarely merit—bring social advancement and prized jobs. The trickle-down of oil money masks the generic failure for a while but ultimately undermines diversification and sound development in the economy—as well as accentuating a crass inequality. Autocracies forge a devil's bargain with radical Islamists and their epigones of terrorist killers, from al Qaeda to Hezbollah, to deflect their efforts away from Arab regimes and onto Americans and Israelis. All the talk of a once-glorious Baghdad, an Arab Renaissance in the thirteenth century, or a few Aristotelian texts kept alive in Arabic still cannot hide the present dismal reality—and indeed is being forgotten because of it.

Millions in the Arab street now enjoy merely the patina of Western culture—everything from cell phones, the Internet, and videos—but without either the freedom or material security that create the conditions that produce these and thousands of other such appurtenances. The result is that appetites and frustrations alike arise faster than they can be satisfied with available wealth—or constrained by the strictures of traditional and ever-more-fanatical Islam. Americans now accept all this and snicker at the old Marxist and neocolonialist exegeses that claim that the British, the Americans, the French—or little green men on Mars—are responsible for the Middle East mess.

Illegitimate governments—whether Arab theocracies, monarchies, dictatorships, or corrupt oligarchies—rely on state police and their labyrinth of torture and random execution to stifle dissent. Filtered popular frustration is directed toward Israel and the United States—as the martyrs of the West Bank are the salve for anger over everything from dirty water to expensive food. Millions of Muslims collectively murdered by Saddam Hussein, Milosevic, the Taliban, the Assads, Qaddafi, and an array of autocrats from Algeria to the Gulf seem to count as nothing. Persecuted and often stateless Muslims without a home in Kurdistan or Bosnia gain little sympathy—unless the Jews can be blamed. It is not who is killed, nor how many—but by whom: one protester in the West Bank mistakenly shot by the IDF earns more wrath in the Arab calculus than ten thousand butchered by Saddam Hussein or the elder Assad.

Before 9/11, the West, in a variety of ways, had been complicit in all this tragedy, and either ignored the alarming symptoms or, worse still, aided and abetted the disease. Oil companies and defense contractors winked at bribery and knew well enough that the weapons and toys they sold to despots only impoverished these sick nations and brought the *Dies Irae* ever closer. "If we don't, the French surely will" was the mantra when bribery, Israeli boycotts, and questionable weapons sales were requisite for megaprofits.

Paleolithic diplomats—as if the professed anticommunism of the old Cold War still justified support for authoritarians—were quiet about almost everything from Saudi blackmail payments to terrorists and beheadings to mass jailings, random murder, and disfigurement of women. Political appeasement—from Reagan's failure to hit the Bekka Valley after the slaughter of U.S. Marines, to Clinton's pathetic responses to murdered diplomats, bombings, and the leveling of embassies—only emboldened Arab killers.

Judging magnanimity as decadence, the half-educated in al Qaeda embraced pseudo-Spenglerian theories of a soft and decadent West unable to tear itself away from thong-watching and Sunday football. Largesse in the halls of power in New York and

Washington played a contemptible role, too—as ex-ambassadors, retired generals, and revolving-door lawyers created fancy names, titles, and institutes to conceal what was really Gulf money thrown on the table for American influence.

On the left, multiculturalists and postcolonial theorists were even worse, promulgating the relativist argument that there was no real standard by which to assess Third World criminality. And by mixing a cocktail of colonial guilt and advocacy about the soi-disant "other," they helped to create a politically correct climate that left us ill prepared for the hatred of the madrasahs. Arab monsters like Saddam Hussein sensed that there would always be useful idiots in the West to march on their behalf if it came to a choice between a Third World killer and a democratic United States. More fools in the universities alleged that oppression, exploitation, and inequality alone caused Arab anger—even as well-off, educated, and pampered momma's boys like Mohamed Atta pulled out their Korans, put on headbands, and then blew us and themselves to smithereens, still babbling about unclean women in the last hours before their rendezvous in Hell.

So the general symptomology, diagnosis, and bleak prognosis of this illness in the Middle East are now more or less agreed upon; the treatment, however, is not. Arab intellectuals—long corrupted by complicity with criminal regimes, and perennial critics of American foreign policy—now suddenly look askance at democracy, if jump-started by the United States. American academics, who once decried our support for the agents of oppression, now decry our efforts to remove them and allow something better.

What in God's name, then, are we to do with this nonsense?

We seek military action and democratic reform hand-in-glove to end Islamic rogue states and terrorist enclaves—not because such audacious measures are our first option (appeasement, neglect, and complicity in the past were preferable), but because they are the last. Go ahead and argue over the improbability of democracy in the Middle East. Reckon the horrendous costs and unending commitment. Cite the improper parallels with Germany and

Japan until you are blue in the face. Stammer on that Baghdad will never be a New England town hall.

Maybe, maybe not. But at least consider the alternatives.

Hitting and then running? Did that in Iraq in 1991—and Shiites and Kurds hated us before dying in droves; Kuwaitis soon forgot our sacrifice, and we spent $30 billion and 350,000 air sorties to patrol the desert skies for twelve years. Afghans gave no praise for our help in routing the Soviets, but plenty of blame for leaving when the threat was over. Establish bases and forget nation-building? Did that too once, everywhere from Libya to Saudi Arabia, and we still got a madman in Tripoli and 60,000 royal third cousins in Riyadh.

Turn the other cheek and say, "What's a few American volunteers killed in Lebanon or the Sudan when the stock market is booming and Starbucks is sprouting up everywhere?" Did that also, and we got 9/11.

Pour in money? Did that for a quarter-century; but I don't see that the street in Amman or Cairo is much appreciative about freebies, from tons of American wheat to Abrams tanks.

Get tough with Israel? Taking thirty-nine Scuds, pulling out of Lebanon, offering 97 percent of the West Bank, and putting up with Oslo got them the intifada and female suicide bombers.

The fact is that the *only* alternative after September 11 was the messy, dirty, easily caricatured path that Mr. Bush has taken us down. For all the reoccurring troubles in Afghanistan, for all the looting and lawlessness in the month after the brilliant military victory in Iraq, and for all the recent explosions in restaurants, synagogues, and hotels—we are still making real progress.

Two years ago the most awful regimes since Hitler's Germany were the Taliban and the Hussein despotism. Both are now gone, and something better will yet emerge in their place. The American military has not proven merely lethal, but unpredictable and a little crazy into the bargain.

Two years ago the world's most deadly agent was an Arab terrorist; now it is an American with a laptop and an F-18 circling above with a pod of GPS bombs.

Two years ago nuts in caves talked about Americans who were scared to fight; now the world is worried because we fight too quickly and too well. There are no more videos of Osama bin Laden strutting with his cell phone trailing sycophantic psychopaths. Yasser Arafat is no longer lord of the Lincoln bedroom, but shuffles around his own self-created moonscape.

Two years ago Syria and Lebanon were considered sacrosanct hideouts that we dared not enter, or so a sapling ophthalmologist from Syria threatened us. Today we tell the custodians of terror there to clean it up or we will—and assume that eventually we must.

Two years ago—and I speak from experience—faulting our corrupt relationship with Saudi Arabia brought mostly abuse from hacks in suits and ties in Washington and New York; now defending that status quo is more likely to incur public odium.

Two years ago the Cassandra-like trio of Bernard Lewis, Daniel Pipes, and Fouad Ajami were considered outcasts by disingenuous but influential Middle Eastern Studies departments; now they, not the poseurs in university lounges and academic conferences, are heeded by presidents and prime ministers.

No, we are making progress because we have sized up the problem, know the solution, and have the guts to press ahead. No one claimed all this would be easy or welcome. But like Roman senators of old with each hand on a fold of the toga, we offer choices. We hope that there are still enough people of goodwill and sobriety in the Middle East to rid themselves of the terrorist killers, and thus select a freely offered, Western-style democracy over the First Marine Division, a thousand-plane sky, and some thirty acres of floating tarmac.

Written on April 21 and published in
NATIONAL REVIEW ONLINE *on April 23, 2003.*

III

SUPPORTING ISRAEL?

Poor Israel. Its enemies, like ours, employ suicide murdering, are often fueled by Islamic fundamentalism, and do not embrace freedom, democracy, or an equality of the sexes. And yet Israel's shared Western heritage often did not win it support in Europe and/or even at times in the United States. In fact, the opposite was true. Precisely because it was a Westernized power it exercised economic and military influence otherwise not explicable by its small population and territory—and thus won disdain rather than respect as an overdog, a postcolonial power, an American surrogate, or a modern-day Crusader state. Indeed, its very reservoir of strength seemed to allow some critics who wished to win Arab approval the luxury of advocating unrealistic policies that would hurt but, they felt, not necessarily destroy Israel.

The hostility shown Israel by its enemies seemed explicable not simply by disputes over land but also by the Arab world's unfree nature: state-controlled media focused on "the Jews" and "the Zionist entity," rather than the failure of inept and corrupt governments to account to a captive people why its own standard of living was so dismal. But what explains why its so-called friends in Europe were suddenly so hostile, especially in a post-9/11 landscape that made all states especially wary of any society that embraced suicide murdering?

And, finally, why did the United States, which correctly saw that there was no reasoning with an autocratic theocracy in Afghanistan or maniacal dictatorship in Iraq believe that Israel should adopt an opposite course in dealing with someone like

Yasser Arafat? Being "either with us or with the terrorists" did not always seem to quite apply when it was a question of the Middle East "peace process."

A recurrent theme of these essays was not merely that support for Israel made strategic and practical sense, but that it was also a moral referendum on ourselves, especially when the population, oil, and terrorism so characteristic of the Middle East called for a more cynical reexamination of American national interest.

10

‹✦≡◉〓✦›

Why Support Israel?

IT WOULD CERTAINLY BE EASIER NOT TO

The Muslim world is mystified as to why Americans support the existence of Israel. Some critics in the Middle East excuse "the American people," while castigating our government. In their eyes, our official policy could not really reflect grassroots opinion. Others misinformed spin elaborate conspiracy theories involving the power of joint Mossad-CIA plots, Old Testament fundamentalists, international bankers, and Jewish control of Hollywood, the media, and the U.S. Congress. But why does an overwhelming majority of Americans (according to most polls, between 60 and 70 percent of the electorate) support Israel—and more rather than less so after September 11?

The answer is found in values, not in brainwashing or because of innate affinity for a particular race or creed. Israel is a democracy. Its opponents are not. Much misinformation abounds on this issue. Libya, Syria, and Iraq are dictatorships, far more brutal than even those in Egypt or Pakistan. But even "parliaments" in Iran,

Morocco, Jordan, and on the West Bank are not truly and freely democratic. In all of them, candidates are either screened, preselected, or under coercion. Daily television and newspapers are subject to restrictions and censorship; "elected" leaders are not open to public audit and censure. There is a reason, after all, why in the last decade Americans have dealt with Messrs. Netanyahu, Barak, and Sharon—and no one other than Mr. Arafat, the Husseins in Jordan, the Assads in Syria, Mr. Mubarak, and who knows what in Lebanon, Algeria, and Afghanistan. Death, not voters, brings changes of rule in the Arab world.

The Arab street pronounces that it is the responsibility of the United States—which gives money to Egypt, Palestine, Jordan, Afghanistan, and others, has troops stationed in the Gulf, and buys oil from the Muslim world—to use its influence to instill democracies. They forget that sadly these days we rarely have such power to engineer sweeping constitutional reform; that true freedom requires the blood and courage of native patriots—a Washington, Jefferson, or Thomas Paine—not outside nations; and that democracy demands some prior traditions of cultural tolerance, widespread literacy, and free markets. Moreover, we give Israel billions as well—but have little control whether they wish to elect a Rabin or a Sharon.

Israel is also secular. The ultra-Orthodox do not run the government unless they can garner a majority of voters. Americans have always harbored suspicion of anyone who nods violently when reading Holy Scripture, whether in madrasahs, near the Wailing Wall, or in the local Church of the Redeemer down the street. In Israel, however, Americans detect that free speech and liberality of custom and religion are more ubiquitous than, say, in Saudi Arabia, Iran, or Palestine, and so surmise that the Jewish state is more the creation of European émigrés than of indigenous Middle-Eastern fundamentalists.

Pluralism exists in Israel, rarely so in the Arabic world. We see an Israeli peace party, spirited debate between left and right, and both homegrown damnation and advocacy for the settlers outside

the 1967 borders. Judaism is fissured by a variety of splinter ortho-
doxies without gunfights. There are openly agnostic and atheistic
Israeli Jews who enjoy influence in Israeli culture and politics. In
theory, such parallels exist in the Arab world, but in actuality rarely
so. We know that heretical mullahs are heretical more often in
London, Paris, or New York—not in Teheran or among the Taliban. No Palestinian politician would go on CNN and call for Mr.
Arafat's resignation; his opposition rests among bombers, not in
raucous televised debates.

Israeli newspapers and television reflect a diversity of views,
from rabid Zionism to almost suicidal pacifism. There are Arab-
Israeli legislators and plenty of Jewish intellectuals who openly
write and broadcast in opposition to the particular government of
the day. Is that liberality ever really true in Palestine? Could a Palestinian, Egyptian, or Syrian novelist write something favorable
about Golda Meir, hostile to Mr. Assad or Mubarak, or craft a systematic satire about Islam? Past experience suggests such icono-
clasts and would-be critics might suffer stones and fatwas rather
than mere ripostes in the letters to the editor of the local newspapers. Palestinian spokesmen are quite vocal and unbridled on
American television, but most of us—who ourselves instinctively
welcome self-criticism and reflection—sense that such garrulous-
ness and freewheeling invective are reserved only for us, rarely for
Mr. Arafat's authority.

Americans also see ingenuity from Israel, both technological
and cultural—achievement that is not reflective of genes but rather
of the culture of freedom. There are thousands of brilliant and
highly educated Palestinians. But in the conditions of the Middle
East, they have little opportunity for free expression or to open a
business without government bribe or tribal payoff. The result is
that even American farmers in strange places like central California
are always amazed by drip-irrigation products, sophisticated water
pumps, and ingenious agricultural appurtenances that are created
and produced in Israel. So far we have seen few trademarked in
Algeria, Afghanistan, or Qatar.

There is also an affinity between the Israeli and Western militaries that transcends mere official exchanges and arms sales. We do not see goose-stepping soldiers in Haifa as we do in Baghdad. Nor are there in Tel Aviv hooded troops with plastic bombs strapped to their sides on parade. Nor do Israeli presidents wear plastic sunglasses, carry pistols to the UN, or have chests full of cheap and tawdry metals. Young rank-and-file Israeli men and women enjoy a familiarity among one another, and their officers are more akin to our own army than to the Republican Guard, Hamas, or Islamic Jihad.

The Israelis also far better reflect the abject lethality of the Western way of war. Here perhaps lies the greatest misunderstanding of military history on the part of the Arab world. The so-called Islamic street believes that sheer numbers and territory—a billion Muslims, a century of oil reserves, and millions of square miles—should mysteriously result in lethal armies. History teaches us that war is rarely that simple. Instead, the degree to which militaries are Westernized—technology that is a fruit of secular research, group discipline arising from consensual societies, logistical efficiency that derives from capitalism, and flexibility that is the dividend from constant public audit and private individualism—determines victory, despite disadvantages in numbers, natural resources, individual genius, or logistics.

We hear a quite boring refrain from enraged Palestinians of "Apache helicopters" and "F-16s." But in the Lebanese war of the early 1980s we saw what happens in dogfights between advanced Israeli and Syrian jets in the same manner Saddam's sophisticated weapons were rendered junk in days by our counterparts. So Israel's power is more the result of a system, not merely of imported hardware. The Arab world does not have a creative arms industry; Israel does—whether that be ingenious foot pads to wear while detecting mines or drone aircraft that fly at night over Mr. Arafat's house. If the Palestinians truly wished military parity, then the Arab world should create their own research programs immune to religious or political censure, and ensure that students are mastering calculus rather than the Koran.

Nor are Americans ignorant of the recent past. The United States was not a colonial power in the Middle East but developed ties there as a reaction to, not as a catalyst of, its complex history. Israel, on the contrary, was both created and abandoned by Europeans. The twentieth century taught Americans that some Europeans would annihilate millions of Jews—and others remain unwilling or unable to stop such a holocaust. We sensed that the first three wars in the Middle East were not fought to return the West Bank, but to finish off what Hitler could not. And we suspect now that, while hundreds of millions of Arabs would accept a permanent Israel inside its 1967 borders, a few million would not—and those few would not necessarily be restrained by those who did accept the Jewish state.

Somehow we in the American heartland sense that Israel—whether in its GNP, free society, or liberal press—is a wound to the psyche, not a threat to the material condition, of the Arab world. Israel did not murder the Kurds or Shiites. It does not butcher Islam's children in Algeria. Nor did it kill over a million on the Iranian-Iraqi border, much less blow apart Afghanistan, erase from the face of the earth entire villages and their living inhabitants in Syria, or turn parts of Cairo into literal sewers. Yet both the victims and the perpetrators of those crimes against Muslims answer "Israel" to every problem. But Americans, more than any people in history, live in the present and future, not the past, loathe scapegoating and the cult of victimization, and are tired of those, here and abroad, who increasingly blame others for their own self-induced pathologies.

The Europeans are quite cynical about all this. Tel Aviv, much better than Cairo or Damascus, reflects the liberal values of Paris or London. Yet the Europeans rarely these days do anything that is not calibrated in terms of gaining money or avoiding trouble—and in that sense, for them Israel is simply a very bad deal. All the sophisticated op-eds about Islamic liberalism cannot hide the fact that Europe's policy in the Middle East is based on little more than naked self-interest. If Israel were wiped out tomorrow, Europeans would ask for a brief minute of silence, then sigh relief, and without a blink roll up their sleeves to get down to trade and business.

Our seemingly idiosyncratic support for Israel, then, also says something about ourselves rather than just our ally. In brutal Realpolitik, the Europeans are right that there is nothing much to gain from aiding Israel. Helping a few million costs us the friendship of nearly a billion. An offended Israel will snub us; but some in an irate Muslim world engineered slaughter in Manhattan. Despite our periodic tiffs, we don't fear that any frenzied Israelis will hijack an American plane or murder Marines in their sleep. No Jews are screaming at us on the evening news that we give billions collectively to Mubarak, the Jordanians, and Mr. Arafat. And Israelis lack the cash reserves of Kuwait and Saudi Arabia, and they do not go on buying sprees in the United States or import whole industries from America. So the reason we each support whom we do says something about both Europe and the United States.

Instead of railing at America, Palestinians should instead see in our policy toward Israel their future hope rather than present despair—since it is based on disinterested values, which can evolve, rather than on race, religion, or language, which often cannot. If the Palestinians really wished to even the score with the Israelis in American eyes, then regular elections, a free press, an open and honest economy, and religious tolerance would do what suicide bombers and a duplicitous terrorist leader could not.

Written on February 2 and published in
NATIONAL REVIEW ONLINE *on February 4, 2002.*

11

Israel's Ajax

THE TRAGEDY OF MR. SHARON

Sophocles once wrote a magnificent play about the Greeks'
greatest fighter at Troy after Achilles—Ajax, as irreplaceable in
war as he proved expendable in peace. During the struggle for
Troy, the Greeks were often saved by the towering, clumsy "don-
key." Without the dash of a youthful, handsome Achilles or the
divine dispensation of a crafty Odysseus, Ajax battered down the
Trojans, fighting out of a sense of duty, personal honor, and perhaps a sheer love of combat.

Yet once the victory was obtained, danger past, and spoils
allotted, the more politically astute and glib heroes—like Odysseus
and the sons of Atreus—came away with all the honors and prizes.
In a fit of madness, Ajax killed himself—bewildered that the race
goes not to the swift, and the memory of men is short and of the
moment. In the increasing democratization of fifth-century B.C.
Athens, the playwright Sophocles was apparently captivated by a
few old warhorses still in his midst who had once built Athens by

blood and toil—and yet were clearly unfit for the nuances and subtleties of the duplicitous politics of the contemporary free-wheeling assembly.

Films such as *High Noon* and *Hombre* draw on elements of the classical tragic hero, the man who does society's dirty work but receives no accolades for his sacrifice—and as often as not ends up as publicly shunned as he is privately admired from a safe distance. Clint Eastwood's Dirty Harry films played on the theme of an over-the-top and often out-of-control cop who bent the rules to thwart evil as he saw it. Shane was a similar figure. The solitary and much-needed gunman saved the homesteaders from the cattle barons; yet his skill at killing murderers ensured that such a danger-ous gun-toting firebrand had no real role amid the very peace he alone had created.

Of course, Sophocles and Hollywood did not invent such fig-ures; rather, their art was modeled after the rare mavericks who occasionally come into and out of democratic cultures—men who are blunt, unsubtle, uncompromising, and deadly in their anger. William Tecumseh Sherman was such a figure. Brilliant but pur-posely uncouth, his fiery rhetoric ("I can make this march, and make Georgia howl") and brutal marches terrified enemies, fright-ened his superiors, ended the war—and earned him eternal hatred for saving far more lives than he took.

It was probably fortuitous that the undiplomatic Patton died in December 1945, after his work at destroying Nazi Germany was done—but before his lunatic fire-and-brimstone clichés repelled the country he had helped save. His boasts that his GIs would "cut up" "Krouts" played well during the war. But after his enemies were vanquished, the media increasingly found his rhetoric dated—if not downright inflammatory in peacetime.

Others as raw come to mind—Arthur "Bomber" Harris and Curtis LeMay. The former resurrected a morbid British Bomber Command, burned down Hamburg and Dresden, helped to wreck the German economy, and was lauded during the conflict for the outright carnage he inflicted on England's fascist enemies, who were butchering thousands each day of the war. After 1945 it was a different story. The portly general was quietly ostracized during the peace as more an unpleasant Neanderthal with the blood of children on his hands than the king's valiant warrior.

Over his long career, Curtis LeMay said ghastly things ("We're going to bomb them back into the Stone Age")—and sometimes did the same. Taking his magnificently designed, high-tech B-29s down from a safe 30,000 feet to firebomb at low levels, he dropped leaflets of warning and then burned down Japan's major cities—in the "collateral" damage killing innocent civilians, combatants, and factory workers alike indiscriminately, as well as wrecking Japanese communications, rail works, and storage facilities. During the war he was seen as a genius who saved millions of lives who would have been lost in the anticipated and much-dreaded long land war against a fully armed and stocked pristine Japan—a dictatorship whose cititzen munitions workers were abetting the killing of thousands of American soldiers in the Pacific and far more innocents in China, Korea, and the Philippines. In peace, the cigar-chomping LeMay became the model for the repugnant and mad General Buck Turgidson of Stanley Kubrick's *Doctor Strangelove,* who bragged of Armageddon ("only ten to twenty million Americans killed, tops").

Ariel Sharon is a similar figure. His past is checkered. Critics cite his negligence in not restraining Lebanese militias from massacring Palestinians. His former opposition to peace accords has emboldened settlers and given encouragement to dangerous zealots and radicals. Opponents remember all that and more—forgetting that in 1967, and especially 1973, his service to Israel was heroic and lifesaving. Five years ago no sane person in Israel imagined that the widowed, obese, sweating, blunt-speaking, untelegenic bulldog would ever be prime minister; five years from now no sane person will ever quite believe he actually was. But now? At this moment of Israel's greatest peril? Israel is lucky to have the likes of him—one last time.

Without Israeli retaliation, Saddam Hussein rained Scuds into Tel Aviv to the cheers of Palestinians (who apparently hoped their payloads were gas-laden, as promised); the unilateral withdrawal from Lebanon brought not the hoped-for peace but the shelling of Israel proper; and the giveaway at Camp David offered almost all of the West Bank and instead sired the intifada—all that implanted the impression to many in the region not that Israel was magnanimous but, rather, tired, dispirited, and ready to call it quits. And so the utopians, peacemakers, and conciliators, for all their forbearance, got the murder-bombers—planned deliberately after Camp David, but blamed on Mr. Sharon's single visit to the Temple Mount.

Despite being besieged by murder-bombers and hounded by the Europeans, the United Nations, and many in our State Department, Mr. Sharon nevertheless did what all such gunslingers do. He said "No more," and plowed into the West Bank to hunt down, kill, or capture the culprits. He barked out that he probably should have had Arafat shot years ago. He promised to bring a terrible retribution to the West Bank, which harbored, cheered, and aided killer-bombers. He said all that and more—without makeup, scripts, or damage-control spinners and handlers.

Yet the reality was that his soldiers were far more humane than the Russians, who blew up entire neighborhoods in Chechnya. His men probably killed fewer civilians than did our outnumbered and trapped heroes in Mogadishu. Unlike the Kuwaitis, Sharon did not ethnically cleanse Palestinians; unlike the Jordanians, he did not murder them in the thousands; unlike the Syrians, he did not wipe out an entire town and pave it over; and, of course, unlike the Arab heroes, Nasser and Saddam Hussein, he did not gas civilians.

No, he sent combatants house-to-house, to pry out killers from booby-trapped parlors, into narrow streets where gunmen shot and then ducked into living rooms. No matter—he was Mr. Sharon and his soldiers were Israelis, and so the world damned this new Sherman come alive. A corrupt international community that ignored thousands who were beheaded, incinerated, and blown apart in the Congo, Bosnia, India, and Rwanda has demonized him for a "massacre" in which less than a hundred Palestinians were killed in efforts to apprehend the murderers among them.

Sharon expected all that condemnation and worse, but cared little, knowing that his duty and his proper role, at this time and at this moment, were to reestablish the first principle of Israel's existence: attacks on the Jewish state will invoke reprisals of such magnitude that no one will dare again murder or maim its citizens in peace. The world believes he is a little mad; but the world also trusts that when the murder-bombing starts up again, he will go back in to root out murderers and make clear to their supporters, both tacit and open, the bitter wages of sanctioning mass killing.

Pessimists now claim that the situation in the Middle East is the worse for "Mr. Sharon's War." Pundits proclaim nightly on the purported Sharon "fixation" and "feud" with Mr. Arafat. Again, the weary warrior is an easy target of the blow-dried, chattering classes—aged, plodding, with heavily accented English, in poor health, and solitary. Indeed, Sharon seems to belong better with a shovel and wading boots on his farm, or astride a tank, than trying to conduct a press conference in a cheap blazer with an ample belly.

Yet the truth we dare not speak is that had not Mr. Sharon acted, we would have seen another hundred or so suicide bombings by now, hundreds more blown-up Jews, the increasingly frightening reality that Israel would not or could not act—and a corrupt international community's sigh, about butchered Israelis, that "perhaps it had to come to this." Due to Mr. Sharon's resolve, his absolute disdain for the amoral posturing of European statesmen (who really do have the blood of Bosnians and Kosovars on their hands), his unconcern for the venom of the Arab world, and the irritation of the United States, Israel is more, not less, safe; and peace for all concerned is more, not less, likely.

Now in his mid-seventies, Sharon will be lucky to get six months of retirement back on his farm for his trouble. When he goes, Americans will sigh with relief. Most Israelis will learn that peacemaking will come easier for his absence. The Europeans, in time, will be wily enough to say, "Sharon did it, not the Israelis." And so in his lifetime, Mr. Sharon will get no credit and much blame. At home most of his rivals who follow him to craft a peace will soon conclude that "Sharon was right, but his methods were not nuanced"; the best he can hope for abroad is something like, "Well, the Palestinians asked for Sharon when they started murdering women and children."

No one will admit that Sharon's war-making was necessary to save lives and establish peace, and far more humane than the fighting that is characteristic of the Russian, Indian, and Pakistani armies—and all the Arab militaries, without exception. You see, Sharon is an Ajax. And all we "civilized" and "sophisticated" armchair critics can find personal redemption and smug self-righteousness in demonizing such men—but only when their necessary work is done and we are no longer being blown to bits.

Written on April 21 and published in
NATIONAL REVIEW ONLINE *on April 23, 2002.*

12

<hr/>

On Hating Israel

What We Know but Can't Say Out Loud

Europe, the United Nations, many elites in America, and, of course, the entire Arab and Islamic worlds, are against Israel. Their venom arises from three pretexts.

1. Occupation?

Israel purportedly occupies land that is not theirs, a travesty said to be wholly unique on the world stage, and so deserving of special and universal condemnation. Yet, *contra* the Palestinians' constant lament, there is a great deal of occupied territory in the world today—tragedies that completely evade the moral radar of the United Nations and are unimportant to any of the self-proclaimed moralists of the Arab world.

Since 1974, a good part of Greek Cyprus has been under Turkish control, the homes and property of the Greek-speaking Cypriots confiscated, the native population expelled, and the island partitioned. The entire country of Tibet has been annexed by China, quite illegally and without much complaint from any besides a few in the United States.

What happened to Lebanon? The Syrians have occupied the entire country, where Palestinians find themselves helots and the Lebanese themselves are little more than butlers to their Syrian overlords. Kurdistan is the property of three different countries; the Balkans are a mess with literally millions of ethnic Slavs, Albanians, Serbs, and Greeks living in lands controlled by others. A quarter million, not three thousand, have died there in the last fifteen years. What gives Russia the right to hang on to Japanese islands they confiscated in the closing weeks of World War II? Terrorist organizations—similar to Hamas and Hezbollah—in Ireland and Spain seek similarly to blow people up to claim for themselves an autonomous and hereditary homeland.

What is different in many of these cases is that the Tibetans did *not* try to invade China on three occasions. Greek Cypriots did *not,* in a series of wars, try to push all the Turks into the Mediterranean. Nor did the Lebanese seek to storm Amman, lose a war against Syria, and thereby lose the autonomy of their homeland. Clearly there is something else going on in Palestine besides the world's moral indignation over the principle of occupied lands.

2. Borders and Refugees?

Wars have a bad history of displacing residents. I doubt whether millions of Germans will ever get back any of their land in what is now eastern France and western Poland. Thousands of Russians have been finding themselves increasingly unwanted in the Baltic states. Will Ionian Greeks—residents of the western coast of Turkey since the eleventh century B.C.—ever return to their homes after the brutal expulsions of the early 1920s? Millions of Islamic Pakistanis and Indian Hindus find themselves living in artificial countries in which they were not born.

By any fair measure of ancient or modern history, the situation in Palestine is *not* unique. Indeed, Israel is trying to be far more just to its defeated enemies than most victors—whether Turks, Poles, French, or Chinese—have been in the past. I omit questions of body counts and collateral damage. *Pace* the United Nations and the Palestine-propaganda machine, the real killing in the world today is going on in Central Africa, the Amazon basin, the former Soviet Union, and India. What is amazing is not that Palestinians have died in the fighting, but that in comparison to urban fighting in Chechnya, Mogadishu, and Panama, so few have perished. In that regard, Mr. Arafat's invocation of Leningrad or Stalingrad is as historically silly as it is obscene to the memory of those hundreds of thousands who perished on both sides in the winter of 1942–43.

3. Racism?

A constant charge—most recently and repugnantly made by a freed Mr. Arafat—is that the Israelis bear a racial grudge against the Palestinians. He has alleged that, like Nazis, Israelis seek to cleanse non-Jews from the West Bank. The UN itself for years tried to pass resolutions equating Zionism with racism. Yet by any fair measure the Israeli government is light-years ahead of the Arab world in terms of racial and religious tolerance. Privately, Arabs would concede that they are treated far better in Tel Aviv than any Jew would be now in Cairo, Baghdad, Damascus, or Amman. We do not read in the *Jerusalem Post,* as we do in the Arab dailies, that Palestinians are "monkeys" and "vampires." Nor is there a sizable literature in Israel, as there is in the Arab world, devoted to proving their enemies are subhuman. Real racism and hatred exist in this present conflict, but they are expressed almost entirely by Arabs, not Jews. Had a paper in Tel Aviv alleged that Arabs drink blood and are related to primates, the world's outrage would be second only to the moral indignation in Israel itself.

If Israel is guilty of little more than defending itself, and of not allowing its defeated adversaries their land back *until* the Jewish state is guaranteed security, what, then, really *is* at the heart of the world's hatred against the Israelis? The answer is rather transparent and can be summarized easily by five general considerations.

I. Realpolitik

We must never forget the crass self-interest of states—a trait that the Greek historians felt was at the heart of most conflicts, albeit often crudely disguised by pretexts such as "justice" and "fairness." There may be nearly half a billion Arab-speaking peoples. Millions of Islamic citizens reside now in the West. Just a few hundred miles of the Mediterranean separate Europe from medieval regimes in Libya, Algeria, and Syria. The importance of the Arab world vis-à-vis Israel, then, can be gauged in an array of cultural, economic, and political fears and opportunities—from the size of expatriate populations to profits to be made from expansive trade and enormous markets. Were Israel large—say, a nation of 400 million Jews—and the Arabs around them relatively few (perhaps 10 million), then we would see dozens of UN resolutions condemning Mr. Arafat, for everything from murdering U.S. diplomats in the past to his present complicity in ordering suicide bombings.

II. Oil

Somewhere between one-quarter and one-third of the world's oil reserves are beneath Saudi Arabia, Kuwait, and Iraq. For the next thirty years or so, Europe, the United States, and Japan must be concerned with this steady supply of imported petroleum. And while these Western economic powerhouses obviously try to seek alternative suppliers in Russia, South America, and Norway, the fact remains that for the foreseeable future, in such an interconnected global economy, Middle Eastern oil—and its unstable and unsavory caretakers—are essential to the world's economic health. We have seen various efforts by these regimes to disrupt such supplies—from Saudi Arabia's oil embargo of 1974 to Iran's bombing of tankers in the Persian Gulf to Saddam Hussein's torching of the Kuwaiti oil fields—and so realize that prejudices, internecine wars, and inexplicable feuds can at any hour incite all these autocracies. Far easier, and cheaper, to keep silent about their routine horrors, or indeed actively abet their often absurd agendas.

Moreover, the income from oil brings these dictatorships Western technological expertise and military hardware—and, hence, the sympathy of millions in the West, who depend on selling them everything from cell phones and computers to jets and drill bits. The thousands of Europeans and Americans who buy, trade, and ship crude oil can hardly risk the ire of their own benefactors. So they usually cloak their crass utilitarianism in more patriotic slogans of "national interest" and "economic security." Had Israel 25 percent of the world's oil reserves and her Arab neighbors none, the European Union would now be damning the Palestine bombers as the thugs and terrorists they are.

III. Terrorism

The majority of the world's international terrorists of the last thirty years—the very worst killers who blow up international jets, storm the Olympic Games, murder Western diplomats, invade embassies, take hostages, and vaporize civilians at work—have been in the service of radical Islamic and Arab causes. That is not to say that Japanese, Irish, Basque, Malaysian, white racist, and Armenian terrorists have not murdered frequently—only that Arab assassins have been far more likely to attack on a global scale, especially against Europe and America. Since at least the 1967 war, the world has known that supporting Israel might well result in the killing of diplomats, athletes, tourists, and soldiers in their sleep, at the office, and on vacation. In contrast, had the Mossad been murdering Frenchmen, Americans, and Germans all over the world, politicians would now be scrambling to assuage Israeli discontent and seeking to ascertain the "root causes" of such grievances.

IV. Anti-Semitism

We do not quite know why anti-Semitism persists in a supposedly educated and modern Western world at a time when assimilation, integration, and intermarriage are ever more common and a crass secularism has blurred distinctions among the major religions.

Traditional stereotypes and hatred, of course, are always passed on to each new generation; and we must never forget the power of envy that highly educated, competent, and professional Jews incur from the less gifted and less successful. Nevertheless, the current rise of anti-Semitism is quite blatant—especially the shameful blasphemy in the indiscriminate use of the words "holocaust" and "genocide," and in the sudden reappearance of swastikas next to Stars of David. I am a forty-eight-year-old Swedish-American Protestant and have expressed support for Israel for thirty years, but *never once* before had I been asked, "Are you Jewish?" This past year alone, however, that question, usually framed as an accusation, has arisen at least fifty times—along with printed and electronic invective that would make Mr. Goebbels proud.

Here we must be frank: the Arab world bears a great deal of the blame for the current new hatred. Islamic prejudice is the engine that drives European anti-Semitism. The state-run newspapers in Egypt and Saudi Arabia are no different from those in Germany in the 1930s. Saudi diplomats and religious figures unapologetically voice loathing right out of *Mein Kampf,* itself a bestseller in parts of the Arab world. The truth is that had the Palestinians been attacked and won four wars against the Israelis, and so right now found themselves occupying the State of Israel, much of the world would say, "More power to you for defeating and occupying those pesky Jews."

v. Aristocratic Guilt and the Cult of the Underdog

With few worries about hunger or drudgery, and with ever-increasing material appetites, many Westerners have used that indulgence of affluence to condemn the very culture that produces such a good life. Nihilism, cynicism, and sarcasm are the symptoms we see among our bored and guilt-ridden elite, who belittle both the capitalists who manage their wealth and the arms and backs of the purportedly crass middling classes who actually produce it.

Radical environmentalism, romantic multiculturalism, and authoritarian utopianism all reflect a rather smug idealization of the disadvantaged and of nature in the raw. Central to this creed is identification with the supposedly anti-Western world of the universal downtrodden—and, really, almost anyone or anything else in the past three centuries that has come up against the juggernaut of the dominant culture of Western industrial capitalism.

Thus, for some Westerners, it is not so much the facts of the last fifty years in the Middle East that drives their hatred of Israel. Nor the plenitude of Arabs and paucity of Israelis, nor, perhaps, even worry over the price of gas for their Volvos and SUVs—nor their fear of bombs and germs, nor envy of Jews. Rather, the Palestinians are weak and the Israelis are strong. So—like the hosts of disadvantaged in America—Mr. Arafat and his minions are deserving of injured-party status as their birthright, getting a pass from liberal censure to mouth hatred and prejudice. In turn, the Israelis—almost like white affluent Republicans in America—are thought to be so strong and confident precisely because they are exploiters, and thus are held collectively responsible for the oppression and current plight of their long-suffering "victims."

Partly Marxist, partly ignorant, and mostly naïve, these insufferable and affluent European and American leftists see their solidarity with Palestinians as inseparable from their own embarrassed personas. It is easy, cheap, and safe to right the injustices of the world by marching, shouting, and signing petitions, rather than by living among, marrying, seeing daily, or materially aiding the "other." It can all be done in a few seconds on campus, on television, or in the suburb—without any true self-introspection about what really ensures one's own rather comfortable material existence in the university, media, or government.

The truth is that Westerners' support or hatred for Israel increasingly tells us far more about ourselves than it does about the real situation in the Middle East.

Written on May 5 and published in
NATIONAL REVIEW ONLINE *on May 7, 2002.*

13

Fortress Israel?

SOMETHING THERE THAT DOESN'T LOVE A WALL

President Bush's recent speech outlined well enough the general parameters of peace: Israeli security, a new democratic government in Palestine without Mr. Arafat, return of most of the West Bank, *et al.* Whether such promised autonomy will ensure a cessation of suicide murdering in the here and now is another matter; so is the advice to seek help from the "Arab states" in helping the Palestinian people find a "constitutional framework" and "a working democracy," as well as "multi-party local elections"— inasmuch as *not a single Arab state* would itself allow such things within its own borders.

All that being said, for the time being to implement Mr. Bush's vision there first must be a mechanism to stop the suicide killers, which means either eliminating them in the West Bank or keeping them out of Israel, or both. In response to that dilemma, a little-heralded wall across the so-called Green Line is slowly taking shape, whose ultimate repercussions may be as important as the president's speech.

Walls, of course, are often dismissed as Neanderthal solutions, and have a rather dubious reputation as unworkable, even among military historians and generals alike. The fiery General George S. Patton, as his massive Third Army blasted through the Siegfried Line and romped into Germany in spring 1945, wrote: "Pacifists would do well to study the Siegfried and Maginot Line, remembering that these defenses were forced; that Troy fell; that the wall of Hadrian succumbed; that the Great Wall of China was futile. In war, the only sure defense is offense."

As in the case of André Maginot's vaunted line on the French-German border and the Great Wall of China, such linear fortifications can be bypassed or even attacked from the rear. The Spartans felt walls of all sorts had a bad effect on morale: by refusing to build fortifications around their acropolis, they claimed that for seven hundred years they had maintained an offensive ardor in their youth that provided far better security than a few stacked stones.

Modern diplomats do not like walls either. For them the problem is not that they are ineffective, but that they work too well, ending utopian hopes of eventual reunion between warring parties. They would rather gamble that changed Palestinian hearts and minds, not a bastion of concrete and wire, will save the lives of school-age Israelis.

Consequently, acrimony from almost every quarter has met the news of Israel's bold plan to fortify the so-called Green Line that more or less marks the 1967 borders. The Israelis envision an eventual 225 miles of fence—millions of dollars worth of barbed wire, ditches, occasional parapets of massive concrete, electronic sensors, obstacles, and service roads.

Depending on the wall's ultimate course, two hundred thousand settlers in Judea and Samaria may be on the wrong side of the new Fortress Israel. So is almost the entire West Bank. But instead of being delighted, the Palestinian Authority is fuming. Mr. Arafat has called the construction an "act of racism," adding that the fence is nothing less than "a fascist apartheid measure," one that he "would not accept"—all this from a leader whose media spouts unadulterated daily racism, whose government really is fascist, and who can neither accept nor reject much of anything.

The United States is also wary, on a number of grounds. We are uneasy with such a unilateral, permanent, and nonnegotiable definition of the disputed border. Our State Department feels that the fence brings a finality to the ongoing crisis that gives little hope for eventual brotherly reconciliation. Diplomats apparently seek something in Palestine like the open Canadian-American border, where Palestinians can "resume work and a normal life."

Yet given the nearly daily litany of suicide murdering, the Israeli public supports the barrier, and thus the massive construction project is likely to go ahead. What are we to make of such a crude throwback in human relations, a cordon that conjures a medieval rather than a modern acceptance of the human condition?

First, General Patton was not entirely correct in his assessment of the dismal efficacy of fortified borders. Both the Great Wall of China and Hadrian's Wall in Roman Britain were not meant as absolute lines of resistance, but rather proved often effective in channeling opposition into more defensible passes. Thus the present-day Gaza fence has more or less worked and directed suicide murderers to cross over through less fortified areas—hence the present scheme to rectify those gaps. The Athenian Long Walls tied the city to the Piraeus, and kept the port and city safe for nearly seventy years. Indeed, so fond of fortifications did the Athenians become that they later built walls and forts all over the Attic countryside in hopes of keeping out Spartan and Theban ravagers—mostly with good success. The helot city of Messene, whose extant circuits are the most impressive remains of the ancient world, was kept safe from Spartan aggression by gargantuan towers and bastions. They eventually did normalize relations with Sparta—but never tore down their vast fortifications.

Yet Israel's wall is not strictly military—in the sense of discouraging armored assaults from Jordan or Egypt through the West

Bank. It is being built instead to dissuade civilians, and thus properly must be compared to our own recent and far less impressive fixtures near San Diego. By all accounts, such barricades in California and elsewhere have been remarkably successful in reducing illegal entries—if, unfortunately, channeling aliens to the undefended but far more perilous deserts of Texas and Arizona. Whatever the complexity of evil that marked the Berlin Wall, few believe that more East Germans got out after than before its creation.

Moreover, the delicate equilibrium between assault and defense is never static. Fourth-century-B.C. catapults prompted stouter construction methods that prevailed for a while against torsion artillery until the rise of gunpowder. In turn, earthen embankments, reinforced concrete, and steel often withstood even the heaviest artillery barrages. More recently, even well-armed and -equipped individuals rarely can find success against walls outfitted with new electronic sensors, especially high-voltage fences, and macabre novel brands of razor wire. Gangs, at least for the present, are not easily breaking into American prisons to free their brethren, nor are inmates breaking out to rejoin them.

So whatever one thinks of Israel's easily caricatured and reductionist solution to suicide murdering, there is ample ancient and modern evidence to suggest that such a rampart will be mostly successful in keeping out Palestinian terrorists. The wall will not be breached by land nor subterranean assault, but only through aerial barrages. Yet the firing of such missiles and rockets will only leave the attackers vulnerable to counterstrikes from the Israeli air force. The wall will also have a powerful effect on those Arabs inside Israel, both citizens and resident aliens. The partition will make their daily intercourse with kin on the West Bank far more difficult, and so redefine—and shrink—their own universe to one of being surrounded by Jews rather than of Jews being surrounded by Arabs.

Walls, for better or worse, also bring to disputes both political and moral *clarity*—especially in the manner that they reveal exactly who wants to broach them and in what direction. The Berlin Wall and the DMZ in Korea made it clear that purportedly content

Communists wanted out of their countries more than supposedly exploited Westerners wanted in. Indeed, since a sudden attack was always more likely to come from the Communist Russian or Korean militaries, such barricades were especially revealing: it was more important for the commissars to stop refugees from leaving their own societies than it was to keep free of obstacles the very path of their own planned armored assaults.

The United States and Mexico are often criticized for sharing an ambivalent policy toward illegal immigration: the borders stayed porous as we played down our enormous appetite for unskilled aliens, while they claimed that American, not Mexican, pathology was the engine of mass flight from their beloved motherland.

But the growing fortifications in the American Southwest now reveal that at least officially the United States does not want illegal aliens to broach its borders and that Mexicans most surely do. In the same manner, the new Israeli wall has now brought a great deal of light to the heat of the Middle East. Since the contours of the fortifications probably will be not all that different from the 1967 borders, Palestinians should be rejoicing at being walled off from their hated enemies. But now we are learning that it simply is not so.

While a majority of Palestinians praise their countrymen who sneak into Israel to blow up Jewish women and children, thousands apparently also do not want such murder to result in being completely cut off from the Jewish state—the source of jobs, capital, and ideas that it turns out many Palestinians appreciate.

Mr. Arafat, whose state-run media glorifies suicide murdering more than his aides pro forma denounce it, is aghast for other reasons. With this new fence, he really will have his own private state of sorts—a land cut off from the Jews but with an open border to all his beloved Arab neighbors. His ire, rather than delight, suggests that the Palestinian Authority is parasitic on Israel: It wants an open border with a free, democratic, and economically vibrant neighbor for profit and fun—but it also needs an indefensible populace "a stone's throw away" that it can threaten and from time to time vent frustrations at due to the failure of its own corrupt government. Without accessible Jews, who is Arafat to terrorize or profit from?

The settlers are a different matter; they will soon find themselves like Roman frontiersmen in the age of Augustus on the wrong side of the Rhine or Danube. For better or worse, the Israeli government has de facto now admitted that in the not-too-distant future it can and will defend well only those citizens that reside roughly in the vicinity of the 1967 borders, ending in a blink the idea of a Greater Israel that has a right to considerable biblical lands on the West Bank. History suggests it is better to be behind rather than in front of a border wall.

So the problem with this wall is not that it won't work or solve problems, but that it may do all that and more, all too well. Consequently, expect the barricade to be damned daily even as it inches irreversibly forward.

Written on June 23 and published in
NATIONAL REVIEW ONLINE *on June 25, 2002.*

14

⊷≍⊙⊝⊷

Flunking with Flying Colors

FAILING THE MORAL TEST OF OUR TIMES

The Middle East crisis offers the world an ethical litmus test for our generation in a variety of historic ways. Legitimate arguments can arise about the proper borders between Israel and the proposed independent state of Palestine—no doubt an eventual autonomous realm of somewhere between 92 percent and 97 percent of the present West Bank.

Yet if simple land and the idea of a self-governed West Bank nation were the primary points of contention, then the dispute would have been settled long ago through reasoned negotiations. Israel, after all, for the first third of its sixty-year struggle, had nothing to do with those on the West Bank; and for the last four decades has offered them independence in exchange for recognition, peace, and normalization.

Instead, there is clear asymmetry in the conflict that even transcends the wealth and power of Israel and the relative poverty and impotence of Palestine—and also goes beyond the historical quagmire of two warring peoples juxtaposed a few miles apart. The fault line really is increasingly a moral one, and it should be evident to almost any sane observer. The government of Israel is legitimate and consensual. Thus it is far more likely to enforce agreements than its antagonists in Palestine.

Palestine, by contrast, is a Potemkin democracy, with the sham façade of elections and republicanism but the dreary reality of an uninterrupted dictatorship since its inception under the Oslo accords. Arafat's initial election was rigged, and the absence since then of a real opposition, parliamentary debate, and an independent judiciary proves that—along with the creation of a corrupt clique of hangers-on and often murderous sycophants. The nature of the Palestinian Authority in and of itself lies at the heart of the entire crisis. Of course, there are sober and responsible leaders in Palestine, but they have no chance to come to the fore through a democratic and legitimate process.

Because there is an opposition and a free media in Israel, Mr. Sharon's policies are the subject of constant scrutiny and debate—again, not so with Mr. Arafat's. When an Israeli missile goes astray and kills civilians, an elected government apologizes and the military undertakes an investigation; meanwhile the opposition party gears up to capitalize on such a blunder.

By contrast, when Palestinian murderers butcher innocent civilians in a university, ten thousand turn out in the street to cheer, and a variety of groups claim credit—all either ignored or tacitly condoned by the Palestinian Authority. Imagine the world's reaction if Jews had deliberately blown up dozens of young Palestinian students as they ate in their school cafeteria, prompting a mass demonstration of Israeli glee in the streets of Tel Aviv.

It is popular for the Palestinians to claim that the American-supplied Apaches and F-16s of the Israelis are terrorist weapons, because when the IDF hunts down suicide murderers collateral damage and unintended death often occur. But destruction that is the accidental by-product of rooting out murderers is not the same as intentionally targeting innocent civilians. That key distinction should be recognized by the world community also as one of the key moral tests of our era—as we should have learned from September 11 and its aftermath in Afghanistan.

There are a variety of other macabre differences that are now apparent as well. The mothers of Israeli pilots do not chant hymns of praise and give ecstatic interviews to the world press when they learn that their sons have bombed a residential house and by mistake killed women and children. Not so with the mothers of Hamas, Hezbollah, and other terrorist groups. For nearly two years now we have seen family members of their deceased in spooky asides praising the "martyrdom" of their murderous offspring.

Israeli peace activists and pro-Arafat Arabs are not lynched as turncoats. Dozens of suspected "collaborators" have been so executed without trial on the West Bank. Jewish children do not march in parades with plastic M-16s and helicopters strapped to their tummies; Palestinian kids have been filmed dressed up with toy explosives. Arabs are far safer walking in Israel than are Jews on the West Bank.

Should Israeli soldiers soak their bullets with rat poison, they would find themselves the target of a court martial and UN condemnation. Meanwhile, Palestinians also mix in glass, screws, and scrap metal for good measure with their toxins. Only a few rightists and extremists in Israel have maps that show the West Bank as part of a Greater Israel. In Palestine the schools and government itself issue atlases that show all of Israel absorbed by Palestine.

Besides these obvious contrasts, there is also the relationship between September 11 and the terrorists on the West Bank. Mr. Atta's crew mouthed gibberish not in similar fashion to Jewish extremists but identical to the Islamic fundamentalists who seek jihad, are promised virgins, and win popular acclaim in Arab countries for blowing apart Western civilians. No wonder Israelis mourned September 11, while many Palestinians cheered; the evil of the World Trade Center bombing resonated with the Israeli public even as it was either condoned or praised by the Palestinian street.

The history of the region should bring moral clarity as well. Wars numbers one through three were fought not over Palestine but for the elimination of the Jewish state itself. For two decades Arab countries hated Israel not because the West Bank peoples suffered under Jordanian control, but only because there were any Jews at all in the new State of Israel. Unilateral withdrawal from Lebanon did not bring praise from Hamas and Hezbollah, only contempt. Offers to turn back up to 97 percent of the West Bank were seen as foolish when an intifada could get 100 percent—or more. Iraqi ballistic missiles raining down on Tel Aviv disappointed cheering Palestinians only because they were not laced with germs or nerve gas. All this the world ignores, as it seeks in vain to fabricate a holocaust in Jenin.

For these reasons and more, the current prejudices of the United Nations and the equivocation of the Europeans, who should know better, are nauseating—and in the end simply shameful. In the latter case, the sanctimonious hedging indeed finally becomes too much and is abjectly reprehensible: Europe, after all, is the great, eternal cemetery of the Jewish people, where six million were incinerated through the evil of the Nazis and the complicity of millions of timid and opportunistic other Europeans. In almost every European city, there are no longer Jews but the ghosts and shades of the dead who surely still flutter among the simulacra of their former houses, synagogues, and streets—for the most part now expropriated or obliterated.

Europe, then, because of its own culpability in the extermination, will always have a unique moral responsibility to ensure that once more we do not see Jewish women, children, and old men machine-gunned in sealed buses or blown apart on the street because they are Jewish. The very idea that Saddam Hussein once boasted that his Israeli-bound Scuds were equipped with gas, that today's Palestinian murderers fortify their bombs with chemical poisons, that *Mein Kampf* sells well on the West Bank, and that swastikas now routinely appear at pro-Palestinian rallies *should send shivers up the collective spine of all mindful Europeans.*

But instead, we get evasion at best from the Dutch and Scandinavians, and defiled Jewish cemeteries, random violence, and warnings for Jews not to be so obviously Jewish in public in Austria, France, Germany, and Italy.

Various reasons explain this moral lapse, which—along with the world's past misguided tolerance for and appeasement of Stalin's Soviet Union and its murderous satellites in Europe and Asia—constitutes one of the great ethical failings of the last century in the West.

Oil, of course, explains much. The West has little. The Arabs who pay bounties to the families of the suicide killers have a lot.

Fear should not be underestimated. Many terrorists, whether Palestinian or fundamentalist, whether contemporary or of 1970s and 1980s vintage, found Europe hospitable, precisely because the Europeans were terrified of their threats to kill and maim—especially when they did not possess the requisite military resources to strike back abroad at the countries who sired such killers. Munich and its shameful reaction to a series of hijackings have never quite left the European mind.

Nor should we discount demography and the recent phenomenon of mass immigration from the Islamic countries into southern Europe. In democracies, politicians pay attention even to 10 percent of the electorate—especially when it is known to be mercurial and prone to violence.

Proximity is also a peripheral concern as well. Less than two hundred miles separate Europe from many millions of poor and angry would-be emigrants, who often on arrival and in frustration fan hatred for the very West they so desperately seek to live in.

Because Europe is militarily weak but culturally influential it has put much of its clout and capital into the United Nations, the World Court, and a host of international collective organizations that it sees as precursors to a new utopian world order. But mostly because of the collapse of the Soviet Union and Eastern Europe, it no longer sees any need to work with American interests. Consequently, its own identity and sense of purpose are tied to supporting asinine UN resolutions, to paying attention to the world's lawyers and activists, and to hectoring the United States, no matter how absurd the cause and how really creepy becomes the company Europeans keep. And, of course, anti-Semitism is always lurking in the background as well—the age-old resentment of the clannish Jews, the envy of their talent and material success, and the bitter religious memories that surround the birth of Christianity.

So here we have it: fear and profit, the one leading the other, argue for appeasing the Palestinian terrorists. Nothing other than principle and the burdens of history urge support for Israel in its dire hour of need. So far the Europeans have flunked the test with flying colors—and as a morality tale to guide us, we should remember that abject lapse in all the future questions that involve the Middle East.

Written on August 7 and published in
National Review Online *on August 9, 2002.*

IV

◆⟶◎⟵◆

Anti-Americanism

Throughout the escalating crisis that followed Afghanistan and led to a showdown in Iraq, there arose—or did it reawaken from a brief slumber?—a virulent anti-Americanism, here and abroad. Sometimes we could sense it in the hysterical rants dutifully broadcast on C-Span by a variety of extremist groups, or the anger evidenced by some of the organizers of peace marches, or the strange outbursts of incensed intellectuals and actors. Such feelings were often outside the current political landscape and the general give-and-take between honorable Democrats and Republicans, or even friendly admonitions from well-meaning Europeans. Instead, a certain deductive hysteria became commonplace that started with the a priori idea that whatever America did was de facto wrong. Thus a chain of events was constructed to fit such a preconceived theory: if we, in fact, won in Afghanistan, then Mr. Karzai's Afghanistan was suddenly seen as no better than the prior society under the Taliban. Proven wrong about the promised disaster to come in Iraq, critics insisted that the postbellum chaos was as pernicious as Saddam's rule. And so on.

In the following essays, I explored a number of causes for such a baffling phenomenon that belied the fact that America was acting with the support of its Congress, with unanimity within the executive branch, according to legal auspices, quite successfully against fascists in Afghanistan and Iraq—and, if polls were correct, to the great approval of the American people.

What caused such venom that went beyond reasonable debate about reasonable differences over proposed action in

Iraq? Was it simply the pastime of an out-of-touch elite who
had the leisure and affluence to engage in easy anti-Americanism, either to assuage guilt or find cheap solidarity with a distant other? Perhaps the Vietnam generation saw a Tet redux,
and felt that there was still yet time in one's twilight years to
revisit the drama and romance of the barricades—or, more
legitimately, to avoid another "quagmire." In a post–Cold
War world, without three hundred Soviet divisions a few miles
from Western Europe, was it at last time for Europe to voice its
independence in a manner impossible during the dangerous
years of Russian tanks and missiles? Or did simple envy and
jealousy also play a role: a much weaker Europe carped at the
United States in the same manner as did Mr. Bush's domestic
critics, stung by his popularity and the amazing proficiency
shown by the U.S. military—successful and popular people
and institutions so at odds with their own increasingly ignored
views?

In any case, the issue was not academic. Civilizations
that lose self-confidence and believe that their own social, political, and economic protocols are no different from, and indeed
no better than, those of their adversaries, usually erode from
within. If our own intelligentsia, media, universities, and
artists doubt the morality and efficacy of their own elected and
audited government, and indeed of American values themselves, then why should allies and neutrals have any confidence
in us either?

15

Roots of American Self-Doubt

WHY CAN NO AMERICAN SAY "WHO CARES"?

*N*ewsweek not long ago ran a story WHY DO THEY HATE US? Recently on ABC's *Nightline,* Mr. Koppel interviewed various Middle Eastern talk-show hosts and correspondents and asked earnestly why "America is not liked." CNN interviewed various Palestinian officials who warned that Americans were not popular on the West Bank.

Professors and former "experts" from the State Department write nuanced articles in *Foreign Affairs* and *The New York Review of Books* warning Americans that we must not be too smug in our success—or, God forbid, perhaps embrace "triumphalism." Europeans publish op-eds of equivocation in what students of classical Greek prose style might call the *"men/de"* antithetical mode: *"while on the one hand* it may appear so far that America has been successful . . . , *yet on the other hand* it still must not . . ."

Rarely do our scholars, pundits, and social commentators apologize for completely getting it wrong with their earlier admonitions during the last four months—misjudging the Arab street, the Afghan winter, the Northern Alliance, fighting during Ramadan, U.S. air power, etc. Instead, it is almost as if critics have been emboldened by, rather than ashamed of, their prior misdiagnoses and so have gone on to conjure up an entirely new array of neuroses.

In the midst of one of the most stunning military campaigns in the last half-century, characterized by both the daring and competence of our military, Americans are still advised to be full of doubt concerning the war ahead. We are told that we must supply legal proof that Saddam Hussein was involved in September 11. (A decade-long violation of armistice agreements is still *not* grounds for belatedly precipitating hostilities.) There is continual griping over the temporary escape of Mullah Omar and bin Laden. (Prior warnings about the quagmire of employing U.S. infantry are now replaced by blame for not using enough troops on the ground.) We read stories about the pernicious warlords in Afghanistan. (They apparently appeared post–October 7 and were not there 2,300 years ago when Alexander the Great arrived.) Some admonish America about triggering the India–Pakistan "war" (somehow we "destabilized" the region and so sparked hostilities that have a nasty habit of breaking out about every decade or so) and deplore the rubble of Kabul (the city was a Paris before the American bombers hit Taliban lines).

In September, we were bombarded with scare stories of "seven million starving Afghanis," followed in October by splashy warnings of "thousands killed in collateral damage." November gave us the hysteria that Mr. Ashcroft had usurped the Constitution as "thousands" of Middle Eastern innocents were to be hounded and sent to camps. December ushered in all sorts of shrill complaints that military tribunals had now overturned our hallowed Constitution; warlords were back on the prowl and apparently given life by the "chaos" of our bombing. January is hardly over, and we are to fret about the hoods and Valium given the al Qaeda killers in custody, more so than contemplating all the poor women and children whose brains these killers blew out in

Afghanistan or the Marines who now sleep in dirty and cold fox-
holes outside Kandahar. The hard work that we probably cannot
do—bringing all the murderers to justice in Afghanistan—we conveniently ignore, so that we can concentrate on the easy, cheap—
and meaningless—things that we can accomplish to make us feel
good—like ensuring that trained murderers are not too stressed by
sleeping outdoors for a few days amid the tropical breezes of Cuba.

It all reminds me of the local EPA monitors, who have visited
our farm on burn days to inspect whether our pruning piles have
an occasional "inorganic" wooden two-by-four in them—while
under their noses hundreds drive from town to dump illegally, and
with impunity, their TVs, household chemicals, diapers, and used
furniture in our vineyards. Lecturing and fining law-abiding farmers about silly statutes is easy and ultimately worthless; arresting
furtive dumpers of toxic materials is dirty, difficult, and sometimes
dangerous—and therefore to be avoided.

Those in the media especially seem worried that we are losing
"the public-relations war," although the Muslim world is more cut
off from the world community than at any time in the last millen-
nium. Another common theme is the supposed "unilateralism" of
the United States and our increasing "isolation" from the global
community. Yet both allies and enemies seem to be tilting toward
what they see as a very much stronger United States, more afraid
they will be left out than counted in.

Of course, constant national self-reflection and occasional
uncertainty is a tradition. Western strength and Americans in general have benefited from their trademark moderation and introspection. But what lies behind this vast chasm of reality and
perception—the distance between what most Americans know to
be true and the glumness that they hear hourly from their elites?
Why are we in such doubt, worried more about what the Muslim
world thinks of us rather than we of them? Why have we not seen
one American offer back a "Who cares?" or "Too bad."

Is it the burden of our Puritan past, the old New England idea
of continual struggle to perfection, so that with proper education

and training we might master ourselves and then show (or force) others how to be as moral as ourselves? In that view, we can never be too pure or zealous in correcting even the trivial wrongs of the world. Or, in contrast, perhaps Vietnam shattered our self-confidence, despite three subsequent decades of relative prosperity and military successes? Or is the problem confined to our elite pundits, mostly in their late forties to sixties, who reflect the ascension of the 1960s generation, so confident in their own moral compasses, so eager to attribute the world's unhappiness to the root causes of American racism, sexism, or imperialism?

Exalted income, status, and the coasts seem to be breeding grounds for hypercriticism and self-doubt. Those who hammer nails—unlike lawyers in New England or Los Angeles—have more worries each hour than the brand of mosquito repellant issued to al Qaeda terrorists in Cuba. Few from the interior of the country—working-class, rural, or even those still caught in the whirlwind of middle-class suburban life—doubt American resolve and power. They have seen our ability firsthand and are confident in what they can do themselves—whether that entails building a house in a few weeks, bringing a cotton crop in, or serving fifteen tables in a thirty-minute rush hour. Most of these Americans are distant from Europe and thus indifferent to public opinion from the Continent. Rather than making them obtuse, this isolation ensures that those in the heartland are in a sense less neurotic than those in the media, entertainment, and politics on the two coasts—hardly worried at all what a French journalist or some crazy British Socialist writes about Guantanamo Bay. People in El Paso or Des Moines don't care much whether carping Europeans visit American universities, review books, or talk glibly on international television, and instead have an instinctual confidence that the humane and competent war we have waged in Afghanistan could not be replicated by any European power.

Our most visible doubters also reveal a peculiar lack of knowledge about history—and, in particular, political, diplomatic, and military history. Does their trepidation about this war perhaps reflect the reading and educational tastes of the last two decades, when history itself was deemed a construct, a mere reflection of the power machinations of a grasping few? In this present conflict, perusal of Tacitus, Ammianus Marcellinus, Bede, Machiavelli, Gibbon, Momsen, Oman, or Prescott—or any other classic narratives of political and military history—would offer far more prescience than would anthropologists, sociologists, gender-studies gurus, or even historians who "do" social history, such as analyses of women's underwear or the story of sitcoms.

A half-century of anthropology, after all, would suggest to us that burqas and clitoridectomies are just "different" or perhaps comparable (or even superior to) Western fashion and custom. Traditional history, on the other hand, argues that women across time and space, like men, struggle to be free, not mutilated, and to be treated as equals.

But many prominent Americans and Europeans also display an even more disturbing cynical attitude toward what we are doing—which perhaps can be summed up as the arrogance of the Enlightenment. This is the idea that all man's sins, all nature's problems, and all the complexities of the cosmos can be alleviated by the god Reason, which they, almost alone, have embraced. They assume that if Americans were just properly educated and trained, then we could insist on 100 percent excellence in this war—as if all wars are between absolute good and absolute evil, rather than a perennial struggle between the far better against the far worse, in which brutality like Dresden, Hiroshima, or Tet is to be avoided but nevertheless is not uncommon.

There are plenty of dangers in this constant expression of self-doubt, along with our national obsession about the inconsequential coupled with unconcern for what is critical. We are engaged in a multifaceted and completely unpredictable war. Ours is now a high-stakes contest that will change the makeup of the current world; it requires not only all our full attention to what is important but also a degree of self-confidence in our ability and right to conduct the struggle itself. Our allies are looking to us to assure

them we have a vision for the Middle East that is better—not perfect, but better—than the conditions there now that led to three
thousand dead in America. Our enemies wax when we hesitate,
wane as we show confidence, power, and justice in our cause. And
neutrals simply watch us, gauging the right moment either to join
in or bail out, damn or praise us, release or round up terrorists.

So let us have some perspective, admit we are human, not
divine, and show self-confidence in what we know from the past,
rather than foreboding about what is unknown in the future.
Should there be a thousand traitorous Johnny Walkers in deten-
tion, the minutiae of their cases should not warrant more concern
than would the life of a single Marine; and if there should be ten
thousand terrorists detained in Cuba, I would not care as much
about all their beards being shaved off as the safety of a single
American pilot.

Written on January 23 and published in
NATIONAL REVIEW ONLINE *on January 25, 2002.*

16

⊷═◉═⊶

Misunderstanding America

WE'RE NOT THE ONES WITH THE PROBLEMS

In the last six months we have witnessed an unprecedented level of hostility voiced toward America by an array of European intellectuals, EU officials, and those in the media, from London to Rome. At a time of war we expect such enmity from our enemies in the Middle East. Americans are accustomed to such opportunistic broadsides from Cuba and China—and of course venom from the lunatic states of North Korea, Libya, Iran, and the like. Yet it is unnerving to hear constant European recriminations over everything from Guantanamo Bay and our injunction of the word "Axis" to plans to topple Saddam Hussein and preserve Israel.

As sort of an informal survey, I counted talking heads that I have listened to recently on public and cable television. In the last five weeks, I have heard eight from India, and six from Russia. All were reasonable, supported more or less the efforts of the United States to combat terrorism, and seemed genuinely to appreciate American institutions. In contrast, the last thirteen European allies

109

I saw—French officials, British journalists, and EU bureaucrats—have uniformly voiced dissatisfaction with America. In some cases they express an almost visceral dislike of the United States. Perusal of some European magazines and newspapers reveals a similar continuum of disdain.

There are two general themes to their unhappiness—apart from simple envy. First, European criticism is, without a doubt, deeply embedded in aristocratic socialism. We Americans somehow are purportedly cutthroat and exploiting in our manner of capitalism and yet manage to allow our unwashed, crass, and parochial classes to define our culture. Do they hate us for trampling upon our less fortunate—or allowing our less fortunate to trample high culture and so dominate the American landscape, from McDonald's, Wal-Mart, and Britney Spears to Oprah, NASCAR, and Jerry Springer?

Second, the Europeans also don't have a clue about America's world role—past, present, or future. And their ignorance has manifested itself in a variety of ways throughout this crisis. Everyone from Swedish relief officials to Bono whines that in proportional rather than absolute amounts of foreign aid, we Americans are tightfisted and do not give generously to the Third World countries. Forget the billions that we do hand out—and whether such blanket donations without prerequisite conditions of Westernization make countries like Egypt, Palestine, North Korea, and Pakistan worse rather than better. Instead consider that Americans, unlike Europeans, spend billions in defense that in real terms are not directly tied to the security of the United States but rather ensure global trade, tranquility, and security.

Just how much "foreign aid" is a multibillion-dollar carrier battle group worth, when it patrols the Mediterranean or the Sea of Japan and so has the effect not of stealing foreign resources but rather of ensuring that Turks and Greeks are not at war, that Koreans do not blow each other up, or that China keeps away from Taiwan and Japan? Unlike simple food or money, this type of "foreign assistance" is quite risky to its benefactors—and more likely to be resented, caricatured, or misrepresented. Sending in an air wing to Kosovo can save thousands; sending in the Red Cross or the UN, tragically, cannot. GPS bombs, not Amnesty International, are more likely to keep killers away from Big Ben and the Vatican. Should we not deploy carriers, frigates, and planes the world over, both the Europeans and the Third World would not enjoy a stable global community, but one that would either sink into the chaos of a Mogadishu, Monrovia, or Kabul, or find its stability only in the law and order of a Baghdad, Peking, or Havana.

Nor do Europeans understand that the United States is, rightly or wrongly, engaged in one of the most radical experiments in immigration and assimilation since the Irish arrival during the great famine over a century ago. We may well have eight to ten million legal and illegal immigrants from Mexico inside our borders. Here in California some cities—like my hometown and dozens nearby—have seen their populations swell to between 70 and 90 percent Hispanic immigrants. Some studies suggest 80 percent of the arrivals, in large part from Oaxaca and Michoacan, have no formal education past the eighth grade. Of all those born in Mexico who now reside in California, only 60 percent will finish high school. In the California State University system, the largest university in the world, 47 percent of all incoming students must take remedial classes.

And how has the United States dealt with millions of aliens from the Third World crossing its borders illegally? Despite the rhetoric of the race industry, it has been mostly humane in its great experiment to transform millions that had no opportunity to become literate into American naturalized suburbanites in a generation. The entire survival of our immediate neighbor Mexico is built on two assumptions: billions in cash remunerations will be sent back by its citizens living illegally in the United States, and millions of them will leave and head north rather than march en masse on Mexico City to seek redress of grievance. Taken in that context, the United States is not merely giving billions of dollars in foreign aid the world over, but in fact trying to vent the social unrest of much of Mexico and Central America—in the same way that we were the safety valve for Europe for much of the nineteenth century. Let Italy, Holland, or Austria allow ten million from Bangladesh, Nigeria, or Mexico cross their borders rather than merely send food and medicine abroad.

Europeans also have a strange way of looking at the history of the twentieth century. Just because on two occasions they have wrecked their civilization and suffered greater tragedy than we is no reason to forget the origins and remedies of those great calamities. Let us remember that Germany, Austria, France, and England almost ruined Western culture between 1914 and 1918. Only the belated entry of a million American soldiers stopped the bloodletting. Two decades later, deviant states in Italy and Germany nearly ruined the West a second time—in the process executing six million of Europe's finest citizens. Western Europe—the bedrock states of the EU of Holland, France, and Belgium—could do little and capitulated in a matter of weeks. All were liberated only due to the efforts of muscular and unsophisticated Americans. I suppose that concern with Europe is why we said "Hitler first," even though it was the Japanese, not the Nazis, who had attacked us directly and were the most immediate threat.

There is no need to recount the half-century of the Cold War. Despite the shrill nonsense of Euro-Communists and Socialists, few doubt that had America not stood firm in creating NATO, the entire continent would have been conquered in the manner of Eastern Europe. Then there are the minor affairs of the Berlin Airlift and the American assurance to risk New York and Washington to stop Soviet armor from reaching Bonn and Paris, or American support for the reunification of Germany when both France and Russia were opposed. The British created Israel, and then bailed with the rest of Europe when it became clear that continued support would endanger the friendship of their former colonial subjects—now full of oil and terrorists—in the Gulf, Syria, Egypt, and Iraq. The Europeans most recently sat paralyzed in fear as 250,000 of their neighbors were butchered in the former Yugoslavia—and that was *after* Soviet tanks were being melted for scrap.

So there is a sad pattern to this sad century. We did not beg to get involved in two world wars. The Soviet Union was no threat on land to us. We didn't know much about the Middle East or the Palestinian problem or Serbia. But somehow we certainly were needed for something by someone to prevent a catastrophe.

The Europeans apparently talk only to our elites on the East Coast, who in turn apparently worry whether they are treated politely or rudely in London or Paris. But the vast majority of Americans simply could not care less. They do not think Kmart or Target are crass; they eat fast food instead of hour-long lunches because they work at hectic forty-to-fifty-hour-a-week jobs that would send much of Europe into a revolution. They are trying to assimilate millions of some of the poorest people in the planet into their culture—a far more daunting task than reuniting East and West Germany.

In this regard, Europe should pay closer attention to America's demography, as well. Some of us teach classes made up of 60 to 70 percent from immigrant students from Mexico, the Punjab, or Southeast Asia. These newcomers have scant immediate cultural or emotional ties with Europe. Even two decades ago, during the Falkands War, all my Hispanic friends in our local community were vehemently cheering on Argentina, and damning rumors of American assistance to England. By 2050, a quarter of the population will be of Hispanic heritage; perhaps another 20 percent Asian and African-American. Their view of Europe will be predicated on its attitudes in the here and now, not on a reservoir of goodwill based on a common emotional bond or ethnic heritage.

Yet in the past six months, our European allies have been frittering away almost all of America's past positive sentiments toward the Continent. After the European reaction to the aftermath of September 11, I doubt seriously whether America would wish to intervene as we did in 1999 in Kosovo. Should there be chaos in the Aegean, should there be a falling-out between Russia and Eastern Europe, should there be a missile attack on a European capital from Iran or Iraq, should China make demands on the EU, there would now be *zero* support in the United States for the use of American troops abroad. As we have seen—thanks to Europe—Article V of the NATO Charter now means little, if anything. Nor is this growing reluctance to aid Europe a return to American isolation or know-nothingism. Americans, by contrast, feel strongly about their obligations to Japan and Latin America, and their thawing relations with India and Russia.

So the problem is not with us but with the Europeans. And if the dividends of their new utopian and increasingly unfree EU are what we've seen in the present crisis, it may well be that we can only remain friends by being allies no longer.

Written on February 23 and published in
NATIONAL REVIEW ONLINE *on February 25, 2002.*

17

—⊶◦═◦⊷—

On Being Disliked

IT'S AN AMERICA THING

A number of advisory groups are now working to improve the image of the United States abroad, in particular to "get the word out" to the Arab world that America is not really the Great Satan of censored Middle Eastern media. These are important tasks, and all Americans should hope that our best and brightest can be enlisted in the effort in "global communications" to provide balanced reporting about the United States. Yet I do not think in the end even the most comprehensive and best-intended media campaign will have much effect in making such peoples fond of us—at least publicly.

The problem is not that we are imperialistic, ruthless, murderous, and oppressive toward allies and neutrals, but, in fact, mostly the opposite. We welcome rather than suppress criticism. Despite our enormous military advantages we do listen to and, as disinterested brokers, try to mediate a variety of complaints—Indians versus Pakistanis, Greeks against Turks, Spanish, and Moroccans.

Foreign critics realize that their grumbles are heard, and often published in American journals and newspapers.

Our recent interventions abroad are rarely to gain territory or lucre, but rather, as we saw from Panama to the Gulf, to put down dictators who are robbing and killing their own people and threatening neighbors to the extent that the entire stability of a region is threatened. It is hard to see how the much-criticized operations in Grenada, Haiti, Somalia, or Kosovo gained the United States much profit or valuable territory.

Coupled with these high-profile and often caricatured efforts to mediate, adjudicate, and intervene are the unique position of the American economy and the ubiquitous culture of the United States. Both are as preponderant on the world scene as are our military forces. You see today small children high-fiving one another in rural Greek villages, and University of Texas sweatshirts in the Amazon basin. Crass TV reruns of *Gilligan's Island* and *The Love Boat,* bad 1970s movies, near-pornographic fashion magazines, and the Internet—all of that and more smother indigenous culture worldwide. And this regrettable domination is not accomplished by some sinister corporate conspiracy. But much worse, it is a natural result of the very egalitarian and democratic logic of American popular culture—an insidious addiction that is designed to appeal to the widest popular audience without prerequisite education, training, or knowledge.

Our own elites whine that we have dumbed everything down to the lowest common denominator. Maybe, but the world's billions have responded by voting with their feet, pocketbook, and remote control for almost everything American. It is precisely this media and consumer tidal wave, when coupled with the omnipotence of the American military, that has an ambivalent effect on most in the world—one that plays out on the personal level absurdly as a mixture of desire for all things American together with shame for that very craving.

Martina Navratilova slurs her adopted America by suggesting it is not unlike former Communist Eastern Europe. Yet she apparently has not yet returned to even her freed country over a decade after it was liberated—largely through a half-century of dogged American opposition to murderous communism.

Thousands of Palestinians are desperately trying to immigrate to the United States, and finding it difficult since their usual route of transit, the hated Tel Aviv airport, is now closed to them. Such would-be refugees may voice overwhelming support for Saddam Hussein, celebrate the news of September 11, and in polls attest their dislike of America. Yet, given the chance, thousands would gladly move to the country they profess to despise. And why not? Where else would they have freedom to say what they please, pursue their dreams of economic security—and protest that their newly adopted country is both amoral and shortsighted in its Middle Eastern policy.

The current issue of *Journal of Palestine Studies* has a splashy ad for a new sympathetic history of Hamas—an official terrorist organization according to our own State Department. Before we get too worked up over this and its other nonsense, we should remember that the entire journal is published only through the auspices of the state-subsidized University of California Press. Critics may praise our enemies and rail against our government—but they still don't turn down help from our state-funded universities, even when the state of California is on the verge of bankruptcy. Again Palestinians profess Arab solidarity and voice anti-Americanism; yet they are not immigrating to Kuwait, which once ethnically cleansed 300,000 of them after the Gulf War, but instead seeking to open businesses in the Bronx.

I recently perused the catalogue of a University of California–Santa Barbara campus and discovered sixty-two classes in Chicano Studies with titles like "Methodology of the Oppressed"; "Racism in American History"; "Popular Barrio Culture"; "Chicano Spanish"; "Chicana Feminisms"; "Body, Culture, and Power"; and so on. Thematic in these classes is that America is a rather hateful place that has made life horrific for Hispanic immigrants. But I also live in a state where millions of undocumented aliens from Mexico reside, and millions more want in—despite the purported sins so amply documented by tenured professors. A few of our elites say America is a rather bad place; millions of poor abroad disagree and apparently instead think Mexico is.

A Greek member of parliament from the Socialist and often stridently anti-American PASOK party recently retired. The news accounts noted that she was a former Harvard professor. Such a contradiction between the life one actually lives and professes is not an anomaly when we realize that the first family of Greek anti-Americanism, the Papandreous, have a long and close relationship with the United States—one manifested over generations by them working, living, teaching, and going to school in America.

But, then, apparently Mr. Musharraf's own son also likes us. Until September 11, Mr. Musharraf had pretty much let Pakistan be overrun by murderous fundamentalists who professed undying hatred for America. One wonders if that included the city of Boston, where the younger Musharraf is employed. Even Saddam Hussein's stepson was found in the United States, and unofficial reports circulated that a few offspring of both the Taliban and the mullahs in Iran were living in America. We, of course, also remember that dozens of close family members of our archenemy Osama bin Laden lived in the Northeast. Their renegade brother pledged to kill every American on sight; did his threats apply only to passport holders or random resident strollers in Boston like his own kin?

Anti-Americanism is as deeply psychological as it is politically motivated. Many observers of the phenomenon have commented that such hostility, especially in Europe, arises out of envy and jealousy. Of course it does, but the animus is still deeper and all the more virulent because it is a war of the heart versus the head.

Professed hatred toward America for millions too often cloaks an inner desire for the very culture of freedom, material security, and comfort of the United States—like Saudis smirking over bin Laden as they push their carts in faux-American supermarkets among Pepsis and Sugar Smacks. In that regard, it all reminds me of tenured academics who send their kids to private schools, vacation in Europe, and live in tasteful tree-lined suburbs—and then in the lounge damn the very institutions that have provided their universities with such bountiful capital to make their lives so comfortable. They are perennially unhappy because what they castigate has given them everything they treasure, and they are either too weak—or too human—to confess it.

What can we do to rectify this illogical dislike of the United States? If the histories of the Athenian, Roman, and British empires—all of them far more aggressive, imperialistic, and uncompromising than us—offer guidance, not that much. If we can believe Thucydides, Tacitus, and Churchill, earlier powers accepted human nature for what it was—mercurial, emotional, contradictory, self-centered, and deeply paradoxical—then shrugged and went on with their business.

Rather than creating new programs to teach others about America, I would prefer that our government instruct Americans about the exceptional history of America, reinaugurate civic education in the schools, explain that racism, sexism, and prejudice are endemic in the human species—but under the American system of government can be identified, discussed, and then ameliorated. If we could instill in our citizens a tragic rather than therapeutic sense of the world, they would understand that utopia is not possible on this earth but that the Constitution and institutions of the United States are man's best hope for eradicating the evil and ignorance that plague us all. If we could do all that, then Americans might project a sense of self-confidence in their history and values that would admonish others that we are proud of, rather than ashamed of, being different—and that we care far more about the principles for which we fight than the applause of the day from the fickle, insecure, and mixed-up.

So, yes, we must remind the Arabs that we saved Muslims, from Afghanistan and Kosovo to Somalia and Kuwait. Yes, we must reiterate that we are at odds with dictatorial Mr. Arafat and Mr. Hussein, not with the Palestinian and Iraqi peoples, that we want democracies for them, not their land or money. And, yes, we should explain to the world why UN resolutions do not represent collective wisdom but often the reinforced biases and private agendas of dozens of autocratic, theocratic, and tribal regimes who vote only in New York, never at home. And if we are more imaginative still we can point out that the American fleet keeps the peace cheaply for others in the Pacific and Mediterranean, that American companies and universities provide the world with life-saving medicine, medical treatments, and critical technology. And so on.

But ultimately we must expect that the anger of many millions will remain, because the pathology lies unresolved and deep within them, not us.

Written on July 30 and published in
National Review Online *on August 2, 2002.*

18

I Love Iraq, Bomb Texas

With this past autumn's discussion in Washington over what to do about Iraq, there arrived also the season of protests. They were everywhere. In the national newspapers Common Cause published a full-page letter, backed by "7,000 signatories," demanding (as if it had been outlawed) a "full and open debate" before any American action against Iraq. More radical cries emanated from Not in Our Name, a nationwide "project" spearheaded by Noam Chomsky and affiliates, which likewise ran full-page advertisements in the major papers decrying America's "war without limit," organized "Days of Resistance" in New York and elsewhere, and in general made known its feeling that the United States, rather than Iraq, poses the real threat to world peace.

At one late-October march in Washington there were signs proclaiming I LOVE IRAQ, BOMB TEXAS, and depicting President Bush wearing a Hitler mustache and giving the Nazi salute. In the dock with America was, of course, Israel: on university campuses,

demands circulated to disinvest from companies doing business
with that "apartheid state"—on the premise, one supposes, that a
democratic society with an elected government and a civilian-
controlled military is demonic in a way that an autocratic cabal
sponsoring the suicide murder of civilians is not. Writers, actors,
and athletes revealed their habitual self-absorption. The novelist
Philip Roth complained that the United States since September 11
had been indulging itself in "an orgy of national narcissism,"
although he also conceded, reclaiming his title as the reigning em-
peror of aesthetic narcissism, that immediately after the fall of the
Twin Towers, New York "had become interesting again because it
was a town in crisis"—a fleeting, final benefit to connoisseurs of
literature from the death of thousands. Barbra Streisand, identify-
ing Saddam Hussein as the dictator of Iran, faxed misspelled and
incoherent but characteristically perfervid memos to congressmen,
while Ed Asner, of sitcom fame, threatened publicly to "lose his
soul" if we went into Iraq.

The Hollywood bad boy Sean Penn, not previously known for
harboring a pacifistic streak, demanded that the president cease his
bellicosity for the sake of Penn's children. Traveling abroad, the
actress Jessica Lange pertly announced: "It makes me feel ashamed
to come from the United States—it is humiliating." And the jet-
setting tennis celebrity Martina Navratilova, who fled here to
escape Communist repression and has earned millions from corporate sponsors, castigated the repressive atmosphere of her adopted
homeland, a country whose behavior is based "solely on how
much money will come out of it." And so forth. Harbingers of this
sort of derision were, of course, on view a year ago, in the period
right after September 11 and well into the campaign against the
Taliban in Afghanistan. Thus Michael Moore, currently making
the rounds plugging his movie *Bowling for Columbine,* and a sympa-
thizer of Not in Our Name, bemoaned the 9/11 terrorists' lack of
discrimination in their choice of target: "If someone did this to get
back at Bush, then they did so by killing thousands of people who
did not vote for him!" Norman Mailer, engagingly comparing the

Twin Towers to "two huge buck teeth," pronounced their ruins "more beautiful" than the buildings themselves.

In the London *Times,* the novelist Alice Walker speculated whether Osama bin Laden's "cool armor" might not be pierced by reminding him of "all the good, nonviolent things he had done." There was the well-known poet who forbade her teenage daughter to fly the American flag from their living-room window, the well-known professor who said he was more frightened by the speech of American officials than by the suicide hijackers of 9/11, and the well-known columnist who decried our "belligerently militaristic" reaction to the devastation of that day. Not all the criticism of the American response to terrorist cells and rogue governments has partaken of this order of irrationality; serious differences, responsibly aired, are also to be found, including in newspaper ads. But in the year since the slaughter of September 11, there emerged an unpleasant body of sentiment that has little or nothing to do with the issues at hand but instead reflects a profound and blanket dislike of anything the United States does at any time.

For a while, the *New Republic* kept track of this growing nonsense by Western intellectuals, professors, media celebrities, and artists under the rubric of "Idiocy Watch," and the talk-show host Bill O'Reilly is still eager to subject exemplars of it to his drill-bit method of interrogation. The phenomenon they represent has been tracked daily by Andrew Sullivan on his Web log and analyzed at greater length by, among others, William J. Bennett (in *Why We Fight*), Norman Podhoretz (in "The Return of the 'Jackal Bins,'" *Commentary,* April 2002), and Keith Windschuttle (in "The Cultural War on Western Civilization," *New Criterion,* January 2002), the last of whom offers a complete taxonomy of schools and doctrines. And yet the sheer strangeness of the overall enterprise, not to mention its recent proliferation and intensification, would seem to merit another look.

Some general truths emerge from any survey of anti-American invective in the context of the present world conflict. First, in each major event since September 11, proponents of the idea of

American iniquity and Cassandras of a richly deserved American doom have proved consistently wrong. Warnings in late September 2001 about the perils of Afghanistan—the peaks, the ice, the warring factions, Ramadan, jihad, and our fated rendezvous with the graveyard of mighty armies gone before us—faded by early November in the face of rapid and overwhelming American victory. Subsequent predictions of "millions" of Afghan children left naked and starving in the snow turned out to be equally fanciful, as did the threat of atomic annihilation from across the border in Kashmir. No sooner had that theater cooled, however, than we were being hectored with the supposed criminality of our ally Ariel Sharon. Cries of "Jeningrad" followed, to die down only with the publication of Palestinian Authority archives exposing systematic thievery, corruption, and PA-sanctioned slaughter.

During the occasional hiatus from gloomy prognostications about the Arab-Israeli conflict, we were kept informed of the new cold war that was slated to erupt on account of our cancellation of the antiballistic-missile treaty with the defunct Soviet Union; of catastrophic global warming, caused by us and triggering floods in Germany; and always of the folly of our proposed intervention in Iraq. That effort to remove a fascist dictator, we are now assured (most tediously by Anthony Lewis in *The New York Review of Books*), is destined to fail, proving instead to be a precursor to nuclear war and/or a permanently inflamed Arab "street." On the other hand, a successful campaign in Iraq, it is predicted, will serve only to promote America's worst instincts: its imperial ambition, its cultural chauvinism (a/k/a hatred of Muslims and Arabs), and its drive for economic hegemonism (a synonym for oil). Those who oppose preemption warn on Monday that the Iraqi dictator is too dangerous to attack and shrug on Tuesday that he is not dangerous enough to warrant invasion. Take your pick: easy containment or sure Armageddon.

The striking characteristic of such judgments is that they, too, are wholly at odds with the known facts. Confident forecasts of American defeat take no notice of what is the largest and best-trained military in history, and fly in the face of recent American victories in the Gulf War (where, at the time, Anthony Lewis likewise predicted quagmire and disaster) and Kosovo, both achieved at the cost of scarcely any American casualties. Alleged American hatred of Muslims hardly comports with our record of saving Kuwaitis from fascist Iraqis, Kosovars and Bosnians from Christian Serbs, or Afghans from Russian Communists and then from their own Islamist overlords, all the while providing billions of dollars in aid to Egypt, Jordan, and the Palestinian Authority. It was Jordanians and Kuwaitis, not we and not Israelis, who ethnically cleansed Palestinians; Iraqis and Egyptians, not we, who gassed Muslim populations. And it is to our shores that Muslims weary of Middle Eastern despotism are desperate to emigrate.

Is there a consistent theme here? We are talking, largely though not exclusively, about a phenomenon of the aging left of the Vietnam era and of its various progeny and heirs; and once upon a time, indeed, the anti-American reflex could be linked with some rigor to the influence of Marxism. True, that particular religion, at least in its pristine form, is just about gone from the picture these days. Some of its fumes, though, still linger in the doctrines of radical egalitarianism espoused by postmodern relativists and multiculturalists and by now is instilled, in suitably diluted and presentable form, in several generations of college and high school students. Hence, for example, the regular put-down of George W. Bush as a "Manichean"—for could anything be more self-evidently retrograde than a view of our present conflict as a war of good versus evil, or anything more simplistic than relying on such "universal" arbiters of human behavior as freedom, pluralism, and religious tolerance?

Eschewing any reference to truths of this kind, adherents of postmodernist relativism assess morality instead by the sole criterion of power: those without it deserve the ethical high ground by virtue of their very status as underdogs; those with it, at least if they are Westerners, and especially if they are Americans, are ipso facto oppressors. Israel could give over the entire West Bank, suffer ten thousand dead from suicide bombers, and apologize formally for its existence, and it would still be despised by American and

European intellectuals for being what it is—Western, prosperous, confident, and successful amid a sea of abject, self-induced failure. One is bound to point out that as a way of organizing reality, this deterministic view of the world suffers from certain fatal defects, primarily an easy susceptibility to self-contradiction.

Thus, a roguish Augusto Pinochet, who executed thousands in the name of "law and order" in Chile, is regarded as an incarnation of the devil purely by dint of his purportedly close association with the United States, while a roguish and anti-American Castro, who butchered tens of thousands in the name of "social justice" in Cuba, is courted by congressmen and ex-presidents even as Hollywood celebrities festooned with AIDS ribbons sedulously ignore the thousands of HIV-positive Cubans languishing in his camps. Kofi Annan gushes, Chamberlain-like, of Saddam Hussein, "He's a man I can do business with," while the ghosts of thousands slain by the Iraqi tyrant, many of them at his own hand, flutter nearby; for this, the soft-spoken internationalist is lionized. Few have exploited the contradictions of this amoral morality as deftly as Jimmy Carter, who can parlay with some of the world's most odious dictators and still garner praise for "reaching out" to the disadvantaged and the oppressed.

As president, Mr. Carter evidently was incapable of doing much of anything at all when tens of thousands of Ethiopians were being butchered; but as chief executive emeritus, he has managed to abet the criminal regime of North Korea in its determination to fabricate nuclear bombs and lately, having been rewarded with the Nobel Peace Prize, has brazenly attempted to thwart a sitting president's efforts to save the world from the Iraqi madman. But all such contradictions are lightly borne. Since, for our postmodern relativists and multiculturalists, there can be no real superiority of Western civilization over the available alternatives, democracy and freedom are themselves to be understood as mere "constructs," to be defined only by shifting criteria that reflect local prejudices and tastes.

Like Soviet commissars labeling their closed societies "republics" and their enslaved peoples "democratic," Saudi officials assert that their authoritarian desert monarchy is an "Islamic democ-racy"—and who are we to say them nay? ("To my ear," the *New York Times* columnist Nicholas Kristof helpfully explains, "the harsh [American] denunciations of Saudi Arabia as a terrorist state sound as unbalanced as the conspiratorial ravings of Saudi funda-mentalists themselves.") In Afghanistan, the avatars of multicultur-alism and utopian pacifism struggled with the facts of a homophobic, repressive, and icon-destroying Taliban, but emerged triumphant: according to their reigning dialectic, the Taliban still had to be understood on their own terms; only the United States could be judged, and condemned, absolutely. As for the roots of elite unhappiness with America, this is a subject unto itself. It would hardly do to reduce everything to a matter of psychology: a whole class of unhappy individuals motivated by resentment over the failure of their society to fulfill their own considerable aspira-tions. Nor does it quite satisfy to say more globally, and theoreti-cally, that they suffer at several removes from the paradoxes of the radical Enlightenment: the unquestioned belief that sweet reason alone, in the hands of its proper acolytes, and yoked to commen-surate powers of coercion, can remake the world. But we need not discount other and much simpler factors—like the law of the pack.

As in the medieval Church or among Soviet apparatchiks, the pull of group speak is always strong among compliant and oppor-tunistic elites. For today's intellectuals, professors, and artists, being on the team pays real dividends when it comes to tenure, promo-tion, publication, reviews, lecture invitations, social acceptance, and psychic reassurance. And the dividends are compound: one is a lockstep member of one's crowd and one enjoys the frisson of dis-sidence, of being at variance, but always so comfortably at vari-ance, with one's benighted fellow citizens. Our unprecedented affluence also explains much, although its role as a facilitator has been relatively scant in most discussions of anti-Americanism that I have seen. The plain fact is that civilization has never witnessed the level of wealth enjoyed by so many contemporary Americans and Europeans. Vast groups are now able to insulate themselves from the age-old struggle to obtain food, shelter, and physical security from enemies both natural and human. Obesity, not starvation, is our chief health problem; we are more worried about our 401(k) portfolios than about hostile tribes across the border. What does this have to do with the spread of anti-Americanism?

Homegrown hostility to American society and the American experiment is hardly a new phenomenon, but in the nineteenth century it tended to be limited to tiny and insulated elite circles (see the writings of Henry Adams). Now it is a calling card for tens and hundreds of thousands who share a once-rare material splendor. That brilliant trio of Roman imperial writers, Petronius, Suetonius, and Juvenal, warned about such luxus and its effects upon the elite of their era, among them cynicism, nihilism, and a smug and crippling contempt for one's own. An ancillary sort of unreality has emerged in modern Western life alongside the reduced need to use our muscles or face physical threats.

In a protected world, Saddam Hussein comes to seem little different from a familiar angry dean or a predictably moody editor, someone who can be either reasoned with or, if necessary, censured or sued. In this connection, it is not surprising that those most critical of America are not the purported victims of its supposedly rapacious capitalist system—farmworkers, car mechanics, or welders—but more often those in the arts, universities, media, and government, who have the time and leisure to contemplate utopian perfection without firsthand and daily exposure to backbreaking physical labor, unrepentant bullies, or unapologetically violent criminals. For such people, the new prosperity does not bring a greater appreciation of the culture that has produced it but rather enables a fanciful shift from thinking in the immediate and concrete to idle musings of the distant and abstract.

For many, today's affluence is also accompanied by an unprecedented sense of security. Tenure has ensured that tens of thousands of professors who work nine months a year cannot be fired for being unproductive or mediocre scholars, much less for being abject failures in the classroom. In government at every level, job security is the norm. The combination of guarantees and affluence, the joint creation of an enormous upper-middle class, breeds a dangerous unfamiliarity with how human nature really works elsewhere, outside the protected realm.

Such naïveté engenders its own array of contradictory attitudes and emotions, including guilt, hypocrisy, and envy. Among some of our new aristocrats, the realization has dawned that their own good fortune is not shared worldwide and must therefore exist at the expense of others, if not of the planet itself. This hurts terribly, at least in theory. It sends some of them to their fax machines, from where they dispatch anguished letters to *The New York Times* about the plight of distant populations. It prompts others, more principled and more honorable, to work in soup kitchens, give money to impoverished school districts, and help out less fortunate friends and family. But local charity is unheralded and also expensive, in terms of both time and money. Far easier for most to exhibit concern by signing an ostentatious petition against Israel or to assemble in Central Park: public demonstrations that cost nothing but seemingly meet the need to show to peers that one is generous, fair, caring, and compassionate. As if that were not hypocrisy enough, those who protest against global warming, against shedding blood for oil, or against the logging of the world's forests are no less likely than the rest of us to drive SUVs, walk on hardwood floors, and lounge on redwood decks. Try asking someone awash in a sea of materialism to match word with deed and actually disconnect from the opulence that is purportedly killing the world and its inhabitants.

Celebrity critics of corporate capitalism neither redistribute their wealth nor separate themselves from their multinational recording companies, film studios, and publication houses—or even insist on lower fees so that the oppressed might enjoy cheaper tickets at the multiplex. Jessica Lange and Alec Baldwin so hate George W. Bush that Lang is delighted to have an opportunity to leave America, and Baldwin threatened to leave our shores—promises, promises. An even less appetizing quality of the new privileged is their palpable and apparently unassuageable envy. Intellectuals and people in the arts are perennially surprised—no, outraged—to find that corporate managers and Rotary Club businessmen, with far less education and infinitely less taste than they, make even more money. To the guilt they feel over what they have is therefore added fury at those who not only have more but seem to enjoy it without a necessary and concomitant sense of shame. Worse yet, because America is still a plutocracy where riches and not education, ancestral pedigree, or accent bring status, it can be galling for a sensitive professor of Renaissance literature to find himself snubbed at dinner parties by his own university's president in favor of the generous but (shall we say) less subtle owner of a chain of Taco Bells. From there it is but a step to seeing the face of that same smiling and unapologetic plutocrat before him whenever he gazes upon the likeness of George W. Bush or Richard Cheney.

This brings us to another element of the new anti-Americanism. All of us seek status in accordance with what we feel we have accomplished or think we know. This naturally selfish drive is especially problematic for radical egalitarians, who must suppress their own desire for privilege only to see it pop out in all sorts of strange ways. I do not mean the superficially incongruous manifestations: Hollywood actors in jeans and sneakers piling into limousines, Marxist professors signing their mass mailings with the pompous titles of their chairs, endowed through capitalist largesse, or the posh Volvos that dot the faculty parking lot. Rather, I have in mind the pillorying by National Public Radio of those who say "nucular" for "nuclear," the loud laments in faculty clubs over the threats posed to rural France by McDonald's, and all the other increasingly desperate assertions of moral and cultural superiority in a world where meaningful titles like earl, duke, and marquis are long gone and in theory repugnant. "Axis of evil? Totally banal," scoffed Felipe Gonzalez, the former prime minister of Spain, not long before his own country swaggeringly recaptured an uninhabited and rather banal piece of rock that had been briefly snatched by Morocco. The superciliousness of the educated knows no end, and may even betray a final anxiety.

One million bachelor's degrees are awarded in this country each year, but under the new therapeutic curriculum there is little to guarantee that any of the holders of these certificates can spell a moderately difficult English word or knows which dictator belongs to which enslaved state. And what is true of students is too often true as well of their pretentious professors, as can be seen whenever Noam Chomsky pontificates about war ("Let me repeat: the U.S. has demanded that Pakistan kill possibly millions of people . . .") and in place of references to historical exempla or citations from the literature raves on with "as I have written elsewhere," "there are many other illustrations," "as would be expected," "it would be instructive to seek historical precedents," "as leading experts on the Middle East attest," and all the other loopholes and escape clauses that are the mark not of a learned intellectual but of a calcified demagogue. But who has time to acquire expertise or exhibit patience with human frailty?

The innate limitations of mortals matter little to our irritated utopians, nor can moral progress ever be rapid enough to keep up with a definition of perfection that evolves as quickly as the technology of cell phones. That Afghanistan a mere year after the fall of the Taliban is not yet as tranquil and secure as New England proves that our postbellum efforts there are not much better than the Taliban. "No one," asserts Edward Said, "could argue today that Afghanistan, even after the rout of the Taliban, is a much better and more secure place for its citizens." No one? That we once aided Saddam Hussein is a supposedly crippling fact of which we are reminded ad nauseam, as if, not before but after the Gulf War, France, Russia, and Germany did not proceed to sell him the components for weapons of mass destruction, or as if we ourselves did not once give the Soviets a third of a million GMC trucks to thwart Hitler, only to see them used in the Gulag. But in the perfect world of America's critics, if Barbra Streisand can fly to Paris in four hours and fax her scrambled thoughts in seconds, and if Gore Vidal from his Italian villa can parse sentences better than the president of the United States, then surely we are terminally culpable for not having solved the globe's problems right now.

Is it because these elite Americans are so insulated and so well off, and yet feel so troubled by it, that they are prone to embrace with religious fervor ideas that have little connection with reality but that promise a sense of meaning, solidarity with a select and sophisticated group, moral accomplishment, and importance? Is it because of its very freedom and wealth that America has become both the incubator and the target of these most privileged, resentful, and unhappy people? And are their perceptions susceptible of change? If the answer to the first two questions is yes, as I believe it is, then the reply to the third must be: I doubt it.

The necessary correctives, after all, would have to be brutal: an economic depression, a religious revolution, a military catastrophe, or, God forbid, an end to tenure. At least in the near term, and whether we like it or not, the religion of anti-Americanism is as likely to grow as to fade. But it can also be challenged. The anti-Americans often invoke Rome as a warning and as a model, both of our imperialism and of our foreordained collapse. But the threats to Rome's predominance were more dreadful in 220 B.C. than in A.D. 400. The difference over six centuries, the dissimilarity that led to the end, was a result not of imperial overstretch on the outside but of something happening within that was not unlike what we ourselves are now witnessing. Earlier Romans knew what it was to be Roman, why it was at least better than the alternative, and why their culture had to be defended. Later, in ignorance, they forgot what they knew, in pride mocked who they were, and, in consequence, disappeared. The example of Rome, in short, is an apt one, but in a way unintended by critics who use passing contemporary events as occasions for venting a permanent, irrational, and often visceral distrust of their own society. Their creed is really a malady, and it cries out to be confronted and exposed.

Written in November and published in
the December 2002 issue of COMMENTARY *magazine.*

19

Evil over Good

THE WAGES OF DEAD-END LOGIC

We are on the eve of a controversial war in the Middle East. So you'd think that opponents of the war could bring to the fore principled arguments, both moral and practical—ones that would enrich the national debate and raise important issues of general concern.

Instead—if yet another of the recent protests in Washington is any indication—there is little offered but the old hypocrisy, shrillness, and carnival absurdity. Signs proclaimed EVIL OVER GOOD. Ramsey Clark was still screaming on cue for the impeachment of the president; the provocateur Al Sharpton was presented as an exemplar of racial harmony. Support was again asked for the cop-killers H. Rap Brown and Mumia Abu-Jamal (honorary citizen of Paris). A vociferous minister reprimanded demonstrators for putting a few coins, not many bills, in his tithe buckets—while affluent suburbanites nodded as Imam Mousa, the Islamist, called for "revolution" throughout the United States, which in theory might even reach their outer boroughs of Maryland and Virginia. Honorable antiwar protestors showing up at a rally sponsored by such leaders would be like critics of racial quotas allowing David Duke to organize their protests.

What, then, exactly is the problem with the opposition to the war? Why is there not an idea to be found? Is it because the protestations of the present antiwar movement rest on dead-end logic?

No Blood for Oil?

Under a favorable scenario of a new reform government in Iraq, oil production will rise to over three million barrels. That would help to allow the world price to decline, or at least stabilize. Such price continuity will help billions worldwide beyond our shores— as well as earn revenues for the *people* of Iraq. Does Exxon really want lower prices and a state-run oil company under civic audit at last controlling the vast petroleum reserves of Iraq? Are Texas oil-company executives clamoring for consensual government in the Gulf or are they big supporters of Israel?

Those most worried about American military force being used to remove Saddam Hussein may well not be D.C. protesters but international oil companies who apparently are jittery that in a postbellum climate there will be too much Iraqi oil under a stable peace—or contrarily scared that their joint-venture infrastructure and investment abroad will be endangered when the shooting starts. Only the continued existence of Saddam Hussein means that none of his oil revenue goes to the people—as the world's oil supply remains tight, wells are relatively safe, and energy-corporation profits stay ample.

Despite the rhetoric that the United States never intervenes for principled or even illogical reasons, America lately has not been using its military power for clearly demarcated economic self-interest. Indeed, if there were one constant that characterizes American policy in the last two decades, it surely was *not* greed for oil—which was not anywhere to be found in Grenada, Panama, Somalia, Kosovo, Bosnia, or Afghanistan. Thirty-seven thousand

Americans are not in Korea for gasoline; the strike of Venezuelan conservative elites might draw sympathy from their kindred souls in Washington, but it is sending gas prices through the roof.

No War?

It is hard to know whether the current war protesters are simply anti-Bush or genuine pacifists. But in either case, if they sincerely wish the United States to renounce force in both Iraq and Korea, then they must accept the moral—and most immediate—corollary of such a position: calls for the immediate withdrawal from the no-fly zones and South Korea. Signs should read: LET THE KURDS BE, or LEAVE THE DMZ. Under such pacifist logic, without gun-toting American imperialists, the Kurdish republicans would be safe from Saddam's resumption of gassing and bombing, and the Korean democrats secure from 10,000 artillery pieces to the north.

Our Enemies Are Victims?

Throughout the Cold War the resonance of the anti-American and antiwar movements was predicated on the utopian pretensions of communism. Commissars were usually savvy enough to masquerade dictatorships as mass liberation movements professing fraternity, egalitarianism, and social justice.

But North Korea is truly a satanic place, where two million starve in order to build and maintain 3,000 tanks, 600 guided missiles, and 2,000 warplanes. Saddam Hussein's Iraq is a simulacrum of the Third Reich. Antiwar activists are thus confronted with the reductionist fact that their opposition to the United States finds resonance with unsavory characters who likewise oppose Washington—whether fascists in Iraq or Stalinists in Korea. The contradictions get worse if we throw in the hot-button issues of sexism, racism, and homophobia. The Taliban and Saddam Hussein, not elites in suits and ties in DuPont Circle, are guilty of those transgressions—at least if burqas, genocide, and summary executions are any indications.

And who are those "brothers and sisters" abroad expressing solidarity with the protesters in Washington? In fact, there were kindred, simultaneous demonstrations on the same day by paid lackeys in Baghdad (organized by Oday, Saddam Hussein's son and a renowned pacifist), old-style Soviet Stalinists waving the hammer-and-sickle in front of the American embassy in Moscow, and Islamic fundamentalists in Cairo.

Arab Sensitivity?

The Arab street can be characterized by two general principles: anti-Americanism and unhappiness with the Middle East's failed and dictatorial governments. Fair enough. But what happens when those twin targets of popular discontent are themselves at variance?

If the United States—albeit sometimes belatedly—is committed to remove fascists like those in Afghanistan and Iraq, and is increasingly pressuring the Saudis, Kuwaitis, and the Egyptians to initiate domestic reforms, will the Arab street evolve in its thinking or instead demonstrate for no future elections in Riyadh, more torture in Baghdad, and the status quo in Cairo? If $3 billion of annual aid to Egypt, Jordan, and Palestine; help for Kosovars, Somalis, Kuwaitis, and Afghans; and open American borders for immigrants from the Middle East earn us such hostility, then what would the opposite policies do? And should we find out?

Empire?

Are we really a hegemon that must intrude into countries all over the world? In a post–Cold War age of twelve mobile carrier battle groups, hundreds of submarines that are being reoriented to a variety of new tactical missions, missile defense, and the spread of democracies, the American military—as we learned from its expulsion from the Philippines—will not dissolve if it is asked to leave from various conventional bases abroad. Gone is the habitual American worry of the 1970s about the need for anti-Soviet home ports. It is replaced by a sort of resignation that host countries should do what they wish—and in response we will adapt and continue as we can.

So instead of European elites constantly hectoring the United States about its Imperial Roman aspirations, their governments should simply match their rhetoric by asking us to vacate Western Europe. Pronto! The United States is not holding back Germany from its "German way." There are places for American ships besides Crete—and the Aegean can be patrolled well enough by joint Greek-Turkish NATO fleets.

Thousands of Americans on the tip of the spear in South Korea, if asked to depart by Seoul, will be only too happy to get out of the way of nukes across the DMZ. The American public will be delighted by the subsequent savings—and relieved even more that they are not pledging San Francisco for the security of Seoul. Anti-Americanism apparently has resonance in German and South Korean elections, but when such nationalist administrations have power, they strangely are not so ready to follow through on their campaign rhetoric.

9/11

The new Bush administration began 2001 promising not to emulate the near yearly interventions abroad of the Clinton idealists— no more nation-building in Somalia, no more human-rights watching in Haiti, no more peacemaking in the former Yugoslavia, and a comprehensive reexamination of the expensive and thankless policing of Iraq. Indeed, the standard pre-9/11 critique of the Bushites was their lapse into the old-style Republican neo-isolationism—not a propensity for utopian interventionism or imperial overstretch.

So take away 9/11 and there would be no U.S. troops poised to go to Baghdad and Mullah Omar would still be pontificating on al-Jazeera. Neither the American government nor the American people had any desire to send troops overseas had not three thousand been slaughtered. The truth is that the left's failure to note the importance of 9/11 in the present crisis, or, worse, to say that it is a mere pretext for American fighting abroad does a disservice to the memory of the dead.

The fact is that we have been fighting Middle Eastern terrorists and fascists all along—al Qaeda, the Taliban, Saddam Hussein—who want weapons that can do far more than kill three thousand Americans and level the World Trade Center. Real costs now—not oil profits later—are the elements of our own fiscal reckoning. Rather than killing "millions of innocent Iraqis," millions of innocent Iraqis in Kurdistan—as well as millions more in Korea—are alive only because of the continued presence of American troops. Arab dictatorships hate us even as "friendly" Arab dictatorships increasingly fear our calls for reform.

I suppose to protest against all that, you really do have to carry signs that proclaim EVIL OVER GOOD.

Written on January 22 and published in
NATIONAL REVIEW ONLINE *on January 24, 2003.*

20

Doom, Doom, and More Doom

SHOULD WE TRUST PAST FACTS OR PRESENT HYSTERICS?

What can we expect from the possible invasion of Iraq? Everything in war is of course uncertain—an awful time when the lives of thousands of soldiers hang in the balance, and brutal, dirty events can spiral out of control the moment the shooting starts. Yet we should be careful in once more believing the pessimistic commentators in newspaper ads and on television who are now warning of several "hundred thousands" of dead, of chaos, of mass starvation, and of internecine killing.

"Hundreds" of dead go to "thousands" and on to "millions" in the blink of an eye—not unlike Robert McNamara's fiery warnings to Congress a dozen years ago that "thousands and thousands and thousands" of Americans would surely die in the 1991 Gulf War.

It is not that such boilerplate pessimism is always wrong on the eve of war—who, after all, could have predicted the butcher's bill that came after rosy predictions of quick resolutions on the eve of Bull Run or August 1914? But it is still easier to issue gloomy prognostications than to offer more optimistic appraisals: we humans are by nature afraid of the unknown, and the generic warning of slaughter in war seems to carry more moral weight than suggesting that there is on occasion even a utility or morality in the use of arms to stop evil.

Indeed, those who say Saddam Hussein can be removed without great loss of life are vulnerable to the charge of either naïveté or bloodlust in their belief that the horror of shooting and bombing now will still save far more lives later on. Yet unwarranted gloom in war is *never* proof of morality, nor does optimism in national prowess reveal amorality.

So what does the past tell us? First, we should *not* listen to hysteria. Noam Chomsky spent an autumn warning of "millions" of dead to come in Afghanistan. Wrong. More respected and often reasonable commentators such as William Pfaff ("The utility of the bombing is hard to defend. It was believed able to bring down the Taliban government, but that is not happening") and R. W. Apple ("Afghanistan as Vietnam"/"Signs of progress are sparse") assured us that after a few days of fighting in Afghanistan we were in a quagmire. Wrong again.

For much of the fall of 2001, I listened to and often debated a number of commentators who pontificated about the high peaks and the "Afghan winter," Ramadan, the Russian and British empires, the Arab street—about almost anything but the respective histories and efficacies of the American and Taliban military forces. And rather than being contrite about their error in predicting American slaughter in Afghanistan, our critics have moved on to Iraq to find renewed opportunity to vent their almost religious cultural pessimism.

Recently Hans von Sponeck, the former UN humanitarian coordinator in Iraq, assured us that the United States "will lose the war. This will be World War Three." And after warning us that there is little chance of a swift and easy victory in Iraq, Immanuel Wallerstein of Yale predicts that the "most likely" scenario is "a long exhausting war." But even that may be too optimistic, since "losing, incredible as it seems (but then it seemed so in Vietnam too) is a plausible outcome, one chance in three."

Instead of listening to this dejection, we should examine the thirty-year record of the Iraqi army in a series of wars against the Kurds in the 1960s and seventies, in the Yom Kippur fighting against Israel, in the surprise attacks on Iran and Kuwait, and in the first Gulf War, as well as several barbaric actions against the Shiites.

True, the Iraqi army has shown flashes of dash and organization—it seemed energetic during the first few weeks of its 1988 counterattack into Iran and the 1990 assault on Kuwait. Military analysts, perhaps too charitably, have asserted that the Republican Guard, which was nearly annihilated on February 26–27, 1991, at least held firm, even as many of its tanks were incinerated—reminiscent of the earlier armored brigades that kept charging even as they were obliterated by the outnumbered Israelis on the Golan Heights.

But despite displays of personal courage, the Iraqis as a rule have *not* fought well when confronted by opponents who were not weak or in disarray, as were the shocked Iranians and Kuwaitis. In earlier Kurdish wars, sporadic attacks against Israel, and the first Gulf War, Iraqi performance was generally dismal. And even the sudden infusion of French planes and the training in France of Iraqi aircrews did not mean air superiority over weak Iranian pilots.

In all these wars, command was uneven, morale low, flexibility and initiative of officers uninspiring, weapons often poorly maintained and not employed as they were designed to be used—the wages of a dictatorial society, where tribalism, not meritocracy, governs promotions, pay is low, enlisted military service earns little status, men fight out of fear rather than with a sense of freedom and initiative, and technology is imported rather than the natural dividend of a modern approach to research, development, and manufacturing.

That the whole Arab world translates fewer books each year from English than does Greece really does affect how well its armies use their purchased advanced weapons. Military parasitism works well enough with small rifles, terrorist bombs, and rockets; but with large assets such as planes, tanks, and ships their proper deployment, maintenance, and optimum tactical use all require a preexisting infrastructure that is not so easily bought or copied.

The geopolitical situation does not favor the Iraqi military either. There will be no Soviet or Chinese advisers fighting for Saddam Hussein; nor are nuclear-armed patrons threatening us with Armageddon should his armies collapse. For all the talk of jihad, even zealots have no desire to die for the Iraqi gulag. Privately, those in the Arab street are mostly angry at us, the infidel, for preempting what they themselves would like to have done.

In contrast, the United States during the last two decades—in the first Gulf War, Panama, Serbia, and Afghanistan—has shown itself adept in almost every aspect of difficult and challenging operations: excellent morale, flexibility in command, and superb use and maintenance of sophisticated and always-evolving weapons. And when it has had problems—tactical confusion in Grenada, the placement of unarmored troops into urban ambushes like Mogadishu—American troops nevertheless fought superbly.

Add to the equation the recent history of American-Iraqi fighting in 1991, when hundreds of thousands of Iraqi conscripts surrendered without firing a shot. American soldiers without much battle experience did more damage to the Iraqi military in one hundred hours than Iran did in eight years. Such memories are still deeply branded into the Iraqi military. Since 1991, Anglo-American aircrews have owned over two-thirds of Iraqi airspace—and know more about it than do Saddam's pilots themselves. This time the war is not over a dictator's withdrawal from Kuwait, but the transformation of an autocracy into consensual government that will promise that its country is no longer a haven for frightening weapons and terrorists.

In 1990 Saddam believed that he could fight a conventional war, wrongly surmising that the terror and attrition that worked once in Iran would frighten a United States wary after Vietnam.

This time he knows that a "mother of all battles" is impossible, but instead worries about what he saw in Serbia and Afghanistan. He takes some confidence only in the American surprise and shock in Mogadishu and on September 11, and wobbliness in Europe, but is still not so unhinged as to believe that an Iraqi military victory is possible.

In sum, in a strict military sense, *if* the Iraqi army—there is no real navy or air force—fights, it will do so as poorly as it has in the past against any good force that it cannot surprise. But we should also remember that in fighting a series of wars, Saddam Hussein has shown a preference for the unconventional and even nightmarish: taking human hostages during the prelude to the 1991 war; putting women and children into the bunkers of the military elite; launching Scuds into Israel, Teheran, and Saudi Arabia; torching the Kuwaiti oil fields; sending gas shells and high-voltage electrical currents against the Iranians; and suddenly slaughtering Shiites and Kurds once American officials allowed Iraqis to fly armed aircraft immediately following the armistice.

We should anticipate, then, that a few Scuds (which are not supposed to exist) will be sent into Israel as well as launched into Kuwait. Chemical and biological weapons (which, again, are not supposed to exist) may be attached to missiles or shot out of some artillery shells at initial marching columns. Like the Scud that hit American troops in Saudi Arabia, some Americans could fall.

And Saddam Hussein may well resort to torching or sabotaging his own oil fields, mining the streets of Baghdad, and even executing many of his own people, as in 1991. If there are no foreigners to serve as human shields, his own citizens may do well enough to deflect shrapnel from his generals—to be broadcast back immediately by the epigones of Peter Arnett. The al Qaeda–Iraqi liaisons (which are not supposed to exist) might have made predetermined arrangements for hitting Americans at home with gas or germs. Saddam Hussein, environmentalists now forget, created the worst oil slick in history—a 200,000-barrel-a-day, 240-square-mile mess—to foul the coast of Saudi Arabia. And he may try again. These are all frightening scenarios, but they will still not alter the military realities that will ensure Saddam Hussein's quick demise without great loss of life.

If we ponder the recent past, I would think that all of Iraq outside Baghdad will be overrun in a matter of days—to the cheers of most of his citizenry. The capital will fall later, but the timing of its liberation will be calibrated on mostly humanitarian rather than military considerations—American caution over walking into a possibly booby-trapped city and the need to avoid killing captives of Saddam Hussein. *So if it comes to war, we will win and most likely win quickly.* We will be safer—and Iraq immediately a better place—for our efforts. And we can at least say that we did not leave a madman with frightening weapons in an age of mass murder for our children to deal with.

Culture—not race, not nationality, not numbers, not chance—more often determines the long-term efficacy of a military. That being said, in the here and now morale and élan play a great role in every particular campaign and hinge on the nature of the cause and the mission. In the present war, our military fights better than Saddam Hussein's, but we also seek liberation rather than conquest, and wish to cleanse a country of dangerous weapons, terrorists, and a bloodthirsty dictator.

Yet no one would believe these lessons of the past if they watched the current television commercials or listened to Nelson Mandela or the doomsday warnings of our actors, novelists, professors, and political activists—all of whom assure us that we are immoral or promise that we will fail miserably should we invade Iraq.

Yet remember, this is also an age of untruth and boutique piety. "Internationalism" and "multilateralism" can mean that Libya, which butchered the people of Chad, adjudicates human rights; that Syria, which practiced genocide, sits on the "Security" Council; and that the two gassers, Iran and Iraq, discuss protocols of illegal weaponry—even as the Nobel Peace Prize goes to the terrorist Yasser Arafat, to a Korean statesman who bribed a mass murderer for the chance at a summit, and to an ex-president who was praised by his benefactors precisely for criticizing his own government at a time of crisis and war.

Strange and depressing times.

So let us trust in reason and history, rather than hysteria and self-righteous bluster.

Written on February 5 and published in
NATIONAL REVIEW ONLINE *on February 7, 2003.*

21

Our Western Mob

FROM THE GRAVEYARD OF KABUL
TO THE QUAGMIRE OF IRAQ
TO THE LOOTING OF BAGHDAD

The jubilation of liberating millions from fascism and removing the world's most odious dictator apparently lasted about twelve hours. I was listening to a frustrated Mr. Rumsfeld last Friday in a news briefing as he tried to deal with a host of furious and crazy questions—a journalistic circus that was nevertheless *predictable even before the war started.*

I thought immediately of the macabre aftermath to the battle of Arginusae in 406 B.C. After destroying a great part of the Peloponnesian fleet in the most dramatic naval victory of the war, the Athenian popular assembly abruptly voted to execute six of their eight successful generals (the other two wisely never came back to Athens) on charges that they had failed to rescue seamen who were clinging to the wreckage.

The historian Xenophon records the feeding frenzy and shouting of the assembled throng. Forget that Sparta felt beaten and was ready for peace after such a catastrophic defeat; forget the brilliant seamanship and command of the Athenian triremes; forget that a ferocious storm had made retrieval of the dead and rescue of the missing sailors almost impossible; forget even that to try the generals collectively was contrary to Athenian law. Instead the people demanded perfection in addition to mere overwhelming success—and so in frustration devoured their own elected officials. The macabre incident was infamous in Greek history (the philosopher Socrates almost alone resisted the mob's rule), a reminder how a society can go mad, turn on its benefactors, throw away a victory—and go on to lose the entire war.

Something like that craziness often takes hold of our own elites and media in the midst of perhaps the most brilliantly executed plan in modern American military history. Rather than inquiring how an entire country was overrun in a little over three weeks at a cost of not more than a few hundred casualties, reporters instead wail at the televised scenes of a day of looting and lawlessness.

I had been expecting at least some interviews about bridges not blown due to the rapidity of the advance. Could someone tell us how special forces saved the oil fields? How Seals prevented the dreaded oil slicks? Whose courage and sacrifice saved the dams? And how so few missiles were launched? Exactly why and how did the Republican Guard cave?

In short, would any reporter demonstrate a smidgeon of curiosity—other than to condemn a plan they scarcely understood—about the mechanics of the furious battle for Iraq? It would be as if America forgot about Patton's race to the German border and instead focused only on Frenchmen shaving the heads of Vichy collaborators, or decided that it had not been worth freeing the Italian peninsula because a mob had mutilated and hanged Mussolini from his heels. Did any remember what had happened to a Russian armored column that tried to enter Grozny to control that city? Did any have a clue what Germany or Italy was like in June 1945?

What was striking about the Iraqi capitulations was the absence of general looting on the part of the victorious army. From the fall of Constantinople to the Iraqi takeover of Kuwait City, winners usually plunder and pillage. American and British soldiers instead did the opposite, trying to protect others' property as they turned on water and power. That much of the looting was no more indiscriminate than what we saw in Los Angeles after the Rodney King verdict, in New York during blackouts, or in some major cities after Super Bowl victories, made no impression on the reporting. Remember, this was a long-suffering impoverished people lashing out at Baathists—not affluent, smug American kids looting and breaking windows at the World Trade Organization in Seattle.

A terrorized people, itself looted and brutalized by fascists for three decades, understandably upon news of liberation feels the need to steal back from Baathist elites and government ministries what had been taken from them. This is not an excuse for general lawlessness, but rather a reminder that freedom for the oppressed sometimes goes through periods of volatility and messiness.

All this was lost on our journalistic elite, who like Athenians of old wished to find scapegoats in the midst of undreamed good news. Dan Rather, for example, finished one of his broadcasts from liberated Baghdad with an incredible "before and after" footage of his entry that should rank as one of the most absurd pieces of the entire war coverage. Tape rolled of his initial drive a few weeks ago to Saddam's HQ, when the roads were once safe from banditry and free of destruction. Then in glum tones he chronicled his harrowing current arrival into Baghdad amid craters and gunfire.

Mr. Rather—so unlike a Michael Kelly or David Bloom— forgot that he was now motoring right smack into a war zone. And he seemed oblivious that just a few weeks ago he had conducted a scripted and choreographed interview with a mass murderer. Consider the sheer historical ignorance of it all: Was Berlin a nicer place in 1939 or 1946? And why, and for whom?

The machinery of a totalitarian society, of course, can present a certain staged decorum for guests who are brought in to be manipulated by dictators. How many were shot in dungeons during his visit, he never speculated. By contrast, the first forty-eight hours of liberation are scary—who, after all, could now put Mr. Rather up at a plush state-run hotel and shepherd him into the posh digs of Saddam Hussein with the security of an armed Gestapo? That the chaos Mr. Rather witnessed was the aftermath of a thirty-year tyranny under which one million innocents have been slaughtered made no discernable impression on him—nor did the bombshell story how the Western media has for years collaborated with a horrific regime to send out its censored propaganda.

Next I turned on NPR. No surprise. Its coverage was also fixated on the looting, and aired several stories about the general shortcomings of the American efforts. Again, forget that a war was waging in the north, that Baghdad was still not entirely pacified, and that there was the example of a normalizing postbellum Basra. No, instead there must be furor that the United States had not in a matter of hours turned its military into an instantaneous police, fire, water, medical, and power corps.

Personally, I was more intrigued that in passing the same reporter at last fessed up that during *all* of her previous gloomy reports from the Palestine Hotel of American progress, she and others had been shaken down daily for bribe money, censored, and led around as near hostages. It is impossible to calibrate how such Iraqi manipulation of American news accounts affected domestic morale, if not providing comfort for those Baathists who wished to discourage popular uprisings of long-suffering Iraqis.

There is something profoundly amoral about this. A newsman who interviewed a state killer at his convenience later revisits a now liberated city and complains of the disorder there. A journalist who paid bribe money to fascists and whose dispatches aired from Baghdad in wartime only because the Baathist party felt that they served their own terrorist purposes is disturbed about the chaos of liberation. Now is the time for CNN, NPR, and other news organizations to state publicly what their relationships were in ensuring their reporters' presence in wartime Iraq—and to explain their policies about bribing state officials, allowing censorship of their news releases, and keeping quiet about atrocities to ensure access.

In general, the media has now gone from the hysteria of the Armageddon of Afghanistan to the quagmire of Iraq to the looting in Baghdad; the only constant is slanted coverage, mistaken analysis, and the absence of any contriteness about being in error—and in error in such a manner that reflected so poorly upon themselves and damaged the country at large at a time of war. It is as if only further bad news could serve as a sort of catharsis that might at least cleanse them of any unease about being so wrong so predictably and so often.

In the weeks that follow, the media, not the military, will be shown to be in need of introspection and vast reform. Partly the problem arises from the breakneck desire of reporters to obtain near celebrity status by causing controversy and spectacle. Many (especially executives) also came of age in Vietnam and are thus desperate to recapture past glory when once upon a time their efforts made them stars and changed our national culture. Reporters are cultural relativists who never ask themselves how many more people are tortured and die because of their own complicity with a murderous regime. Ignorance also is endemic. Few read of history's great sieges and the bedlam that always follows conquest, liberation, and the birth of a new order. Arrogance abounds that journalists are to be above reproach and thus deserve to be moral censors in addition to simply reporting the news.

So while it is censorious of politicians and soldiers, the media is completely uninterested in monitoring its own behavior. Would Mr. Rather have gone to Berlin amid the SS to interview Hitler in his bunker as the fires of Auschwitz raged? Would NPR reporters have visited Hitler's Germany, paid bribes to Mr. Goebbels, and then broadcasted allied shortcomings at the Bulge, oblivious to the Nazi machinery of death and their own complicity in it?

There is also a final reason that explains our demand for instantaneous perfection. It is often a trademark of successful Western societies that create such freedom and affluence to fool themselves that they are a hairsbreadth away from utopia. Journalists who pad around with Palm Pilots, pounds of high-tech gear, dapper clothes, and expensive educations have convinced themselves that if lesser people were as caring or as sensitive as themselves then we could all live in bliss. The subtext of the daily Western media barrage has been that if we were just smarter, more moral, or better informed, then we could liberate a country the size of California in days, not weeks, lose zero soldiers, not 110, and be instantaneously greeted by happy Iraqis who would shake hands, return to work, and quietly forget thirty years of terror as they voted in a Gandhi.

Anything less and Messrs. Rumsfeld, Meyers, Franks, "the plan"—somebody or something at least!—must be held accountable for the absence of utopia.

But that is a word, they should remember, that means not a "good place" but "no place" at all.

Written on April 12 and published in
NATIONAL REVIEW ONLINE *on April 14, 2003.*

V

EUROPE

For much of the 1990s there were signs of growing tension between many European countries—especially France and Germany—and the United States. Sometimes the disagreements were larger than differences over the issues of the day— the Kyoto accords, the International Criminal Court, American capital punishment, or the proposed war against Saddam Hussein—and seemed to hinge on concerns about the very nature of American culture.

Had the times really changed all that much? Thus were new organizations such as the European Union compatible with or antithetical to older ones such as NATO? Why exactly were there nearly 100,000 American military personnel based in Germany and environs over a decade after the collapse of the Soviet Union and almost sixty years following the end of World War II—to protect against external enemies or to prevent the rise of new internal ones? And why did Europeans object to proposed American intervention in Iraq to end a fascist tyranny, but not earlier against a similar monster in Serbia?

Perhaps given the new times it was no surprise to see antiwar demonstrations that were larger in Paris, Berlin, Athens, or Rome than in Damascus, Cairo, or Tripoli. A number of European intellectuals—and, indeed, a few statesmen—voiced patently anti-American sentiments that suggested a deep and underlying suspicion of the United States. Much of this attitude baffled insular Americans who still had distant memories of World War II liberation, the Marshall

Plan, a half-century of deterrence against the Soviets posi-
tioned in Eastern Europe, support for German unification, and
the American intervention in the Balkans to stop a European
holocaust. What accounted for it all?

Did the new suspicion—the goodwill garnered after
September 11 seemed to have dissipated within a year—reflect
the unilateralism of the Bush administration and the presi-
dent's harsh twang, the end of the Soviet threat against West-
ern Europe, anger over American support for the Sharon
government, jealousy over the unchallenged position of the
United States in the post–Cold War era, suspicion that we
were undermining multilateral institutions so vital to Euro-
pean cultural prominence, or worries that the United States
would stir up a terrorist hornet's nest that might well swarm
into mainland Europe?

22

European Paradoxes

THE WAR THAT DIVIDES US

The gulf in understanding between America and its European friends seems to be widening and not entirely a matter of governmental squabbling. Despite the age of globalization and a world economy, and our similar goals of eradicating the terrorists, there are real differences in the perceptions of the current war that do not bode well for the future.

After spending the last two weeks abroad talking to a number of Europeans, I sensed that the constant criticism of the United States that we read in European newspapers and magazines are not reflections of an out-of-touch elite but the general pulse of a complex anti-Americanism that is widely shared among much of Europe's citizenry. At the heart of the misunderstandings are a number of paradoxes in our relationship, wounds whose thin scabs the events of September 11 have ripped open.

Right as Left

Most Europeans voice criticism of America ostensibly from the left. We are allegedly a bully who rashly uses military force in lieu of dialogue, snubbing international agreements on everything from the environment to world jurisdiction over our military's improprieties. Our culture is cutthroat and greedy, as the recent Enron and WorldCom scandals attest. We support right-wing governments such as Israel's and are often in opposition to the aspirations of Third World oppressed peoples, to the authority of the United Nations, and, indeed, to the growth and power of international organizations.

Yet when these criticisms are probed, a startling revelation appears: far from being radicals, Europeans are, in fact, in a fundamental sense more reactionary than Americans. And here things get interesting. In conversations, the Europeans very soon begin to voice all the old right-wing complaints about America that explain why they see our country as so insular, crass, and dangerous: we have no respect for tradition; our movies and television are uncouth; our volatile citizenry is increasingly ignorant, multicultural, and lawless, and so blinkered to the concerns of others. Welcome to radical democratic culture.

So the Europeans have not a clue that we are powerful and influential precisely because, unlike themselves, we truly are a radically revolutionary society—the only one in history in which the hard-working and perennially exhausted lower and middle classes are empowered economically and have fully taken control of the popular culture to create strange institutions from Sunday cookouts and do-it-yourself home improvement to tasteless appurtenances such as Winnebagos, jet skis, and PlayStation IIs.

The Europeans profess that they resent us because of a sinister military-industrial complex that has a stranglehold on American foreign policy, has replaced idealism with Realpolitik, and has illegitimately and selfishly tried to abet exploitative corporations abroad. But upon examination, they freely admit that our idea that money, not education, breeding, and culture, determines success, bothers them. This unease is coupled with the new awareness that Americans—whether hyphenated Americans from Mexico and Vietnam, Hindus, Mormons, blacks, Pentecostals, poor whites, or Puerto Ricans—have no identifiable race, religion, or common bond other than a purportedly shared allegiance to values and ideas.

This new notion of a future United States—with a minority of Euro-Americans and religions other than mainstream Protestantism and Catholicism—unleashed upon the world is a frightening idea to those of largely homogeneous racial stock, itself struggling badly with nascent immigration from impoverished societies. Europeans are as vocal as leftist critics of America as they are silently embarrassed over their rightist disdain for what we have become.

Secret Delight

The second paradox about the use of American power stems from Europeans' defensiveness about their lack of military preparedness. When asked what they would do should the Eiffel Tower or the Vatican be targets, they grow perplexed and defensive. They seem resigned to the fact that they lack the air and sea forces requisite to conduct extended military operations in the Middle East or, in fact, anywhere outside of Europe. Oddly, many instead seem confident that their own professed liberality (in contrast toward the world's general antipathy toward America) will ensure them exemption from illogical hatred.

As one European professional told me, "Paris was there well before American GIs, and it will be there long after them"—a debatable point given the events of 1914–18 and 1940–44. But after the first few minutes of conversation, another admission creeps out. In truth, most Europeans seem privately to look forward to unilateral American action against Iraq. There is a strange sense that they are fed up with the extremist regimes of the Middle East, tired of the secret subsidies from the Arab world to criminals, and deathly afraid of terrorism. While they surely would not be so silly as to lose treasure and youth on such a foolhardy expedition ("A Sicilian Expedition" one professor scoffed of our proposed Iraqi war), and while they will be the first to criticize us should we stumble, there is nevertheless a general feeling that the temperamental, half-crazed Americans are now going to be unleashed to settle accounts for the Western world in general.

Of course, in their view, we are fighting the war against terror crudely, and must be continually monitored and audited by more subtle minds that can guide us through the labyrinth of world politics. Somewhere in all our efforts they suspect also that there must be some unstated and sinister American goal. Still, in the last analysis, there is a certain satisfaction among Europeans that al Qaeda and Iraq have perhaps bitten off more than they can chew and will earn a reckoning long overdue.

Hating What You Want

I heard in conversations often that we are the global menace. "Ask yourself why you are hated" was repeated ad nauseam. Occasionally something like the following was voiced: "The entire world cannot be wrong in not liking you." Often comparisons were made to the empires of the U.S.S.R. and ancient Rome to suggest our hyperpower status is similarly exploitative and thus eventually also will fall. Any memory that America once fought far from home to protect the democratic soil of Europe against Prussian militarism, German and Italian fascism, and Soviet totalitarianism has been long erased.

But, oddly, many Europeans love to visit the United States, have relatives here, or were educated at an American university. Some of the most adamant Socialist critics of America are former residents of the United States who taught in (and often are pensioned from) American colleges and universities.

Part envy, part adolescent resentment toward a supportive but interfering parent, part simple confusion—the Europeans seem to think they are the brain to our brawn, fascinated with our wealth and power but saddened that such splendid assets could not be directed in a more focused and supplicated manner to do the world real good. Just as they were confused about the ultimate source of our economic and military strength, so they have even less insight about the morality of removing murderers like Noriega, the thugs in Grenada, Milosevic, Arafat, and Saddam Hussein. In contrast to Americans, they seem to care more about the procedure than the ultimate result of using force.

So there is a real gut fear that there is something dangerous about us Americans. We are like some frightening virus that bores into the system and takes control of the internal mechanisms, thereby ensuring the zombie its slow destruction. Whether it's the baffling addiction of their youth to violent American video games or their own preference for *Spiderman* over French films, Europeans have to watch themselves around us lest they lose their carefully developed and maintained hierarchies.

Americans are the new Sirens, whose seductive appeal to the appetites might lure even the most resolute Odysseus onto the shoals of self-indulgence and moral corruption. Most Europeans seem to attribute problems with their own children's disobedience, laxity, and listlessness to the poison of American popular culture (what they euphemistically call "globalization")—odd given that Americans, in fact, are not pampered, but work about a month per year longer than Europeans and often expect their kids as adults to work their own way through college or join the military.

On Being Liked

A fourth paradox is the changed American attitude toward Europe after September 11. Before that milestone, Europeans were at least smug that their disdain affected us. Once upon a time—especially in the Clinton administration—we patiently listened to moral lectures, apologized constantly, and tried all sorts of ways to explain our baffling behavior to our moral betters. Europeans felt their ace in the hole was that we really did want to be liked by them and earn their moral approval.

No longer. They fear now that September 11 was a macabre liberating experience for Americans, and realize that we don't much care about European carping when our greatest buildings and best citizens are vaporized. Yet when you tell a European precisely that—and as politely as possible—he is either shocked or genuinely hurt.

Iraq? Stay put—we don't necessarily need or desire your help. The Middle East? Shame on you, not us, for financing the terrorists on the West Bank. The Palestinian Authority and Israel? You helped to fund a terrorist clique; we, a democracy—go figure. Racism? Arabs are safer in America than Jews are in Europe. That 200,000 were butchered in Bosnia and Kosovo a few hours from Rome and Berlin is a stain on you, the inactive, not us, the interventionist. Capital punishment? Our government has executed terrorists; yours have freed them. Do the moral calculus. Insensitive to the complexities of the Middle East? Insist that the next Olympic games are held in Cairo or Teheran, and let a deserving Islamic Turkey into the EU.

What's Next?

Scholars attribute these tensions to the growth of inordinate American military power in the aftermath of the Cold War and the twenty-year boom of the American economy. Yet while it would be foolhardy to join Europe in its utopian, statist, authoritarian, and ultimately dangerous enterprises, we should not ignore their views either. They really do admire us when we act morally. For all their aspersions, they know the Taliban is evil and Mr. Karzai far better. They accept that our bombs, not their greater number of peacekeepers, saved lives and drove Mr. Milosevic out. If we seek to stay on and create a legitimate government in Iraq, they will quietly be pleased when it is all over. And they also acknowledge, albeit privately, that America has some cause to suspect UN actions when authoritarian governments like China are on the Security Council, and lunatic and criminal thugocracies like Libya, Syria, and Zimbabwe vote in the General Assembly on an equal basis with democratic states.

If we can ignore all the grating ankle-biting and hypocrisy, the Europeans must remain our friends because they do see within us a shared moral heritage, and so admire American idealism when it is coupled with real power. In these dark days ahead, it is in our own interest that our efforts against Middle Eastern autocrats always be couched in the language of genuine concern for their captive peoples. Liberation, not aggression, must be our motto. Europe won't like publicly what we do, but privately they will agree that we did what we had to do.

Written on July 27 and published in
NATIONAL REVIEW ONLINE *on July 29, 2002.*

23

※━●◆━※

Good-bye to Europe?

In the aftermath of the catastrophe that struck the United States last September 11, few things can have been more dismaying to Americans than the attitude adopted by many of our closest European allies, whose sympathy for the loss of life was quickly replaced by skepticism, if not outright hostility, toward American motives and American policy. The ensuing months seem only to have heightened rather than diminished their animosity.

In the recent election campaign in Germany, Chancellor Gerhard Schroeder volubly parted ways with us and our proposed "adventure" in Iraq, promising his countrymen a "German way" of dealing with global crises, perhaps oblivious to the unfortunate historical echoes this phrase still awakens among millions of Americans. British Labor politicians, ostensibly worried about a conflagration that would draw the United Kingdom into an unending American-led war in the Middle East, have deprecated George W. Bush as an ignorant simpleton ("The most intellectually backward

American President of my political lifetime," writes Labor MP Gerald Kaufman). French commentators, for their part, are more apt to call Bush a cowboy than Saddam Hussein an outlaw.

If the fear of Russian tanks used to unite America and Europe, are differences over everything from greenhouse gases and Yasser Arafat now to divide us? Josef Joffe, the editor of the German weekly *Die Zeit,* downplayed this already simmering hostility last year in an influential pre–September 11 essay in the *National Interest.* Dismissing European snipings as a species of "neo-ganging up," Joffe noted that most Europeans talk one way but tend to act another, and he recommended that the United States apply a little cosmetic diplomacy to soothe ruffled Continental feathers. But now it is a year after September 11, and the anti-American mood seems quite firmly entrenched, deriving less from anything we have done—Americans have not used their imperial power to acquire territory since the Spanish-American War—than from a perception of who we purportedly are: flag-waving, gun-toting, SUV-driving, MTV-watching, minority-electrocuting, Big Mac–chomping boors running amok in the world.

In the absence of in-depth surveys, it is difficult to gauge the prevalence of unease among our European allies or its incidence across countries, classes, and groups. Most often, evidence of animus comes to us anecdotally—Frenchmen protesting McDonald's restaurants, Greeks booing during a memorial commemorative silence in a soccer stadium at the news of September 11, Berliners demonstrating against President Bush's visit to Germany, and a chorus of pundits warning us against any assault on Saddam Hussein. But we are also reminded that Britain, for example, showed remarkable solidarity with the United States in Afghanistan and might do so again in Iraq, notwithstanding the unprecedented venom that pours forth from much of the English journalistic and academic elite, and at least one Europe-wide poll taken in early September showed conditional support for an invasion of Iraq.

What seems beyond denial is that, from the Atlantic coast to the Balkans, there has been a rise in the level of truculence. Scandinavians to the north seem as mistrustful of the United States as do the

Mediterranean peoples of Greece, France, and Spain. Has a Palestinian child been hit by a stray Israeli missile? American F-16s are to blame. Is Europe racked by floods? They are the effect of global warming, set loose by a Kyoto-boycotting America. In the United States itself, has Mumia Abu-Jamal been condemned as a murderer by a jury of his peers and sent to death row? Paris, in recompense, will make the convicted killer an honorary citizen of the city.

The new anti-Americanism also seems to bridge the usual ideological fault lines. Leftists and socialists indict us for the death penalty, guns, the lack of universal health care, and grasping corporations. Right-wing clerics and nationalists join them in bemoaning the perversion of traditional European culture as the result of American advertising and hucksterism. In Greece, an Orthodox priest can prove more virulently anti-American than a diehard socialist—and for reasons that transcend our having ousted from power his fellow Eastern Orthodox Christian, Slobodan Milosevic. The more the European masses appear to be hooked on American popular culture, the more bitterly their elites decry the United States as the profitable but cynical pusher.

As for governments, no less indisputable is that most of them have greeted with disapproval or distaste nearly every major American foreign-policy initiative of the past two years—our walking out of the Durban conference on racism, our dismissal of the Kyoto accords, our cancellation of the ABM treaty with the former Soviet Union, our reference to an identifiable "axis of evil," our strong support for democratic Israel and disparagement of the corrupt Palestinian Authority, our refusal of International Criminal Court jurisdiction over American GIs, and our advocacy of capital punishment for al Qaeda murderers. The doubts and suspicions expressed by European officialdom encourage more extreme voices to broadcast their invective with a new aggressiveness. Long before September 11, Polly Toynbee, a columnist for the *Guardian,* wrote an essay ("America the Horrible Is Now Turning into a Pariah") concluding that the United States was itself "an evil empire" and a "rogue state" that had to be "reeled in." A week *after* September 11, another *Guardian* columnist assured her readers that

"It is perfectly possible to condemn the terrorist action and dislike the U.S. just as much as you did before the World Trade Center went down."

Conversations with individual Europeans only confirm the attitudes expressed by governments and media. From recent visits to Europe and a number of daily communications from acquaintances abroad, I can attest that many Europeans take an almost perverse delight in the spectacle of a United States so estranged from the universal opinion of mankind and so unpopular from Asia to Latin America. "Welcome to the real world," one Greek academic scoffed to me at dinner, as he explained that Americans cannot "have it both ways, ducking out on UN conferences and then strong-arming allies for your war against terror."

Where does the new anti-Americanism come from, and what does it mean? In an incisive and far-reaching essay that has been much discussed in Europe and elsewhere, Robert Kagan has dissected the growing European antipathy and pinpointed its source ("Power and Weakness," *Policy Review,* June–July, 2002). Fundamentally, Kagan writes, the distrust arises from insecurity and envy that are, in turn, grounded in the present imbalance of military power—an often embarrassing disparity that has driven the much weaker Europeans to look to their own safety in means other than armed strength and, correlatively, to fear and censure the deployment of armed strength by others: mainly, us. "Today's transatlantic problem," Kagan writes, "is not a George Bush problem: It is a power problem. American strength has produced a propensity to use that strength. Europe's military weakness has produced a perfectly understandable aversion to the exercise of military power."

Or as Jesse Helms more crudely remarked of Europe's preference for talk and mediation at the expense of military action, "The European Union could not fight its way out of a wet paper bag."

There is clearly much to be said for this realist reading of the growing crisis. Our planes, carriers, and divisions dwarf theirs; and this asymmetry not only skews our ability to conduct joint operations with Europeans but also creates resentment on their part and superciliousness on ours. Jealousy among states always arises among the weak toward the strong, and so it makes sense that a generalized resentment and its attendant fears, rather than specific gripes over American "exceptionalism" and "unilateralism," could be the true cause of European discontent.

Compounding this umbrage, as Francis Fukuyama has pointed out in a recent public lecture, is surely the fact that Europe's relative impotence has nothing to do with a lack of intrinsic material resources. The European Union will soon outstrip us in the size both of its economy ($10 trillion to our $7 trillion) and its population (375 million to our 280 million). But still it continues to spend only a third the amount of our outlays on defense ($130 billion to our current $300 billion annually and rising). European weapons programs have not been evolving at anywhere near the same pace as nonmilitary research and development, not to mention expenditures on social welfare. Their various national military schools, while illustrious, cannot compare with West Point, Annapolis, and Colorado Springs in size, sense of mission, or resources, much less with our academies' ability to capture the élan of contemporary young Americans. In Europe, military enlistment is not seen as an avenue either toward social advancement or toward national service but as somehow antithetical to the humane and pacific place that the EU is slated by its utopian charter to become.

It is hardly unheard of for states that are themselves well heeled and yet lack commensurate military resources to adopt a lower profile and to use guile, stealth, or money to fend off potential bullies. And so, in lieu of the capacity to airlift divisions to Afghanistan, bomb Iraq from carrier task forces, or present wayward regimes like Pakistan with ultimatums, frustrated Europeans have put their faith, mistakenly or not, in international bodies like the United Nations and the International Criminal Court, while pretending not to notice that American power alone is what has permitted them to dream that they inhabit a global fairyland of reasonable people.

When it comes to what we should do about this growing divide, most thoughtful analysts maintain that it behooves us as a truly mighty nation to act with maturity. Ignoring our allies' ankle-biting and shrill charges of "brinkmanship," we should concentrate instead on areas of real mutual concern and advantage, and encourage the Europeans to build up their own muscle through a greater investment in defense. After all, the argument goes, the bases we maintain in Germany, Spain, Italy, and Greece are critical to the worldwide projection of American power, even as the intellectual machinery of the European press and media is essential to the crafting of popular support in times of crisis. In a spirit of what might be called *puissance oblige,* we should strive to alleviate our weaker allies' fretfulness at the same time that we subtly mobilize them to assume a more assertive role that better serves our mutual purposes.

This argument, to whose sweep I have not begun to do justice, is surely a persuasive one, as far as it goes. But might there be additional and even more fundamental reasons for the perplexing European disavowal of force that so often manifests itself in visceral anti-Americanism? In particular, is it really true that the present tension between the United States and Europe results largely from a disproportion of power, and that the way to mitigate it is to begin to redress the imbalance?

My own feeling is otherwise: that the current state of transatlantic tension, far from being a temporary artifact of power relations, is the more natural condition between us—a strain based on our radically different cultures and histories and hence unlikely to be dissipated by bigger defense budgets there or more sensitive diplomats here. And my guess is that this condition is likely only to worsen.

Forgotten in the present anguish over European attitudes is our own age-old suspicion of the Old Country, a latent distrust that once again is slowly reemerging in the face of European carping. It helps to recall that, for millions of Americans, doubts about Europe were once not merely fanciful but often entirely empirical. In my own hardly atypical family, both Europe and Japan were seen as not very nice places that for selfish reasons started wars, drew us in, and tended to take Hansons and Davises away from their small vineyards and orchards, only to return them a year or two later dead, maimed, or crazed. At family dinners, "Europe" never meant vacations or the grand tour but evoked gruesome stories about poison gas, "rolling" with Patton, or having one's head exploded at Normandy Beach.

To some of us, then, the fifty-year Cold War was not a dress rehearsal for a perpetual American military alliance with Western Europe but another of those emergency life-and-death struggles that necessitated the temporary stationing of American troops on European soil. When the Cold War ended, ten years ago, should this not have brought us back to the more normal condition of the past? Since there was no longer an overwhelming threat to Europe that the Europeans could not handle, was there a need for a formal American presence in Continental affairs at all?

These old American prejudices may no longer be shared by the elites who make our policy, but they are not for that reason to be dismissed. As it happens, such mistrusts are themselves deeply rooted in essential fault lines between the American sense of self and the European. Those differences lie in our separate histories and national characters, our different demographies, our different cultures, our different approaches to questions of class and economic mobility, our different conceptions of the individual and society, our different visions of the good life and of democracy— and our very different attitudes toward projecting outward our versions of freedom. All these historic antitheses may better explain the current acrimony than an imbalance of power, often more an epiphenomenon than the cause of rifts among nations.

Volumes have been written on each of these subjects, but we can agree on the fundamental elements of American exceptionalism. The experience of the frontier encouraged a sense of self-reliance and helped to define morality in terms of action rather than rhetoric. Having no history of monarchy, fascism, or communism, we retain our founders' original optimism about republican government, considering it not only critical to our own singular success but a form of political organization that should be emulated by others. The absence of a common race and religion encouraged us to treasure a necessary allegiance to common ideas and values, an allegiance that has so far outlasted the attenuating doctrines of multiculturalism and "diversity." That refugees from around the world, and especially the unwanted of Europe itself, not only survived in an inhospitable country but created history's greatest civilization in the course of a mere century is testament to the revolutionary success of American democratic culture, a society that today morphs newly arrived Koreans into NASCAR fans, transmogrifies Hmong into country-and-western addicts, and allows the children of illegal aliens to become Ph.D.s, electrical engineers, and newspaper columnists.

An American might well contend on the basis of recent history and the present state of world affairs that his confident doctrine, so often antithetical to Europe's, is by far the superior: far better not only for him, but for the world as a whole. Scholarship and practical experience alike demonstrate why, just as immigrants have consistently voted with their feet by flooding our shores, so, too, have hundreds of millions around the globe, including among Europe's own peoples, voted with their stomachs for the fruits of American material abundance and with their remote controls for the raw energy of American popular culture.

But that is a long argument that we need not stop to adjudicate. The essential point is this: American strength and European weakness are not just a temporary manifestation of our spending more on guns and accepting less in social services, while they insist on state help at the expense of navies and armies. Thanks to our physical size and natural riches, our dizzying diversity, and our belief that success is more often to be predicated on talent and hard work than on ingrained social and class hierarchies, we have become a nation *both* enormously rich and, especially, strong. With military power and economic force in service to singular values and ideas, we could not be cynical or faltering even if we wished to, or at least not for long. Seeing things in black and white is part and parcel of our aspiration to be moral—as much our national glue as our very optimism and aggressiveness.

In short, far more fundamental than the absence of European military resources and its queer ramifications is the issue of *why* we, and not they, have power, and how and why we are willing to use it in ways they would not. If we gave the Europeans fifteen carriers and twenty divisions tomorrow, we and they would still be at odds. Turn over to them our entire multibillion-dollar B-2 fleet and it would be mothballed or sold for scrap while we continued as we could with our incorrigible habit of feeding Somalis, freeing Panamanians, liberating Kuwaitis—and, when necessary, patrolling the Mediterranean. The long list of their complaints against us that I enumerated early on—in essence, grievances against who we purportedly are rather than what we do—unconsciously pays tribute to these indelible facts.

September 11 has awakened America in ways we still are not quite sure of. But as far as Europe is concerned, it seems more than possible that we are coming to the end of a relationship born out of the unusual circumstances of the twentieth century. Our diplomats and politicians, who so often travel to and are educated in Europe, are just now starting to worry about this growing specter of estrangement, but I suspect that large numbers of Americans have not only taken it in stride but accepted it as inevitable.

It makes a certain sense that the EU has staked its future on international accords and its own ability to persuade or cajole frightening regimes in Asia and Africa. One need not be altogether cynical about this: Europe's military unpreparedness is in fact an inescapable problem, and Europeans have plenty to be anxious about. Without the Atlantic and Pacific to serve as buffers, only a few hundred miles separate a largely weak Continent from the lunocracies in Algeria and Libya, while Syria, Iran, and Iraq are within missile range. Rising and unassimilated populations in England, France, and Germany round out the causes of European angst. Still, it is hard to believe that any of these threats could not be handled by a united Europe itself.

As for the dangers from within—lest we forget, another of the purposes of NATO was to inhibit the aggressive impulses of any one European country, especially Germany, against any other, specifically France—here, too, cynicism is uncalled for. Given Western Europe's turbulent past, farsighted diplomats are to be congratulated for uniting such a disparate group of nations under the aegis of some sort of federation, and for avoiding a major war within Western Europe for more than a half-century. But it is hard to believe that, if their achievement is genuine, and not simply the result of a common Cold War enemy, the United States is needed to guarantee it; or that, if it breaks down, the United States would be able to fix it.

Hardest of all to accept in our current circumstances is that our European allies would or could join *us* in any meaningful way in sustained military operations abroad that involve real costs and risks. Indeed, we may be one unilateral action away from the de facto dissolution of NATO. Should the United States end up going it alone in Iraq while Europe remonstrates, and should it succeed both in removing Saddam Hussein from power and in fostering some sort of consensual government there, domestic support among Americans for any future military campaign to aid a European power is likely to be drastically diminished. In such a world, and whatever action we took on our own or with de facto allies, the very idea of Americans ever again leading a NATO crusade to banish a marauder like Milosevic seems preposterous.

The onus to preserve the status quo of the present alliance thus lies not on the American people, who may be returning to a time-honored and reasonable consensus about Europe, but on those, included among them our leaders, who believe Europe still merits a special relationship at all. By any objective standard, we have long ago ceased being members of a true partnership, and it may be time to accept that reality and move on. Who knows? After our separation, when we are no longer sworn allies, we might even become better friends.

Written in September and published in the
October 2002 issue of COMMENTARY *magazine.*

24

Geriatric Teenagers

The Paris–Berlin–Moscow Axis
Needs Some Tough Love

Imagine a continent that collectively budgets very little on its own defense, instead finding protection in a distant and democratic superpower that pays rent for the privilege of basing troops, planes, and ships to stop hooligans—sometimes, as in the case of an embarrassingly impolite Mr. Milosevic, right on Europe's doorstep.

In return, many European elites ridicule American values, naïveté, and insularity—even as their countries have raked in billions of American dollars in trade surpluses and tourism from mostly oblivious, aw-shucks Americans. We self-absorbed, parochial yokels laughed and paid little attention to the fact that some in Europe had forsaken Christianity for this weird, emerging boutique religion of anti-Americanism.

Who could take their ankle-biting seriously? Who, after all, would give up all that they had gotten so cheaply—that dream of all spoiled teenagers: to snap at and ridicule their patient and paying parents, even as they call on them *in extremis* for help whenever the car stalls or the rent is short?

Yet suddenly many Europeans are not talking of "Europe," but telling us instead: "You Americans must be careful in lumping us all together as if there are not real differences among us." Thank the crazed Chirac and his infantile Talleyrand for this new, more nationalist and "non-European" identity now growing among Europeans in the wake of the Iraqi war.

The unease with the Paris–Berlin–Moscow axis is just beginning. In the coming year alone, troves of archives—economic, political, and military—will reveal France to have been more an enemy than a friend of the United States in the present war, and that a legion of German, French, and Russian businessmen, journalists, and politicians were on the Iraqi take, or worse. The duplicity of our so-called friends will make their deceit during the Balkan fiasco look like child's play.

So it would be a terrible mistake to assume that our relationship with "Old Europe" will—or should—so easily get back on track. Our own Washington–New York nexus is assuring us that it was just the generation of 1968 come of age in Europe, and our own clumsiness, that led to the fallout over Iraq—as if Mr. Bush's Texas drawl were the problem.

Yet polls continue to show that at least a third of Frenchmen, Belgians, and Germans don't like Americans, and another third don't trust us. Eight years of Clinton's lip-biting and apologies du jour earned no sympathy, but did win us plenty of contempt. The problems are fundamental and transcend American presidencies.

Let us face reality at least once: we are living in the most precipitous moment of change of the last half-century as we witness a tectonic shift in Europe, one that is realigning the way an entire continent operates.

Such radical changes are not unusual in European history. Remember the first New/Old World transfer of power. The fifteenth- and sixteenth-century Protestant Reformation—coupled with the rise of Atlantic exploration and trade with the New

World and the onslaught of the Ottoman Empire—helped to shift European weight from its classical foundations on the Mediterranean to the new Europe of England, northern France, Holland, and Germany.

Nor are fits of Continental craziness, both real and abstract, even new. Napoleon was willing to risk the lives of millions for the idea of a pan-European dream, its scary, pretentious adages not unlike those now emanating from Brussels or from the mad M. de Villepin. The rise of German Nazism, Italian fascism, and Continental Marxism at times turned Europeans away from the liberal tradition and drew them to darker and more authoritarian promises, with roots from Plato's *Laws* to Oswald Spengler. Too many Europeans still cherish the belief that they are close to an end to war, hunger, want, and meanness—ideals inseparable from a light workweek, cradle-to-grave care, protection by an uncouth American military, and a steady supply of fertile, darker, unassimilated peoples to take out their trash and clean their toilets.

The fact is that the absence of Russian divisions has meant an end to both a common threat and unity with the United States. It is not just that Europeans have forgotten past American help. They resent even the *mention* of past beneficence, and, if history is to be contemplated, prefer to bring up Hamburg and Dresden rather than Auschwitz.

Maybe, as so many rightly remind us, it is our power and their weakness that incite jealousy and necessitate such pretence. It is an age-old phenomenon not unlike the case of the Aegean states of the Hellenic League that preferred to pay Athens with tribute rather than ships for their own protection—and then awoke, furious that the Athenian fleet was establishing its own defense policy, unchecked by multilateral constraints.

Maybe the animus comes from our radically different constitutions and the singular American experience of vast frontiers, immigration, assimilation, and the lack of a national creed or race? Or could it even be because we are optimistic about the future, and believe we can still assimilate our newcomers, grow the economy, expand our military, and promote freedom—even while they fret about stagnant growth, a demographic time bomb, and rising unassimilated minorities. Maybe, too, the angst arises because of the youth of Europe, who desire America's popular and often crass culture enough to worry their older guardians of hallowed values? Who knows? Who cares?

The key now, instead, is to find remedies that are neither too weak nor too strong, and that are aimed at radically reforming rather than simply eradicating shared institutions. We will always be friends and, as democratic liberal societies, must remain partners of some sort. But failure to react would be as disastrous as it has been in the past. First, we must distinguish French, Belgians, and Germans from the rest. The former three, whom we have most helped in the past, not surprisingly are the most duplicitous—resentment also being among the most powerful of all emotions.

Yet if we are subtle, the map soon may reveal who are the real odd men out. Eastern Europe does not share their distrust of America, but is more likely to remember 1939–40, when Germans invaded as the French sat. To the south, Spain and Italy are not sympathetic to either the bullying of Paris–Berlin–Moscow or the unattractive trends in the EU. Nor are the U.K., Holland, Denmark, and Norway at all happy with Mr. Chirac and Mr. Schroeder.

Abroad, good luck to M. de Villepin in his efforts to convince the Arabs his country is either principled or strong. I do not think a Japan, South Korea, or Taiwan cares much for French-German diplomacy to keep their neighborhood safe from nukes. M. de Villepin, who claims he knows something of the latter career of his hero, Napoleon, should remember that nations can survive impotence or immorality—but not both. And that "both" is exactly the dividend of his recent pathetic gambit.

To bring back moral clarity and maturity, we must begin to establish a more reciprocal relationship with the willing. We can start by moving *all* our troops from Germany or relocating them in much smaller pockets in Eastern Europe. This is not just a military

issue; and the generals involved there should bow out and yield to
their civilian overseers, who recognize the larger political and
moral issues at stake. In the post–Cold War era we still need naval
and air bases in the Mediterranean, but not necessarily in Spain,
Italy, Greece, *and* Turkey. We should hold honest discussions with
all four and see who wants us in and who out—and, politely and
with tact, act accordingly.

Given the antics of Belgium with its wild criminal courts and
anti-American rhetoric, it is a cruel joke to house NATO in Brussels. Better to move the headquarters to Warsaw or perhaps Rome.
France should decide whether it is in or out of the alliance, but it
can no longer be both. They, not we, have nearly destroyed NATO
by abusing their own quasi-relationship, and that, too, must end.
They will soon see that the end of the Soviet Union gives us as
many options within NATO as it provides them. So as the alliance
wanes—and all such leagues do, in the absence of common enemies—we should carefully establish bilateral relationships with
those Europeans who know something of the history of the twentieth century. It might be wise also to lift all quotas on skilled
Europeans who wish expedited American citizenship—both for
our own good and to discover how many talented people might
prefer leaving a creeping socialism.

Reform at the UN should be a centerpiece of our new policy.
There is no reason why a billion people of a nuclear, democratic
India, an increasingly confident Japan, or a vast country like Brazil
should not be represented as permanent members of the Security
Council. In addition, we must move to require democratic government for participation in the General Assembly; it makes no
sense to give despots the privileges they don't extend even to their
own people. Let the UN become an assembly of free peoples, and
allow Libya, Syria, North Korea, and Cuba to form their own
United Tyrannies.

We should also seek to merge France's veto power under EU
auspices, as befits the new EU Continental "nation." The input
of a Norway, Denmark, Holland, or Poland alone might make

"Europe" a more credible UN Security Council member. Remember that we have arms and brave soldiers—and a veto in the UN—while France relies on the latter alone. So we ought to be more active in the UN to abstain, veto, or block almost everything France does that we do not find compatible with our interests. Unlike us, they have no alternatives. Perhaps America should start by offering a series of resolutions asking for aid to the Iraqi people, putting the onus of a veto on France—no more backroom deals, flattering, or cajoling to save them from expressing to the world their own naked machinations.

It is time also to quit allowing functionaries like Kofi Annan and Boutros Boutros-Ghali to assume leadership roles in the UN—not when there are real statesmen and moralists of free countries, like Vaclav Havel or Elie Wiesel, who have known hardship and appreciate freedom.

Our ambassadorships to European countries (especially Turkey and Greece) and the Middle East should be carefully examined to ensure that we have resolute, principled men and women there to present our new views forcefully, rather than apologizing for the United States or triangulating within the Bush administration. Now is not the hour for oil men, think-tankers who have taken or will take Saudi money, State Department apparatchiks, or Atlantic Alliance yes-men whose careers are predicated either on pleasing their bosses, making money, or hopping in and out of academia. For these radically new times, we need folk of a different nature, who are convinced the events of the last two years were not an aberration.

We must also warn Old Europe of *our* hesitancy about "intervening" in *their* own purely European affairs. Unsavory characters such as Mr. Lukashenko in Belarus, like past lunatics in Serbia, will always arise. But now they are European problems, requiring the intervention of the German navy and the French army, operating under the shield of the Belgian air force and—who knows?—perhaps Russian command and control.

Cyprus, tension in the Aegean, Turkish EU membership, Gibraltar, North African disputes—all these and more must remain exclusively Europe's quagmires. We wish them well but cannot under the present circumstance hope to send a single soldier to resolve a single one of their own internal crises—unless it involves the safety of our own bilateral allies: perhaps a Britain, Poland, Italy, Holland, Spain, or others in such future coalitions of the willing.

To preserve relationships with our cultural brethren will, oddly, require a lower profile in Europe, and a trust that after sixty years Europeans can arm themselves and take care of their own problems without reverting to their old violent and internecine proclivities.

A final note concerning our NATO diplomats, generals in Europe, and functionaries at the State Department: it would be silly to demonize those who call for changes as if they were naïve or parochial, or worse. It was the old way of doing business that helped bring us to this impasse—whether it be the appeasement of the past decade that so emboldened terrorists and dictators, or the constant flattering of European diplomats in the face of their sustained and often dangerous anti-Americanism.

The world is not as it was: three thousand Americans are dead. We took casualties in Iraq as a result of Turkish-French-German duplicity, and the French government seemed to have almost stronger military associations with Iraq than it did with us. The saner and safer, not the more precipitous, course is quietly but resolutely to change business as usual—and sooner rather than later.

Written on March 30 and published in
NATIONAL REVIEW ONLINE *on April 2, 2003.*

25

⟶⊜⟵

The Old Game

*ONCE UPON A TIME, EVERYTHING WAS
SO NICE AND PREDICTABLE . . .*

Seasoned diplomats lectured that superpowers must act carefully and predictably, allowing friends and enemies to know in advance the parameters of their behavior. A certain caution arose in the United States during the last twenty years that held that we had a special burden not to overreact to provocations and must always work within the framework of multilateral consensus. The conventional wisdom admonished that we were too powerful or perhaps too civilized—or even polite—to respond to every annoyance.

Because our diplomatic experts have so often been graduates of our best universities, they believed that before shooting back it was always wise to examine the social and economic conditions—read Western exploitation—that might have encouraged such anti-American behavior in the first place. Moreover, we usually were willing to implore our clients to let us spend billons of dollars on them and risk in their defense thousands of American lives.

181

We routinely would worry about riling the world in order to put troops in harm's way to protect nations that were privately relieved and publicly hostile. Those voices that urged that it was wiser for America—given the nature of man—to be a little unpredictable, perhaps even volatile at times, and, like the Greeks of old, to punish enemies and help friends, were caricatured as Rambos and simpletons who did not understand the complexities of diplomacy, a supposedly higher art than the rules of the factory, farm, or neighborhood corner.

Unfortunately, the world soon caught on to us predictable and unimaginative Americans and mastered this strange game far better than we ever did. If I had been a terrorist in the 1980s and nineties, I would have sized up the rules of the contest something like this: kill or take hostages at no more than ten or so Americans at a clip, about every other year. Big operations—like killing hundreds of Marines in Beirut or taking embassy hostages in Teheran or blowing a crater in the USS *Cole*—would be possible, but only if they were cloaked in general Muslim radicalism and purportedly independent of state sanction. Or, such mayhem could be carried out on the home soil of an Islamic state without much law and order, ensuring that American reprisals would not be deemed logical by strict cost-benefit analysis. The aim, of course, would be something like a perpetual series of smaller Vietnams—Mogadishus and Haitis where Americans threw up their hands, withdrew, and allowed killers and thugs to drop the pretense of political reform and simply take over. At worst, retaliation might involve a battleship salvo or a few dozen cruise missiles—usually a minor irritant and sometimes valuable for publicity purposes if there were enough collateral civilian damage.

The terrorists' modus operandi sort of worked if you look at the record of American restraint, confusion, and paralysis from Teheran 1979 to September 10, 2001—or until bin Laden got greedy, broke the rules, and killed too many at once, and at home.

If I had been a friendly Middle Eastern head of state who wanted my family, tribe, or clique to continue its despotic rule, I would have trolled for U.S. support by being anti-Communist, pumping oil aplenty, or keeping terrorists from moving in downtown. All that would win me American money, debt relief, trade concessions, military credits, a pass on human-rights abuses, or explicit promises of protection.

Then I would move in the other direction to assuage the domestic anger and frustration that was inevitable under a corrupt and authoritarian regime. I would offer bases, but impose such stringent conditions on their usage that they could not really be employed for major operations in the region and, in fact, would become sources of money and recycled arms—not to mention the state pride that comes when such powerful renters are ordered to stay put and not venture off the premises. Meanwhile, I would send my youth over to the United States to get educated and acquire expertise in the Western material things I wanted, but ensure that they resented their benefactor and decried its decadence and license.

So the Middle East calculus ran something like this: unleash the state-controlled press to attack America and its Zionist puppet and either buy off or subsidize Islamic fanatics to curb their political venom, or at least direct it against the United States. The party line delivered to visiting American diplomats: only with increased financial or military support (as stealthily as possible) and a more "balanced" policy in the Middle East crisis will the "Arab street"—that raging herd that materializes out of nowhere with its effigies, bloodcurdling yells, and perpetual fist-shaking—be neutralized. All this would garner platitudes like "America's traditional friend in the Middle East" or "decades of commitment to security and stability in the region."

This game, too, would have still gone on, had the Saudis not outsmarted themselves by giving too much money to too many killers, or had the censored Egyptian press and mob cut their vitriol to monthly rather than daily doses.

If I were a Western European government in the post–Cold War era, I would slash my arms budget and spend less than 1 percent of

GNP on defense. I would use the savings to increase social entitlements and adopt a utopian worldview befitting both my country's wealth and absence of military power: only in conjunction with the UN, the EU, or NATO should America act militarily; in contrast, Europe should never resort to force, even if it means 250,000 dead just hours from Berlin or Rome. Talk is cheap, arms are not.

To handle the rhetoric of a self-centered population demanding ever more benefits, fewer children, and utopia now, I would seek to blame the United States for everything from racism to pollution, insisting that globalization, militarization, and suburbanization were all more or less imported American pathologies—even as European companies aped American business, advertising, and financial practices to ensure its people commensurate profits. I would damn the United States for backing democratic Israel, and then make huge profits selling everything and anything to Iraq, Iran, or any other cutthroats who could pay.

All this would hinge, of course, on keeping American arms and troops in Spain, Italy, Germany, and Greece to prevent some rogue in a province of the former Soviet Union, a madman in the Middle East, or a murderer in the Balkans from going too far and killing Europeans in Europe—or even blowing up European tourists, ships, and planes abroad.

NATO would always be praised in the abstract, but never used in the concrete. Diplomats would know the script: as millions marched in Paris, Berlin, or Rome against American capitalists, soldiers, or politicians, functionaries would shake their heads and publicly lecture the poor dense Americans—but of course keep the financially lucrative and militarily essential bases and alliances that underpin the whole charade.

So Messrs. Schroeder and Chirac spoiled a good thing by going a wee bit too far, finally convincing even our most diehard NATO apparatchiks and trans-Atlantic attachés that Europe was really a different place after all. How hard it was for them to slither back into the fold, with an American "anti-Europeanism" that ran deeper, and with a longer memory, than the parlor game's smug "anti-Americanism."

If I were a roguish China or Russia, I would count on the premise that the United States wanted a stable world more than I. I would sell arms to lunatics, forget where my own plutonium was, and claim such enormous political and economic problems at home that I could ill afford to be entirely responsible abroad. In a sea of industrial pollution and state-planned environmental desecration I would hector the United States at international conferences about assuming a greater burden to save the planet from people like myself. I would always use force to ensure fealty nearby—a Tibet or Chechnya—but condemn its employment in the abstract, and especially when the United States was involved. I would triangulate with the Europeans, arguing that we all must do our part to force the United States to act more like a world citizen, knowing that if I got out of line, only America, not they, would stand in my way.

The Old Game had so many sly players. Mexico's Vicente Fox was as adept as any. He sent millions of his exploited and impoverished population northward and harangued the United States to treat illegal aliens more humanely than did his own government— all the while hoping to avoid fundamental political and economic reform at home, encouraging Mexican nationals to talk of the "Reconquista" and counting on billions of dollars from expatriates who would romanticize their homeland the further and longer they were away from it.

South Korea, too, played the game. Its youth hit the streets damning America, as a new generation of sunshine diplomats talked grandly of a third way—while 38,000 American sacrificial lambs served as a trip wire on the DMZ. The UN—its elite housed in New York, its membership often undemocratic, its budget inflated—was a real gamer as well, damning this as Zionist, that as imperialist, all the while asking the United States to pay for being a fat target. The world's intellectuals, writers, and journalists were expert players.

Unfortunately, two strange events transpired that should not have, undoing all the old rules. On September 11, 2001, three thousand Americans were murdered en masse at a time of peace— in our planes, in our most iconic buildings, and at the center of

American military power. And worse still for terrorists, faux allies, and triangulators, our president was a Texan inexperienced with the game's nuances—not a liberal Democrat who wanted to be liked abroad or a seasoned Republican congressional alumnus who wanted to preserve the old rules. Stranger still, President Bush surrounded himself with a different kind of person—the kind who, in a crisis, offers one reason why we should act, rather than a thousand Hamlet-like excuses why we should not.

And so, all bets are off. Bases, alliances, institutions, friendships, immigration policy, easily duped Americans—nothing can be taken for granted anymore.

The board has been abruptly wiped clean. The game's up.

Written on June 4 and published in
NATIONAL REVIEW ONLINE *on June 6, 2003.*

VI

THE THREE-WEEK WAR

After a tumultuous national debate over going into Iraq, and indeed acrimony even through the first week of hostilities, when a sandstorm and a brief resupply effort led to charges of "quagmire" and a shortage of American troops on the ground, conventional hostilities ended with the defeat of Saddam Hussein's military at the cost of less than two hundred American and British fatalities incurred during the formal war and the subsequent mop-up operations in the months that followed.

Public opinion proved constant in its support for American action, even as elite commentators experienced deep mood swings in their prognostications of defeat and stasis. The three-week war proved earlier forecasts of doom wrong, but they were almost instantaneously replaced by assertions that our military forces were not necessarily to be praised for their prowess but, rather, that they had enjoyed a cakewalk against an outmanned enemy. Indeed, as I write, sixty Americans have been killed in the hundred days since the cessation of formal hostilities—tragically, a few hundred more will probably become casualties before the end of the occupation—proof in the minds of unabashed pundits that the war is not really over.

It is, and we will within the year put down insurrectionists and terrorists who have no agenda except the despair of acknowledging that there is no future for Saddamites and Baathists in a new Iraq. In the following essays I expressed confidence in often dark times that the American military would prevail and do so quickly, often to criticism from a variety of observers. One skeptical reporter for the Los Angeles Times *who visited my farm over Christmas vacation, on January 3, 2003, seemed to scoff at such optimistic appraisals ("three or four weeks") of a proposed invasion of Iraq. His version of my side of our dialogue went as follows: "I would imagine the United States is going to go in there, and three or four weeks later it is going to be the end of Saddam Hussein and his government. A period of instability may follow but eventually you will have a consensual government" (January 5, 2003, p. A16).*

In another case, however, my instincts were proven wrong in suggesting that the American military would find evidence of weapons of mass destruction shortly after overrunning Iraq. In fact, in the first hundred days no such arsenals were found—only a few documents and anecdotal reports of their prior presence. As of July 4, 2003, we are still not certain whether Saddam's weapons are still ensconced somewhere in Iraq, were destroyed on the eve of the war, or sent out for storage in Syria or worse places still. Yet, because both the Clinton administration and the United Nations had firm intelligence that such weapons existed in 1998, and there have been no documented reports that they were subsequently destroyed even after Operation Desert Fox of 1999, we can only assume that the full tale of their odyssey will emerge only when Iraq is a fully consensual society and the fate of Saddam Hussein finally established—when those intertwined in the arms industry will feel secure enough to come forward.

26

Iraqi Interrogatories

THE USUAL QUESTIONS ABOUT IRAQ

Isn't going into Iraq just a bad idea?

Every war is a bad idea. When are there ever attractive options in risking soldiers in times of national crisis? The last good choice we had was in January 1991, when a huge and victorious American army had a clear road to Baghdad, with a good chance at eliminating a mass murderer who was on the verge of collapse and poised to exterminate innocents.

By contrast, our present dilemma involves something bad or much worse. Yet we must not forget that there still is a great moral difference between the depressing choice of invading and risking American lives, and the much worse policy of doing nothing and waiting to be blackmailed or attacked in the future. Preemption may be saner than reaction.

Does Saddam Hussein really pose a deadly or immediate threat to the United States—and how, as a democracy, in good conscience can we act pre-emptively?

Since September 11 there has no longer been a margin of safety—or error—allowing us a measure of absolute certainty before action. Long gone is the notion that American soil is inviolable or that enemies will not butcher thousands of civilians unexpectedly and in time of peace. All we need to know is that he broke the armistice agreements of the first war, violated the weapons-inspections accords, likes to attack other countries, dallies with terrorists, has nightmarish weapons, and has already fought us once. That he is a dictator, killed thousands of his own people, sought to assassinate a president of the United States, tried to destroy the ecology of Kuwait, and sent missiles into Israel and Saudi Arabia are not misdemeanors.

In fact, consensual governments, from Republican Rome in the Third Punic War through to the present, have often struck first when their strategic or moral interests were felt to be at stake. In Grenada, Panama, Serbia, and Kosovo we preemptively attacked governments that had not directly assaulted us, because they posed perceived dangers to either our own interests or their own people. What discredits the idea of preemption is the combination of failure and amorality—as with the 1956 English-Israeli-French assault on Suez, or the Arab attack in the 1973 Yom Kippur War. By contrast, success and moral right make even the most audacious strikes less objectionable—as in Israel's much-deplored destruction of Saddam's bomb-making nuclear complex or its bombing of terrorist headquarters in Tunisia.

But won't we set a bad precedent? Maybe India or Russia will do the same.

This is the current conventional wisdom repeated ad nauseam. But Russia went into Chechnya regardless of our wishes or example. And India will make a decision to act on the basis of its own self-interest, not whether it can cite "precedent" on the part of the United States. Strong nations evaluate their options from

calculations of self-preservation and morality—choices not necessarily predicated on what the United States must do to ensure its
own security. The invasion of Iraq will have a deleterious effect on
world peace only if it is seen as gratuitous or unnecessary—and
neither presently happens to be true.

So the danger is not preemption per se but bellicosity for no
good reason. We must get away from stereotyped generalizations
and look at specifics. Being inactive in the face of unprovoked
attacks on Americans—the Iranian embassy takeover and the Marine barracks bombing are good examples—can establish precedents just as pernicious. In that regard, President Carter's restraint
in 1980, in combination with a failed raid, was a far more dangerous act than President Reagan's bombing of Libya—and makes his
present moral objections to preempting Saddam as disturbing as
they are hypocritical.

*If we are so worried about Iraq's weapons of mass destruction, why aren't
its immediate neighbors equally concerned?*

What states profess publicly is often at odds with their private
concerns. And it may be that, despite the appearance of Islamic or
Arab solidarity, the autocracies of the Gulf *secretly* wish us to
remove the Iraqi regime against their publicly expressed desires. In
addition, this new assault will not be about the containment but
the removal of Saddam Hussein, and thus will be far more explo-
sive, in a variety of ways, than the last war. A cynic would add that
illegitimate regimes will worry as much about a democratic revolution on their borders as they will about the presence of autocrats.
A humane, secular, democratic, and oil-producing Iraq may be as
dangerous to the interests of the Saudi royal family as is Saddam
Hussein. After all, our moderate despots in the region are not worried that Saddam is a dictator, only that he is a mad dictator.

And Europe? How can we ignore their worries?

We cannot ignore the Europeans and must consult them. Still,
in all honesty, we must also accept that once the EU had placed its
national security in the hands of international accords and the UN,

its members could hardly publicly support us without undermining the very legitimacy of their new utopian protocols. Yet unilateralism is hardly a dirty word; the singular obstinacy of a single country has ended many of the world's great evils. The British took on the slave trade, and later faced Hitler alone for two years. Few thought the United States should station Pershing missiles in Europe to thwart the nuclear intimidation of the Soviets. Had the United States waited for European or United Nations approval last autumn, bin Laden and the Taliban would still rule Afghanistan. Again, the effort to view "unilateral" or "preemptory" as pejorative terms in order to deprecate the use of military force misses the point—it is the moral landscape in which such policies are undertaken, not the singular use of a first strike per se, that determines their legitimacy.

And the UN?

We need not enter into a long discussion about the morality of the United Nations, where murderous regimes like China or Libya adjudicate questions of human rights. Instead we can grant, first, that an international framework to air grievances is salutary. Therefore the fact that the United Nations has passed over a dozen resolutions concerning Iraq that have been ignored—and has had its inspectors expelled—suggests either its unconcern with or impotence in enforcing its own statutes. It is increasingly reminiscent of the League of Nations in the age of spreading fascism and totalitarianism. We must remember that present threats of American preemption—not the Europeans' lectures or General Assembly resolutions—alone are making Saddam Hussein give lip service to inspections.

Aren't we diverting our attention from al Qaeda?

No more so than B-29s were a diversion from B-17s, or than Okinawa can be said to have taken our minds away from the encirclement of Hitler's armies.

Won't Saddam's removal destabilize the region?

Haven't we heard this before? The question assumes that the region is stable now. Yet even if it were, such flux might still represent an improvement over the last fifteen years. A worse scenario would be the creation of an Islamic theocracy, the rise of another dictator, or chaos. Yet we have handled all three before—in Iran, Libya, and Afghanistan and Algeria. And in none of those cases were weapons of mass destruction an issue, as they are now. In postbellum Iraq we seek something like the new government in Afghanistan, the Kurdish nascent efforts at republicanism, perhaps the reformist movement in Qatar, or, ideally, a secularized democracy such as is found in Turkey. We must be prepared to promote some foundations for eventual democracy, with the awareness that even if it fails, we will still be better off than we are with the monster there now.

Won't the Islamic world turn on us?

That constant refrain has now joined the annals of conventional ignorance alongside "the Arab street," "a Ramadan cease-fire," "universal jihad," etc. We should have learned by now that anti-American fundamentalists find resonance with their countrymen only when they are not in power and can distort the people's frustrations with autocrats. When they rule, they fail miserably, and incur hatred for themselves.

Iran and Saudi Arabia are an interesting pair of antitheses, are they not? The former has a hostile regime and a friendly populace; the latter has a purportedly friendly government and a hostile citizenry. Democrats are on the move against fundamentalists in Iran; fundamentalists are on the move against autocrats in Saudi Arabia. Surely that should tell us something—that fundamentalists like autocracy and hate democracy. Dictatorial Pakistan has an Islamic fundamentalist problem; democratic India, with its larger Muslim population, less so. The end of the Cold War, the rise of Westernized Arabs, the spread of democracy, and instantaneous global communications all suggest that we may well be successful in crafting consensual government in Iraq—which could prove the most revolutionary act of the last thirty years. Should this war be couched in terms of the liberation of the Iraqi people, Iraqis may well react in jubilation, as did the Afghans—sending a message that we really are on the side of the region's disenfranchised and not of cabals like those of Arafat, the Saudi sheiks, or the Egyptian strongmen who have looted their countries and jailed and killed dissidents.

But didn't we back Saddam Hussein in his war against Iran?

That is often alleged, but the record suggests that our amorality was more a question of hoping that both sides would wear each other out. Recall that the Iranians had just seized our embassy, taken hostages, and pledged death to Americans; under such circumstances, why wouldn't we gain psychological satisfaction at seeing our enemies attacked, even if by equally odious thugs? Allying ourselves in 1941 with the Soviet Union—a regime that had just killed twenty million of its own people—to stop Hitler was a far greater moral quandary. Giving a third of a million trucks to the architect of the Great Terror and the Gulag seems as morally ambiguous as providing some helicopter training for Iraqi pilots. In war you rarely find allies with clean hands; and so, again, conflict is always a matter of bad and worse choices.

Won't Saddam gas our troops, hit Israel, or send agents to blow up cities in America?

Why not envision even more terrifying situations, since doomsday-forecasting is an endless exercise? We should remember instead Grant's dictum that he didn't want to hear what the enemy would do to him, only what he was going to do to the enemy. I suggest that Baghdad in the next few months will be a much more unsafe place than New York or Tel Aviv. More to the point, our military is already preparing for worst-case scenarios—gas, nerve agents, urban warfare—as are the Israelis, our own FBI and CIA, and our allies in the region.

But how can you be so sure that it will be easy or right to remove Saddam Hussein?

We can't assume anything, since war guarantees nothing—except that many plans go wrong somewhere, at some time, once the shooting breaks out. All we can rely on is the excellence of our troops, the morale of our citizenry, and the principled case of removing fascists with deadly weapons and a track record of aggression—and then hope for the best. War is fraught with peril, but in this case inaction is the far more dangerous option—if not for us, then surely for our children, who will have to live with the nuclear-armed epigones of Saddam Hussein. Our record against Islamic or Arab armies—in the first Gulf War, Afghanistan, or the no-fly zone—is not undistinguished and gives cause for more confidence than despair on the battlefield. And let us hope that, unlike in the first Gulf War, we stay on to ensure the safety and democratic aspirations of Kurds and dissidents, and show that our sacrifice can include causes beyond oil and security.

But why do we have to fight the Iraqi people, who are innocent?

We seek to harm them as little as possible; but we are also not naïve. Either through design, laxity, or fear, they allowed their country to be hijacked by a madman who threatens non-Iraqis. They are as guilty or as innocent as were the Germans under Hitler or the Japanese when Tojo ruled—to be warred against under despots and then immediately aided when liberated. Moreover, human nature being what it is, had Hitler taken Moscow and obliterated London, few Germans would have rebelled but would more likely have flocked into Nuremberg for huge victory rallies. Had their forces won at Midway and slaughtered us on Guadalcanal, the Japanese people would have held massive thank-you demonstrations for their military leaders.

So it is with Iraq: should we fail, we can assume that there will be spontaneous celebrations in which the Iraqi "street" will drag around American bodies and cheer—without any prompting on the part of Saddam Hussein. We need not embrace the idea of collective punishment to accept the truth that sometimes entire peoples can go off the deep end and require military defeat to be brought back out of their trance.

Why pick on Iraq when there are also other members of the axis of evil?
    Well, why not worry also about China, Cuba, world hunger, a new AIDS epidemic, West Nile virus, fatty fast food, and . . .

*Written on September 18 and published
in* NATIONAL REVIEW ONLINE *on September 20, 2002.*

27

Iraq Redux

NOT ANOTHER 1991 GULF WAR

Skeptics warn us that we cannot assume that the next war with Saddam Hussein will be as easy as the last, especially since this time we are after his head, not the liberation of Kuwait. True, there is an array of strategic and tactical differences from a decade ago, but I'm not sure that any of the new realities presage a more difficult task than last time. If anything, the challenge is now clearer, more moral—and more suited to our own unique character and strengths.

We are told that because Saddam Hussein knows that we are after his person, he will do ghastly things in his last hours on the planet. But, oddly, that is not the usual way of mad dictators in their last hours on earth. A doomed Hitler barked to his lieutenants to consider using the gas arsenal, but then balked upon their wise advice that the Allied retaliation would be nightmarish. Doomed Japanese madmen promised kamikaze attacks against the surrender ceremonies in Tokyo Bay before either being rounded up or sulking away. Milosevic talked of bombing nuclear power plants and then was led off in handcuffs.

It is not an easy thing for a madman to pull down the world with him. Too many lackies are not willing to share a führer's fiery *Götterdämmerung* when there is a slight chance of cutting a deal and leaving the bunker alive. We should not even assume that Saddam Hussein in the last seconds of his life will not still ponder some final ruse to save his skin—an eleventh-hour fancy that would be rendered impossible should he use weapons of mass destruction. And his henchmen will want to live in this world rather than join him in the fiery next, and so may not push the button when ordered—especially given American antebellum instructions that life next year can be either okay or very, very bad for them, depending on what choice they make when the bombs fall.

We are also warned that Israel might not be so "reasonable" as in 1991. Good. Knowing Israel this time will strike back hard, rather than being leashed by the United States will make it less, not more, likely that Saddam will strike at Tel Aviv. The entire Iraqi cult of the "39 Scuds" in the decade after the Gulf War teaches us that unanswered attack in the Middle East is the real madness. Enduring missiles in 1991 without reprisals and to the cheers of Palestinians, and then unilaterally withdrawing from Lebanon prompted, not discouraged, the present cycle of violence. The fact that a cornered Saddam Hussein, in desperate need of a cause and an Arab jihad, has so far refrained from striking Israel before we act suggests that he equates such bravado with national suicide.

We are told that conquering Iraq now is much more difficult than liberating Kuwait. Again, the very opposite may be true. Saddam's military is worse, but ours is better than a decade ago and far more confident on the eve of battle. Before 1991 there was Vietnam; Afghanistan presages the present attack. If in 1991 we still suffered from a sense of postbellum Vietnam guilt and uncertainty, the last year after 9/11 has brought us confidence and righteous anger. Saddam Hussein controls only one-third of the Iraqi airspace; two-thirds are now very familiar to an entire generation of

American pilots. In 1991 we had no idea of the extent of his weapons of mass destruction; now we have some idea of their nature and where he is likely to cache them.

Plentiful allies, of course, are reassuring, in theory, but last time the Brits were stellar and the rest were mostly in the way, either haggling for the slots in the victory parade or carping that we could not go to Baghdad. So this time we get the benefits of real fighters without the costs of bringing along onlookers and showboaters. Desperate Kurds and Shiites will prove better freedom fighters in liberating Iraq than opulent Kuwaitis and Saudis were in protecting their gold stashes. Before 1991, Saddam talked of the fearsome Republican Guard, who had fought for a decade in Iran; this time we remember it was about an hour away from annihilation before the American M1s were called off. Like prizefighters, armies that were once badly beaten rarely wish for another licking in a rematch against the same opponent.

In 1991 we talked not of freedom, but dispassionately of fighting for "jobs" and "security," code names both for oil. And we were ultimately embarrassed about leaving a murderer in power who subsequently butchered his own. Most of us felt additional unease about restoring a monarchy in Kuwait and fighting to protect an autocracy in Saudi Arabia. So something about the first Gulf War bothered Americans—suspicions that were only confirmed when unsavory Kuwaiti elites left their American hotels and were given back their country without requests for reform, while a "beaten" Saddam Hussein machine-gunned and bombed civilians, and while Saudi generals pinned medals on one another for being saved by Americans.

Not this time. No one is envisioning anything in postbellum Iraq other than the installation of a consensual government. No American is being told to defend Saudi Arabia or to free Kuwait. Instead, our men and women are being asked to liberate an entire country from a fascist, not merely to protect the oil reservoirs of fundamentalists, anti-Semites, and despots. The cause, in other words, is far nobler this time around, and that perception will have a positive effect on our troops. I do not think that we will see Arab women jailed in a free Iraq for wanting to drive cars in the postbellum jubilation.

Analysts admonish that it is tricky to attack a country without warring against its people, and that it is especially hard to remove its dictator without killing his enslaved. The messy history of the recent years teaches us otherwise. We ousted Milosevic without killing thousands of Serbs, despite a series of tactical and strategic mistakes. And this time no one is calling for a Clintonesque air war with bombs in lieu of ground troops. Panama and Afghanistan proved that we can attack a country, rid it of its thugs, and in the process make life better, not worse, for the people.

Americans were bothered by the "Highway of Death" in 1991 and the scenes of hungry, pathetic conscripts being buried alive beneath tons of sand in the desert. By contrast, this war is focused precisely against the agents, not the draftees, of Saddam Hussein; in 2002 the latter at least will have a better chance of choosing to live on for a better cause rather than to die now for an evil man.

There may well be surprises in store for everyone when the shooting starts in Iraq. But comparison with the first Gulf War suggests cause for present optimism, not despair; and we must not take counsel of our fears. We may be more easily caricatured by both friends and enemies as imperial, interventionist, and unilateralist than last time, but we are also fighting for a far better cause— and in a world that is no longer what it once was.

Written on September 25 and published in
National Review Online *on September 27, 2002.*

28

-→══◎══←-

From Manhattan to Baghdad

ONE ENEMY, ONE WAR, ONE OUTCOME

The monotonous inquiries of the critics resound: "What does Iraq have to do with al Qaeda?" "First Afghanistan, now Iraq—what next?" "Isn't Bush's war endless?" "Aren't we diverting our attention from the war on terrorism?"

On the eve of war with Iraq, we should remember that such uncertainty about enemies, allies, aims, and the scope and duration of wars is typical. That al Qaeda does not meet us with tanks and planes on the field of battle does not mean we do not know who we are fighting and where and how we should do it.

We speak of the "Persian Wars" of 490 and 480–79 B.C. But only later did Herodotus and the Greeks look back on the defeats of Darius I at Marathon (490) and Xerxes at Salamis (480) as related events in one overarching campaign. In retrospect, they saw that these battles were *not* isolated victories over various Persian kings with different agendas, but, in fact, all part of a ten-year struggle to free Greece from Persian despotism. Thucydides wrote of a single, long Peloponnesian War. Most of his contemporaries probably disagreed. Plague, twenty-one sieges, two major hoplite battles, half a dozen sea fights, five invasions of Attica, far-off campaigns, helot insurrection, revolutions from the Ionian to the Aegean seas—how was all that terror and tyranny connected?

So many at the time thought that the Archidamian War, the Peace of Nicias, the Sicilian War, the Pachean War, and the Ionian War were all discrete events. Had all the fighting really been a war of Athens against Sparta—or, at times, Athens against Thebes—and against Sicily, the Peloponnesian States, and Persia? Did the terrorists on Corcyra have anything to do with the Athenian fleet or the Spartan army?

By contrast, Thucydides in a fit of genius understood that a single conflict involved a single theme—radical democratic imperialism pitted against conservative oligarchy. And in his view such fighting went on in a variety of confusing contexts and landscapes until one side capitulated—as Athens in fact did twenty-seven years later. He didn't much care who joined in or where the conflict flared up and died down—only that it was one terrible war "like none other." Whether waged in Sicily, the Black Sea, the western Peloponnese, or outside the walls of Athens, it ended only when the reason for war—Sparta's "fear" of a grasping Athenian empire—no longer existed.

So wars are not only difficult for their participants to envision as simple events; the combatants are not always so easily distinguishable. Britain and America—but not Russia—fought Japan for most of the Second World War. Germany, under a nonaggression pact with Russia, fought England, and only later was defeated with the help of Russia and America. There was no more synchronism between Germany and Japan than among the present Axis of Evil. Russia never invaded Italy. Nor did Germany send troops to the Pacific, nor Japan to Europe. Guadalcanal was part of the same war, as was Stalingrad—just as Anzio was connected to the capture of Copenhagen, the jungle fighting in Burma, and Hiroshima. If all that is not true, then we are wrong now grandly to speak of a

"World War II"—a single conflict that combines the Pacific and European theaters, unified by a common struggle against fascism in its various manifestations in Germany, Italy, and Japan, and started on September 1, 1939, June 22, 1941, and December 7, 1941.

Before we criticize President Bush for "diverting attention" away from the war against al Qaeda, we should pause and at least grant that historians may envision it in quite a different way. It is just as likely that at some future date we will come to see that the war on terror for the United States started on September 11 with the murder of three thousand Americans and the destruction of our planes and iconic buildings in New York and Washington. Then the war moved on to a variety of other theaters in Afghanistan and Iraq—and anywhere else the Islamo-fascists and their sponsors of terror operated or received aid.

"The Taliban War" (October–November 2001) was fought to destroy the Afghan sanctuary of bin Laden and remove the Taliban. It was waged simultaneously with the more insidious and stealthy "War on Terrorism" (September 12 through the present) conducted by police and intelligence operatives to stamp out al Qaeda cells in Europe, Asia, and the United States.

A third, concomitant "Iraqi War" with additional enemies is a further effort to destroy a historical patron of terrorism and his caches of deadly weapons that either have gone or will go to terrorists. Saddam's defeat will end the possibility that his oil-fueled supply of deadly weapons will fall into the hands of al Qaeda and its epigones. His end will isolate and cut off al Qaeda operatives in Kurdistan; it will rid Baghdad of enemies like Abu Abbas (and the ghost of Abu Nidal) as well as various al Qaeda visitors; it will stop bonuses for the suicide killers of Hamas and Hezbollah (who embrace the same modus operandi and similar religious extremism as the 9/11 killers); and it will send a powerful message to states like Iran and Saudi Arabia that subsidizing terrorists who killed three thousand Americans is a very dangerous thing to do.

Just as Italian fascists, Japanese militarists, and German Nazis saw commonalities in their efforts to spread right-wing nationalist rule, so Islamic radicals seek to end Western global influence in similar ways—either through the establishment of Islamic theocracies in the Gulf and other oil-producing countries or loose alliances of convenience with tyrannies like those in Syria, Libya, or Iraq, which can be cajoled, blackmailed, or openly joined with in ad hoc efforts to destroy a hated West.

Fascist states and radical Islamists, in fact, exhibit affinities that go well beyond sporadic and murky ties between such governments and fundamentalist terrorist groups. For one, in a post–Soviet Union world, they all seek weapons of mass destruction to be used as intercontinental blackmail as a way of weakening Western resolve and curtailing an American presence abroad.

For another, their common ideological enemy is liberal democracy—specifically its global promotion of freedom, individualism, capitalism, gender equity, religious diversity, and secularism, all of which undermine both Islamic fundamentalism in the cultural sense and politically make it more difficult for tyrants to rule over complacent and ignorant populations. Third, our various enemies share an eerie modus operandi as well: al Qaeda terrorists blew themselves up killing Americans; so do terrorists on the West Bank—and so does Saddam Hussein send bounties to the families of such killers.

Nihilism—whether in the form of torching oil fields, gassing civilians, crashing airplanes, desecrating shrines, toppling towers, or creating oil slicks—is another telltale symptom of our enemies, as is the perversion of Islam, whether illustrated in bin Laden's crackpot communiqués, the rantings of Hezbollah and Hamas to extend theocracy and kill infidels, or Saddam Hussein's ugly nouveau minarets and holy books written with his own blood.

Muslims from the Middle East are not per se the enemy, but rather those renegade Muslims who use the cover of Islam to rally support for their self-serving politics. After all, without the bogeymen of Zionism and the Great Satan they would have to explain to their own dispossessed why Cairo is poorer than Tel Aviv, why heart surgery is done in London and not Damascus, or why so many Arabs seem to gravitate toward Detroit rather than Baghdad.

Saddam Hussein, al Qaeda, bin Laden, Hezbollah, and others—they all speak in apocalyptic tones about Western decadence, the inability of Americans to take casualties, the need to destroy Israel, and the moral superiority of Islam. They all sprinkle here and there crazy references to crusaders, colonists, infidels, and jihad. They have all fought and killed Americans in the past, and brag that they will do so in the future—whether referring to cooked-up "victories" at "the mother of all battles" or the trenches and caves of Tora Bora.

Their real gripe is that the world is passing them all by—whether we speak in noble terms of the benefactions of globalization such as high-tech medicine and the respect that freedom conveys to the individual, or of the crass schlock of Michael Jackson's globally broadcasted sins and the addiction of video games. The millions of the Islamic world are at last trying to taste some of this far faster than their mullahs and dictators can stop them. So in the warped minds of terrorists and strongmen it is either to blow up a skyscraper or to blackmail the West with germs—or to see the slow strangulation of Islamic fundamentalism and Arab tyrannies through the advent of globalized freedom.

Are we, then, confronted with a clash of civilizations? Not really, but rather with the tottering of the last impediments to the reform of the Arab world before it joins the world of nations and embraces freedom and tolerance, which alone can provide it with security and prosperity. While there are hundreds of thousands of terrorists and state fascists in almost every Arab government, *hundreds of millions of ordinary citizens are watching this war* to see who will win and what the ultimate settlement will consist of. Many, perhaps the majority, may for the moment have their hearts with bin Laden and Saddam Hussein, but their minds ultimately will convince them to join the victors and a promising future, rather than the losers and a bleak past.

The jailing of al Qaeda, the end of the Taliban, and the destruction of Saddam's clique will convince the Arab world that it is not wise or safe to practice jihad as it has been practiced since 1979. Killing American diplomats, blowing up Marines in their sleep, flattening embassies, attacking warships, and toppling buildings will not only not work but bring on a war so terrible that the very thought of the consequences from another 9/11 would be too horrific to contemplate.

Taking on all at once Germany, Japan, and Italy—diverse enemies all—did not require the weeding out of all the fascists and their supporters in Mexico, Argentina, Eastern Europe, and the Arab world. Instead, those in jackboots and armbands worldwide quietly stowed all their emblems away as organized fascism died on the vine once the roots were torn out in Berlin, Rome, and Tokyo. So, too, will the terrorists, once their sanctuaries and capital shrivel up—as is happening as we speak.

Since the Iranian hostage crisis of 1979 we have been caught in a classic *bellum interruptum* that could not be resolved through mediation and appeasement, but only—as we saw on 9/11—made worse. Wars do not end with truces, nor do they start because of accidents or miscommunications. They break out when one side has aggressive aims and advances grievances, whether real or perceived, and feels there is nothing to deter it. And conflicts end *for good* with either victory or defeat. Although we may not see it now, we really are in one war against one enemy—and since we started fighting it, on September 12, we are, in fact, winning and will soon be nearing the end.

Written on February 19 and published in
NATIONAL REVIEW ONLINE *on February 21, 2003.*

29

The Long Riders

HOW DO OUR SOLDIERS DO IT ALL?

The screen graphics, television glitz, punditry, lead-in music—all that hype of the news sometimes disguises the sheer improbability of what we are attempting. Too many forget about the obstacles of time and space altogether. But Iraq is over 7,000 miles away. The weather is windy; sandstorms are common; and sleep is impossible. We are trying to conquer a fascist regime in the Middle East, fighting in a sea of outright enemies or duplicitous friends. The world is turned upside down as a Kuwait is more trustworthy than a France or Germany.

All in the Middle East claim they want democracy; few wish to fight for it; most begrudge those who do. Tactical surprise was lost long ago. In fact, never in the history of military operations have so many troops had to invade so exposed from such a narrow front. Patton yelled to "——— the flanks" and plunge ahead; but even he would never have been so audacious as to send thousands barreling nonstop ahead in a narrow motorized column. It took

Sherman three months to slice through the Carolinas; Patton romped his 400 miles in two months; we are impatient that it might take us five days to cover the same distance to Saddam Hussein's bunker.

Baghdad is their target, but Baghdad is also far away, and the path of desert, marsh, and town is choreographed, and progress televised and watched by the world. Most parents do not leave their teens alone on weekends; but hundreds of thousands of them now are driving tanks and trucks to their rendezvous with the Republican Guard, a modern SS mercenary band of killers and criminals. Missiles that we were assured by the UN did not exist are launched to kill our soldiers—shot down by Patriot missiles we were told would not work. In response, forty-eight hours into a war snarly foreign journalists demand proof of weapons of mass destruction—who we know will be silent when evidence of them appears.

Meanwhile thousands of Americans ride alone on to Baghdad.

Friends like Turkey bar a second northern front; but once our soldiers take on the enemy, they sneak across the border to intimidate Kurds who are at least real allies. Our bombs are among the most selective in the history of warfare, hitting the headquarters of fascist killers, the modern-day equivalents of Hitler, Göring, Ribbentrop, and Himmler—even as Western journalists ask whether we are seeking a repeat of Dresden and Hamburg.

CNN tele-journalists are expelled from Baghdad; and in perplexity (given their own slant and bias) they whine that a suddenly ungrateful Saddam Hussein usually was fairer to them than the United States. Arab papers lie that atomic bombs were used. Hamas calls for suicide murdering. Our own *New York Times's* headlines blare OIL WELLS BURN even as we read that less than a dozen, not 600, are ablaze. Its columnists in a time of war call for the resignation of the secretary of state and claim protesters, not soldiers under fire, are our true heroes. Articles allege that the news is slanted—and in the Pentagon's favor, no less! Most of us in response sigh that at least we are spared from more of the nightly nonsense of Scott Ritter, Dominique de Villepin, and Hans Blix.

And thousands of Americans ride alone on to Baghdad.

The rules of this surreal war are as contradictory as the hoplite protocols of old Greece. We can bomb the headquarters of a terrorist state but not hit anyone but outlaw generals—as if a criminal society exists only because of the evil of a handful of men who must be distinguished at night from a nation of twenty-six million. Trenches of oil are ignited to thwart our laser-guided bombs; civilians are put as shields in harm's way; the sky is lighted up with anti-aircraft fire—but a bomb deflected, a missile sent astray is our fault, not theirs. Thousands of Iraqi soldiers surrender as crowds of civilians cheer; in response, the Arab street at a safe distance threatens us with death, and protesters in free societies slur the liberation of those under fascism. Our soldiers must not die, but nor should they kill, either; instead, they must find a way through lights and fire to scare a Reich into submission.

And thousands of Americans ride alone on to Baghdad.

How do such men and women do such things, against such material, cultural, military, and psychological odds? I don't know. But in the last year all those who have bet against the Americans now riding into the desert—elite journalists, out-of-touch academics, and self-satisfied Europeans—have been consistently wrong in their shrill predictions that we were either incompetent or amoral or would fail.

Why is this so? It is not merely that so many are so ignorant of history, or that most who are degreed and certified are glib and swarmy but not educated. No, the better explanation is that they rarely work among, know, see, or care about the type of Americans now barreling to Baghdad—who are still a different and, I think, a better sort of people.

And now thousands of them ride on to Baghdad.

Written on March 22 and published in
NATIONAL REVIEW ONLINE *on March 24, 2003.*

30

The Train Is Leaving the Station

WILL OUR "FRIENDS" JUMP ON IN TIME?

Wars disrupt the political landscape for generations. Changes sweep nations when their youth die in a manner impossible during peace. An isolationist United States became a world power after the defeat of Japan and Germany, buoyed by the confidence of millions of returning victorious veterans. Even today the pathologies of American society cannot be understood apart from the defeat in Vietnam, as an entire generation still views the world through the warped lenses of the 1960s. In some sense, postmodern quirky France today is explicable by the humiliation of 1940 and its colonial defeats to follow.

So, too, one of the most remarkable military campaigns in American military history will shake apart the world as few other events in the last thirty years. Depressed and discredited pundits now turn to dire predictions of years of turmoil in postbellum Iraq. A lunatic Syria promises a Lebanon to come. Meanwhile we are currently reassured that the Atlantic Alliance is unchanged. The

Washington–New York corridor, in sober and judicious tones, has rightly emphasized to us all that we must work harder to renew our old ties—echoed by their like counterparts in Europe. But it is eerie how the more the experts insist on all these probable scenarios, the more they seem terrified that things are not as they were.

Something weird, something unprecedented, is unfolding, driven by American public opinion—completely ignored in Europe—and the nation's collective anger that Americans are dying by showing restraint as they are slandered by our "friends." Despite the protestations of a return to normalcy, this present war will ever so slowly, yet markedly nonetheless, change America's relationships in a way unseen in the last thirty years.

With little help from Saudi Arabia or Turkey—"allies" and "hosts" to our troops—damned by many of our NATO allies, stymied in the UN, turned on by Russia, opposed by Germany and France, the Coalition nevertheless is systematically liberating a country under the most impossible of conditions. This experience in turn will, oddly, if we avoid hubris and maintain our sanity, liberate us as well.

Far from making the United States hegemonic, the success in Iraq will have a sobering effect on Americans. Contrary to the pundits, the hard-fought Anglo-American victory will not make us into hegemonists, but simply less naïve about tradition-bound relationships and the normal method of doing business. I would expect American military spending to increase, even as *American reluctance grows to get involved with any of our traditional allies.* Given billions of dollars in foreign aid, the past salvation of Europe from the Soviet juggernaut, and a half-century of protection under our nuclear shield, the old way was supposed to work something like the following.

At worst France and Germany would quietly call Mr. Powell. They would explain their predicaments and then abstain at the UN, ensuring passage of a second decree. The traditionally wise and savvy German diplomats—conscious of everything from the Berlin Airlift to the American promise to pledge New York to preserve

Bonn from a Soviet nuclear strike—would cherish American good-will toward the German people, grimace somewhat, and then say something like: "We believe you are wrong; but we are not going to ruin a half-century of mutual amity over a two-bit fascist Iraq. So good luck, win, and let us pray that you, not we, are right—for both our sakes."

A Turkish prime minister would learn from Tony Blair, and thus explain to his parliament the historic and critical relationship with the United States, while vigorously campaigning to win approval for our armored divisions to hit Iraq from the north to help shorten a controversial war.

Mexico and Canada would complain privately, but express North American solidarity. In other words, sober and sane Western statesmen would swallow their pique at a powerful United States acting unilaterally, seek to provide it diplomatic cover, and quietly accept that a removal of a mass-murdering dictator was in all liberal states' interests.

Instead, just the opposite happened, and so we must eventually react to this radical realignment that brought it about.

We can start with those hosts of American military bases. Many Americans are now dead in part because a NATO ally—Turkey—not merely refused its support, but did so in such a long and drawn-out fashion that it is impossible to believe that it was not designed to hamper U.S. military operations. And, of course, Turkey's last-minute refusals to allow transit of U.S. divisions did exactly that by delaying the critical rerouting of troops and supplies to the Gulf.

I would expect that we all will smile, still extend some minor aid, but simmer on the inside and quietly and professionally take steps to ensure that we are never put in such a position again. We should, without fanfare, bow out of Turkish-EU discussions, and let Europe and Turkey on their own decide the wisdom of allowing an Islamic country into the "liberal" European confederation. The EU can handle Cyprus. Who knows, maybe Brussels will be forced to reward Turkish recalcitrance toward America with renewed subsidies and membership—and who cares? So in the eleventh hour of this war, the democratic government of Turkey must pass some decree, if only symbolic, that they value our friendship and wish us to win in Iraq.

Ditto the erosion with the Saudi Arabian relationship, even if, as I expect, we will soon hear from their sheiks with various proclamations of liberalization and greater freedom for their unfree. Bases that earn us enmity cannot be adequately used when Americans die nearby, and are expensive political liabilities, are not military assets. And the paradox grows worse when bases exist through the pretexts that they in part help to protect a host country that does not wish to be protected.

We should smile, profess goodwill—and then withdraw *all* American troops from Saudi Arabia as soon as events settle down in Iraq, reassessing in a post–Cold War, post-9/11 world our entire relationship with that medieval country. After all, we buy oil from the worst of all dictatorships in Teheran and the people there like us better than do the Saudis, precisely because we are not complicit in their government. The Saudis, of course, could still catch the train as it leaves the station, close the madrasahs, and join the twenty-first century—but it is their call, not ours.

We are told that an Israeli-Palestinian solution will restore our good name in the Middle East. Maybe. But like the past spectacle of Palestinians cheering news of the three thousand American dead, the recent West Bank volunteers who wish to go to Baghdad to blow up more Americans and protect another Arab fascist don't play well in the United States—and make us wonder what our hundreds of millions of dollars in aid for the Palestinian Authority are for.

We must maintain cordial relations with Russia—but Russia has never had an accounting with the tens of thousands of Communist apparatchiks still in place throughout the present government. This was a country, after all, that to the silence of the Arab and European worlds killed thousands of Muslims in Chechnya, rooted for the mass murderer Milosevic, allowed weapons to be sold to Saddam Hussein that would be used to kill Americans, and thwarted all our efforts in the UN. Surely it is time for sobriety and circumspection in everything we do with them.

If we thought Turkey's recent turnabout was depressing, imagine a South Korea when that crisis heats up, as thousands in Seoul take to the street to protest our presence as such citizens are hours away from being annihilated by North Korean artillery. As soon as possible we should begin discussions about carefully drawing down troops and relocating them far to the south to compose a "strategic reserve" as tens of thousands of wealthy, brave South Korean teenagers assume their exclusive place on the front line to protect their own motherland from Korean Stalinists. And if we cannot convince China that it is time to rein in Pyongyang's nukes, then we should throw up our hands and let Tokyo, Seoul—even Taiwan—do what is necessary to provide for their own strategic deterrence.

In the neighborhood of the battlefield, Iran is in a unique position. The illegitimate government will have to tell its own restless population why the liberation of Iraq next door is a bad thing. The unfortunate Iranians, scarred by a dirty war with Saddam Hussein, weary of mullocracy that they brought in themselves, will not be unhappy that the soldiers a decade ago who slaughtered them are losing, and the changes that are coming across the border are what they themselves want.

Syria, the embryo of most terrorist groups and the occupier of Lebanon, still issues empty threats. For all the scary rhetoric and promises of worldwide jihad, an impotent Syria must be terrified of the consequences should it send direct aid to Saddam Hussein. It is a historical rarity that 300,000 United States troops are at last fighting an Arab dictator with 70 percent of the American people's support—and losing far fewer personnel than were slaughtered in one day in their sleep in a barracks in Lebanon.

And then there is the madness of Europe. It is time to speak far more softly and carry a far larger stick. France may be right that we all have really come to the end of history—and so we should give them an opportunity to prove it, to match deed with word by being delighted as we withdraw troops from Germany. Germany may or may not be embracing the frightening old nationalist rhetoric—but, again, that will be France's problem, not ours. Let us hope that the more sober in Germany can still grasp at what Mr. Schroeder has nearly thrown away, and see that few superpowers have given it so much and asked for so little in return—and genuinely wish it to do well.

But again it is their call, not ours. We do not have to withdraw from a dead NATO, but we should simply grin and spend as much on it as Europe does—and so let it die on the vine. How could we be allies with such countries as France and Germany when sizable minorities there want a fascistic Saddam Hussein to defeat us?

There is not much need to speak of the governments of Canada and Mexico. More liberal trade agreements and concessions with Mr. Chretien are about as dead as open borders are with Mr. Fox. It is the singular achievement of the present Canadian government to turn a country whose armed forces once stormed an entire beach at Normandy and fielded one of the most heroic armies in wars for freedom into a bastion of anti-Americanism without a military. Both countries are de facto Socialist states, and the Anglo-French pique we see in Europe exists right across our northern borders in miniature. Anyone who looked at the papers in Mexico City could rightly assume our neighbors' elite preferred an Iraqi victory.

And so where does all that leave us? Contrary to the conventional rhetoric of pessimists ("The world hates us"), we may well be in a stronger position than ever before. Russian arms, German bunkers, and French contracts will become known in Iraq and will be weighed against America's use of overwhelming force for a moral cause in a legal and human fashion against a barbaric regime. The Middle Eastern claim that we won't or can't fight on the ground is a myth. And America, not the Orwellian Arab street, is the catalyst for democratic reform. Looming on the horizon are Iraqi archives, the textual evidence of weapons of mass destruction, and a liberated populace that Europe would have otherwise left well enough alone to profit from its overseers.

The United Nations has lost its soft spot in the hearts of Americans and is more likely to appease dictators than aid consensual governments. The general-secretary should be scrambling madly before the armistice to win our good graces—never has American support for the UN been lower, even as a UN resolution has never been better enforced at almost no cost to its general membership. The debate has now spun out of control and questions not merely our own membership but also the very propriety of the residence of the General Assembly headquarters in New York.

And as for Britain, Australia, Spain, Denmark, Italy, and a host of Eastern European countries who are rolling down the tracks with us, waving to the exasperating at the station, we have to show them as much appreciation for their stalwart courage as we do abject disdain for the duplicity of their peers behind.

The world is upside down and we should expect some strange scenes of scrambling in the weeks ahead as side-glancing diplomats and nail-biting envoys flock to Washington to meet with Mr. Powell, who, far from fearing those recent idiotic calls for his resignation, will in fact emerge as one of the most effective and powerful secretaries in recent history. Such are the ironies of war.

It will all be an interesting show.

Written on March 22 and published in
NATIONAL REVIEW ONLINE *on March 24, 2003.*

31

·◦─═◦◐◦═─◦·

Don Rumsfeld,
a Radical for Our Time

The Taliban defeated without American infantry, and at a cost of fewer than ten U.S. fatalities? Ten thousand Special Operations troops turned loose to work independently in northern Iraq? Not one traditional armored division on the ground near Baghdad? Thousands of GIs rumored soon to be redeployed out of Germany? Troops in the DMZ eyeing transfer southward to Pusan? Past draftees characterized as not as effective as present volunteer professionals? A secretary of defense going head-to-head with seasoned and cynical Washington reporters—and coming off as their moral and intellectual superior?

These are all aspects of the same fundamental question: What exactly is going on with the American military? Not since Secretary of War Edwin M. Stanton poked his head into every department of the Union Army and Robert McNamara tried to apply corporate business procedures to the Pentagon bureaucracy has a U.S. official exercised such political and military influence as

Donald Rumsfeld. But while Stanton was politically inept and McNamara failed at war, so far—twenty-seven months into his tenure—Rumsfeld is showing every sign of success. At home, he is steamrolling angry generals and balky diplomats; on the battlefield, he has crushed the Taliban and Saddam Hussein.

But what exactly is Rumsfeld's vision for the future of the U.S. military? The public is unsure, because an array of critics—out of either self-interest or simple ignorance—has caricatured his attempt to reform the armed forces. Their reservoir of ill will broke out into hysteria during the race to Baghdad, when a pause in fighting—occasioned by horrendous weather conditions and necessary resupply efforts—touched off an eruption of anti-Rumsfeld rhetoric among a few retired generals who had found employment as TV pontificators. Before 9/11, Rumsfeld's efforts to refashion the American military were largely ignored; but they are now being showcased on the world stage, and will be judged on their effectiveness.

One key Rumsfeld accomplishment is to have devised a new role for the Army. It is a serious mistake to suggest, as some have, that Rumsfeld favors the Navy, Air Force, and Marines; in fact, his reforms will probably enhance the Army's ground forces. His approach has already paid off in the Iraq war: the Army's Special Forces, the 101st and Eighty-second Airborne Divisions, and the Third Mechanized Division played a crucial role in the victory. (It was not Rumsfeld but the Turks who thwarted the efforts to open a northern front with at least two more Army divisions. And the Fourth Infantry Division has arrived in Iraq on plan and on time, not, as some assert, because of a desperate call-up.)

But while the Army's Bradley fighting vehicles and Abrams tanks were vital in smashing Iraqi defenses and preventing Mogadishu-like nightmares, other things were equally important: the speeding motorized convoys that bypassed initial resistance; the air drops; the irregulars who organized the Kurds; and the small squads of highly trained skirmishers who proved masterful house-to-house fighters. In other words, Rumsfeld's plan was creative and successful: rather than send out tens of thousands of traditional soldiers behind a wall of armor—which would have been a logistical nightmare, requiring perhaps a year or more to assemble in a vulnerable, confined place—Rumsfeld allowed the Army to undertake new responsibilities well beyond its traditional role. The Army has been on the cutting edge in mobilizing and deploying the indigenous forces that have been critically important in our recent Middle East wars. Furthermore, thanks to instantaneous electronic communications between ground forces and pilots, the new Army is not replaced by, but rather essential to, successful air operations.

There remains a need for traditional armored and infantry divisions, but not in the old numbers required to fight two traditional wars simultaneously against Soviet-style ground forces. We would surely need tons of steel and shells to stop a North Korea–style onslaught; but to ensure that such a war is not lost at its very beginning, we will need lighter, more mobile forces that can be rushed to hot spots until the heavy muscle arrives.

In a few months, analysts will begin to appreciate the true audacity of Operation Iraqi Freedom. The Army had access to firepower to a degree never before seen. No tactician has yet quite figured out the force-multiplying effect of quickly achieved air superiority, GPS-guided munitions, and on-the-ground spotters; but surely the destructive power of A-10 fighters, helicopters, and carrier- and land-based bombers that were in service to small Army tactical units was worth the equivalent of a thousand tanks. Furthermore, the operation took a number of (successful) tactical risks to satisfy myriad political objectives. For example, long, vulnerable supply lines made it possible for U.S. forces to advance rapidly to Baghdad, and thus take momentum away from a growing global antiwar movement; and the dearth of prebattle bombing ensured a relatively sound infrastructure for rebuilding.

Rumsfeld has discovered how to use the Army in a better way than had been possible before; his analysis of the relative merits of draftees and professional soldiers shows an equally clear apprehension of military reality. His comparisons may have been inelegant, but his larger thesis—that the effectiveness of highly trained, highly motivated soldiers cannot be measured in mere numbers—is surely correct. The stories and pictures of soldiers running into burning trucks to save valuable equipment, of the wounded shooting from stretchers, and of women of supply units emptying their magazines before capture suggest that the present generation of professional troops is lethal in ways we can only begin to appreciate.

Indeed, something strange is happening to the American soldier, almost as if current popular culture were being married to nineteenth-century notions of heroism and sacrifice. Europe, where military service is looked upon with distrust and rarely seen as either consistent with national values or a means of personal advancement, is shocked to see young kids with Ray-Ban sunglasses driving multimillion-dollar tanks, and artillery emblazoned with slogans like "Bad Moon Rising" and "Anger Management."

It is this weird alignment of rap music, counterculture adolescent fashion and diction, and popular movies and videos with selfless and heroic action that so astounds the world. Generals of all races give crisp briefings; Arab-American Marines boast of liberating a Muslim city; women brag of flying three combat missions per day; and bearded, hippie-looking Green Berets on horses prefer the company of medieval tribesmen as they radio in bombs from billion-dollar Stealth bombers. This all suggests that the U.S. military is not so much insidious as postmodern. For someone who dresses so formally and insists on protocol, Donald Rumsfeld, it turns out, is actually quite a radical and has helped to turn our military into something that values efficacy and performance far more than habit, tradition, and procedure.

Just two years ago, the slur against today's infantry was that it was "without a mission." No one would have expected that Army to prove itself a proper successor to General Patton's lightning-quick strike force of central France in 1944. That General Tommy Franks's plan is now called Pattonesque—and that our new generals are compared to America's most audacious warrior—is ironic but understandable, and thanks are due in large part to Rumsfeld.

So he's been a military innovator. But hasn't Rumsfeld played an intrusive and disruptive role in foreign affairs? Wrong again. Here, too, his policy is one of shrewdness, prudence, and realism. The net result of Rumsfeld's military strategies will be greater political autonomy and flexibility for the United States—without the traditional dependency on host countries. And surely this idea—of a powerful America that can act without granting political concessions to Germany, Turkey, or South Korea—is what really bothers our allies. In this regard, however, nothing could be more unfair than to typecast Rumsfeld as a willy-nilly interventionist, who in some romantic fashion wishes to put footprints down everywhere abroad to impose democracy. If Rumsfeld's new, more cost-efficient military comes of age, it will be both more muscular and more independent, and thus shift the onus of strictly regional defense to our allies.

In any case, what is the exact value of bases in such places as Saudi Arabia and Turkey, when they require political concessions and cannot be fully exploited? When a politically hostile Germany boasts that it allows us to use its airspace, and that it guards our bases, which are purportedly guarding *it,* or when spoiled South Korean youth perpetually damn us for fomenting trouble with an unaggressive North, we clearly need to do some rethinking. In this context, it is perfectly logical for Rumsfeld to be the chief promoter of missile defense, which would liberate us from being held hostage politically by ostensible allies.

The State Department may have resented Rumsfeld's quip about an "Old Europe," and his association of Germany's antagonism with the anti-Americanism of our traditional foe Libya, but once again irony abounds: no secretary of defense in modern history has done more than Rumsfeld to strengthen the hand of our diplomats. Because he has essentially ended the Powell Doctrine of cautious intervention—using overwhelming force for limited objectives, and with a quick exit strategy—Rumsfeld has brought a certain unpredictability to American foreign policy. And it is precisely this willingness to act alone that will in turn encourage a new maturity abroad, and expedite the war against the sponsors of terror.

"You can't defend," he remarked in an interview about terrorism, "except by offense." It is not so much that he wishes to invade
Iran, Syria, or North Korea as that he wants to make it clear that
the United States can in theory now act precipitously, yet on principle, to thwart totalitarians and terror states—without a great deal
of dependence on traditional bases, allied contingents, or the con-
sent of the United Nations. The days of a static big target of
American troops being blown up in Lebanon or Saudi Arabia
without reprisals are over. Our enemies' fear may prompt political
reform, or at least second thoughts on sponsoring terrorism—
which, in yet another Rumsfeld irony, will eventually make the use
of military force less likely.

It may well be that Colin Powell has more diplomatic leverage
than any secretary of state in recent memory precisely because the
new military can move so rapidly and unexpectedly with lethal
power—a fact that will bring him a host of obsequious foreign visitors. And of course Rumsfeld's blunt language about controversial
nomenclature like the Axis of Evil—"I think putting the micro-
scope, the floodlight, on what is going on in those three countries
is just enormously valuable for the world"—allows Powell to triangulate: he can press straddling states to deal with him now, or
Rumsfeld later.

What is the source of Rumsfeld's independence and steeliness
in the face of criticism? Plutarch, of course, would respond:
"character" and "age." And there is much to be said for both.
Rumsfeld's dossier—Princeton, naval aviation, congressional service, an array of presidential appointments, and personal wealth
derived from successful corporate leadership—suggests that he
doesn't much need or want anything from anybody. He has known
disappointment—an aborted presidential bid and participation in
Bob Dole's inept 1996 campaign—and realizes that Washington
fame is fickle, often undeserved, and deeply resented.

That at a robust seventy Rumsfeld doesn't care to flatter or
network gives him enormous credibility—and an affinity for
bringing in bright, independent people like Paul Wolfowitz and

General Myers without fear or jealousy. He is neither a young, ambitious McNamara, swept up in the culture of the best and brightest, nor a worn-out Stanton. Add to that his wealth of experience—including being under attack in Beirut (in 1983, when he was President Reagan's Mideast envoy) and at the Pentagon (on 9/11)—and you have at least a partial explanation why he has been so often right: about the need for an ABM program, about intervention in Afghanistan and Iraq, and about deployments abroad to battle al Qaeda operatives from the Philippines to Yemen. As a Thucydidean, he accepts the role of power; he knows that until the nature of man changes, regimes in the Middle East will respect our force as much as our values.

But there is a final wild card at play, not just where Rumsfeld is concerned but in the administration as a whole. Rumsfeld, as both a Princeton graduate and a naval pilot, is familiar with—though neither envious nor in awe of—the eastern elite that so dominates our universities, government, and media. Like Bush, Cheney, and Rice, who have all either attended or taught at top schools, the former Illinois congressman acknowledges the intellectual richness of our great universities but nevertheless seems more at ease with the sounder practical judgment of Middle America—and is more than willing to bristle and snap at what he perceives as an overly cynical and skeptical cadre of brainy but foolish people.

His résumé reads like a counter-dossier to the 1960s and seventies. Even his speech—replete with "by golly" and "my goodness"—proclaims that the 1950s can endure, oblivious to the chaos: "I've always enjoyed life, no matter what I'm doing. I like people and I like ideas, and I've got a lot of energy, fortunately."

What does the future hold for Rumsfeld himself, and for our new high-tech military? I imagine he will probably retire at the conclusion of President Bush's first administration, once the war on terror that he has fought so successfully has wound down. His legacy will be a far more sophisticated, more motivated armed force, staffed by confident, well-spoken officers who lead a spirited cross section of American youth. The very idea of entirely separate and feuding branches of the military is coming to a close, as the Navy, Army, Air Force, and Marines all—at times—both fly and fight on the ground, under synchronized command. War itself is undergoing a moral reappraisal, as military conflict is shown to save more lives than allowing mass murderers—Milosevic, the Taliban, or Saddam Hussein—to ply their trade of death without consequences.

Rumsfeld didn't create this renaissance in a mere two years. But at a time of war and uncertainty he did give those with such missionary zeal and vision the confidence and support they needed to come forward out of the halls of the Pentagon to pursue their reforms. And he did bring back a confidence that militaries ultimately exist not just to launch cruise missiles but to fight—and to win. And for that alone we are in debt to this controversial, opinionated man, in ways that will not be fully understood for years to come.

Written on April 26 and published in
NATIONAL REVIEW *on May 5, 2003.*

32

~=◎=~

Postbellum Thoughts

The First Peacekeeper Division?

The complexities of Panama, the Gulf War, Kosovo and Bosnia, Afghanistan, and the Iraqi War involved not just military challenges but postwar reconstruction and global opinion-making as well. In part, our problem arises from our very success and the intrinsic power of the American military. We can take out rogue regimes within a matter of days or weeks without inflicting the level of pain, injury, and humiliation on enemy forces that traditionally rids opponents of any lingering doubts about the end of the old order and the onset of the new. In short, *we win so quickly that some of the losers inevitably do not quite concede that they were really defeated.*

As was the case in Afghanistan, our victory in Iraq was achieved so quickly that most enemies were more likely to run or surrender than fight, thus allowing a number either to drift back within the civilian landscape or fool themselves into thinking we were far from being exacting victors. What a funny world for a soldier fighting Americans: one day, in a trench, you stand the chance of getting blown to smithereens by a GPS bomb; the next, after surrendering, you are ensured of impunity in a street rally to throw rocks at Americans before international cameras.

To meet such challenges, perhaps it is time to create a permanent division-strength body of peacekeepers, police, and civilian reconstructionists. Their duties would be to follow the military into captured enemy cities and, within a matter of days, if not hours—rather than the current months—hunt down government criminals in hiding, keep order and security, provide the populace with food and water, resurrect infrastructure and utilities, and begin near-immediate resumption of television, radio, and newspapers.

In theory, such a corps would include a variety of company-sized cohorts, from snipers and police to electricians and constitution-framers—and their tasks would be coordinated with the antebellum bombing-planning. They would be the true "shock and awe" corps, restoring order so quickly after the dissolution of enemy forces that enemy opportunists and agents would simply have no time to organize and manipulate the inevitable confusion in the months of political instability that ensued.

A Truth-in-Broadcasting Statute

We need legislation requiring journalists and reporters to publicly disclose the financial and political arrangements that they agree to in order to broadcast or write from belligerent regimes at a time of hostilities. Nothing in the recent war was more appalling or unethical than the censored reporting that emanated from the Palestine Hotel. Only after Baghdad fell did millions of listeners and readers discover that their purveyors of information had been semi-hostages, controlled by "minders"—and willing to pay daily bribe money for the privilege of divulging half-truths and releasing misleading accounts. Had their audiences known fully about *all* such concessions in advance, they might have been better equipped to assess the "truth." At the least, we can ask that American citizens not pay extortion money to enemy governments in a time of war. It is disturbing enough that none of our journalists in Iraq questioned Baghdad Bob's veracity in their nightly reports, but even more troubling to realize that their danegeld helped to subsidize his rantings.

A Defense Cultural Advisory Board

The military needs to create a civilian cultural advisory board as a supplement to those committees concerned with technology and policy. Such scholars and intellectuals sympathetic to the military might develop policies and procedures to identify problems inevitable in the use of military force in a postmodern, therapeutic society. Scholars, for example, could have advised the military about the complexities that surrounded potential damage to cultural sites in Baghdad. Their duties could be both proactive—creating guidelines about protecting archaeological sites, dealing with cultural issues, and cultivating intellectuals, dissidents, and ministry officials—but also reactive, when tragedies like the destruction of priceless icons unfold.

Untold damage was done to our cause by the hysteria surrounding the looting of the Iraq National Museum in Baghdad. Officers on the scene made the case well enough that men under fire can hardly be transmogrified into museum guards, and that enough vandalism was done to a variety of petroleum installations and refinery offices to give the lie to the canard that we "saved the oil and let the museum be looted." But a board of scholars could also have explained to the public that it is rare for a liberated people to ransack their own treasuries: such worries historically have surrounded the occupying force, from the fall of Constantinople (1453) to Berlin (1945) to Kuwait City (1990).

They could have also gotten the word out that archaeologists are not de facto superior beings: those who worked in the museums of Iraq were by nature precisely those who kept most quiet about Saddam's own theft of antiquities and his use of national shrines for despicable contemporary propaganda purposes. Like the "thousands" dead in "Jeningrad" that soon were reduced to fifty-two fatalities in a firefight, the "178,000" destroyed priceless icons are slowly being downsized to a few hundred—and were mostly lost through the complicity of the Baathists themselves. And those rogues in the Antiquities Ministry who oversaw Saddam's malicious and criminal "reconstruction" of Babylon—garish desecrations that made Arthur Evans's misadventures at Knossos, or the Italian temple rebuilding in the occupied Greek islands during World War II, seem like child's play—did far more damage to the cultural heritage of Iraq than the (mostly professional) thieves' premeditated heists in Baghdad.

The Primacy of Politics

The military's newfound mobility and flexibility are taking on more than merely tactical importance. The key in the twenty-first century will be the American armed forces' ability to project military power quickly almost anywhere across the globe—without granting humiliating political concessions or paying bribery to purported hosts, allies, and international institutions.

Large bases such as those in Germany, Turkey, and South Korea should be broken up, relocated, removed, or scattered into smaller, less intrusive arms caches and depots with less-noticeable footprints. Aerial tankers, transport planes, and helicopters must be designated highest-priority to ensure that assets can be deployed and maintained autonomously for extended periods.

A new criterion for basing should be as much political as geostrategic, inasmuch as the two are now inseparable. A Diego Garcia may be less ideally located than are bases in Turkey, Greece, or Saudi Arabia, but in the long run it entails fewer actual costs. In the Cold War, carriers were deprecated by submarine advocates as "sitting ducks"; today they are properly seen as priceless acres of sovereign American territory that can be shifted to any theater on the globe. In short, a critical question should be demanded of any new technology, strategy, or organization: To what degree does it enhance the ability of the United States to resort to military power *without* dependence on foreign governments (allied or otherwise) or multinational institutions?

Moving Beyond the UN

As long as UN action is predicated on the majority votes of illiberal regimes, or the single veto of undemocratic states like China, or the obstructions of envious, fourth-rate powers like France, it will remain either a debating society or a manipulative mechanism to thwart *anything* the United States does. It was about as effective in monitoring Saddam Hussein as the International Olympic Committee was in stopping the routine torture of the Iraqi Olympic team. While we should seek drastic reform—admitting India, Japan, and Brazil to the Security Council; promoting statesmen reputed for their defiance of authoritarian governments as candidates for the secretary generalship; insisting on democratic government as a requisite for full voting membership in the General Assembly; and distributing France's Security Council veto across the entire European Union—we will probably have no alternative but to seek more permanent relationships with a coalition of the willing.

Eventually, some astute diplomat is going to make the obvious observations that English-speaking nations like the United States, Australia, Britain, (Western) Canada, and India have defied popular wisdom and retained common cultural and historical affinities that only become more apparent in times of conflict—and could form the basis for a more permanent and formal alliance.

Final Observations

On a personal note, this column marks the end of my year-long tenure as Shifrin Professor of Military History at the U.S. Naval Academy and a return to a rather isolated farm in Selma, California. My first memory upon arrival in Annapolis on August 8, 2002—a time of Washington doom and gloom—was picking up a copy of *Foreign Policy* and reading the cover story ("The Incredible Shrinking Eagle: The End of Pax America"), in which readers were assured by Immanuel Wallerstein that "Saddam Hussein's army is not that of the Taliban, and his internal military control is far more coherent. A U.S. invasion would necessarily involve a serious land force, one that would have to fight its way to Baghdad and would likely suffer significant casualties."

As an outsider, the most notable impressions I have had since arriving are of the surprising degree of self-criticism of the U.S. military and its willingness to welcome both internal and outside audit—and thus its abject contrast with two equally formidable institutions, the media and the universities, which really are shrinking and have indeed suffered "significant casualties" to their reputations. Again, it is far easier to be a liberal in the supposedly authoritarian military than to be a moderate or conservative on a college campus; students are more likely to be segregated by race in the lounges and cafeterias of "progressive" universities than they are in the mess halls of aircraft carriers.

In the past year I have met midshipmen, Air Force cadets, colonels at the Army War College, officers in the Pentagon, air and naval crews at sea, reserve and retired officers, and a variety of civilian defense analysts. Very few were triumphalist about their singular victories in Afghanistan and Iraq; instead, they were eager to dissect past plans, identify lapses, and encourage candid criticism—both operational and ethical.

Rather different from all that are the New York and Washington press corps and the culture of most universities. Many elites in these two latter institutions have throughout this crisis revealed lapses in both ethics and common sense. There is a general lack of contrition (much less apology) by prominent columnists and talking heads about being so wrong so often in editorializing about the war. Partnerships with fascist regimes were embraced by major American news networks—and at home, elite critics got into bed with pretty awful antiwar organizations whose true agenda went well beyond Iraq to involve subverting the very values of the United States.

The media needs to ask itself some tough questions about its own rules of engagement abroad, the use of bribe money, and the ethical and voluntary responsibility of its pundits and writers to account to their readers, when they have for so long consistently fed them nonsense and error. Universities, in turn, must ask themselves fundamental questions about tenure and teaching loads: Why does tuition consistently rise faster than inflation? Why is free speech so often curbed and regulated? And why did so many prominent professors, during the past two years, in a time of war, say so many dreadful things about their own military—from general untruths about "millions" of starving, refugees, and dead to come, to the occasional provocateur applauding the destruction of the Pentagon and wishing for more Mogadishus?

Compared to all that, I prefer trees and vines.

Written on May 7 and published in
NATIONAL REVIEW ONLINE *on May 9, 2003.*

VII

⊷≈◉⇇

A NEW FOREIGN POLICY?

After September 11 there grew a need to awake from the slumber of the last decade and go to war with the agents of terror in a way we did not after the killing of Marines in Lebanon, the attacks on our embassies, the murder of Americans in Saudi Arabia, the first World Trade Center bombing, the near sinking of the USS Cole, and so on.

Yet that new embrace of engagement was not the product of some neoconservative conspiracy—indeed, President Bush campaigned on a platform of avoiding numerous deployments overseas. Rather, the hunt for terrorists and the elimination of regimes that facilitate terror and destruction—all aimed at avoiding another September 11—brought Americans into new roles all over the globe. It was not so much that Americans wished this new role of a hyperpower, but, rather, that the abrupt collapse of the Soviet Union left the United States in a singular role neither foreseen nor necessarily welcomed.

Given the vehement criticism of incursions in Afghanistan and Iraq from our allies in Europe, neutrals in the Middle East, and observers from China to South America, it seemed necessary for a reexamination of American foreign policy in a manner not seen since the close of World War II. But a new generation of critics has forgotten that there was a deep strain of isolationism in the American people, coupled with a recognition that such emotion could not in and of itself drive our foreign policy. So perhaps there was a balance *to be struck between engagement and isolationism, a muscular engagement of sorts that allowed us to pursue national interests but without the traditional dependence on bases and multilateral contexts that so often hampered the range of American options.*

33

A Funny Sort of Empire

ARE AMERICANS REALLY SO IMPERIAL?

It is popular now to speak of the American "empire." In Europe particularly there are comparisons of Mr. Bush to Caesar—and worse—and invocations of all sorts of pretentious poli-sci jargon like "hegemon," "imperium," and "subject states," along with neologisms like "hyperpower" and "overdogs." But if we really are imperial, we rule over a very funny sort of empire.

We do not send out proconsuls to preside over client states, which in turn impose taxes on coerced subjects to pay for the legions. Instead, American bases are predicated on contractual obligations—costly to us and profitable to their hosts. We do not see any profits in Korea, but instead accept the risk of losing almost 40,000 of our youth to ensure that Kias can flood our shores and that shaggy students can protest outside our embassy in Seoul.

Athenians, Romans, Ottomans, and the British wanted land and treasure and grabbed all they could get when they could. The United States hasn't annexed anyone's soil since the Spanish-American

237

War—a checkered period in American history that still makes us, not them, out as villains in our own history books. Most Americans are far more interested in carving up the Nevada desert for monster homes than in getting their hands on Karachi or the Amazon basin. Puerto Ricans are free to vote themselves independence anytime they wish.

Imperial powers order and subjects obey. But in our case, we offer the Turks strategic guarantees, political support—and money— for their allegiance. France and Russia go along in the UN—but only after we ensure them the traffic of oil and security for outstanding accounts. Pakistan gets debt relief that ruined dot-coms could only dream of; Jordan reels in more aid than our own bankrupt municipalities.

If acrimony and invective arise, it's usually one way: the Europeans, the Arabs, and the South Americans all say worse things about us than we do about them, not privately and in hurt, but publicly and proudly. Boasting that you hate Americans—or calling our supposed imperator "moron" or "Hitler"—won't get you censured by our Senate or earn a tongue-lashing from our president, but is more likely to get you ten minutes on CNN. We are considered haughty by Berlin not because we send a Germanicus with four legions across the Rhine but because Mr. Bush snubs Mr. Schroeder by not phoning him as frequently as the German press would like.

Empires usually have contenders that check their power and through rivalry drive their ambitions. Athens worried about Sparta and Persia. Rome found its limits when it butted up against Germany and Parthia. The Ottomans never could bully too well the Venetians or the Spanish. Britain worried about France and Spain at sea and the Germanic peoples by land. By contrast, the restraint on American power is not China, Russia, or the European Union, but rather the American electorate itself, whose reluctant worries are chronicled weekly by polls that are eyed with fear by our politicians. We, not them, stop us from becoming what we could.

The Athenian *ekklêsia,* the Roman senate, and the British Parliament alike were eager for empire and reflected the energy of their people. By contrast, America went to war late and reluctantly in World Wars I and II, and never finished the job in either Korea or Vietnam. We were likely to sigh in relief when we were kicked out of the Philippines, and really have no desire to return. Should the Greeks tell us to leave Crete—promises, promises—we would be more likely to count the money saved than the influence lost. Take away all our troops from Germany and polls would show relief, not anger, among Americans. Isolationism, parochialism, and self-absorption are far stronger in the American character than desire for overseas adventurism. Our critics may slur us for "over-reaching," but our elites in the military and government worry that they have to coax a reluctant populace, not constrain a blood-drunk rabble.

The desire of a young Roman quaestor or the British Victorians was to go abroad, shine in battle, and come home laden with spoils. They wanted to be feared, not liked. American suburbanites, inner-city residents, and rural townspeople all will fret because a French opportunist or a Saudi autocrat says that we are acting inappropriately. Roman imperialists had names like Magnus and Africanus; the British anointed their returning proconsuls as Rangers, Masters, Governors, Grandees, Sirs, and Lords. By contrast, retired American diplomats, CIA operatives, and generals are lucky if they can melt away in anonymity to the Virginia suburbs without a subpoena, media exposé, or lawsuit. Proconsuls were given entire provinces; our ex-president Carter from his peace center advises us to disarm.

Most empires chafe at the cost of their rule and complain that the expense is near-suicidal. Athens raised the Aegean tribute often, and found itself nearly broke after only the fifth year of the Peloponnesian War. The story of the Roman Empire is one of shrinking legions, a debased currency, and a chronically bankrupt imperial treasury. Even before World War I, the Raj had drained England. By contrast, America spends less of its GNP on defense than it did during the last five decades. And most of our military outlays go to training, salaries, and retirements—moneys that support, educate, and help people rather than simply stockpile weapons and hone killers. The eerie thing is not that we have thirteen massive five-billion-dollar carriers, but that we could easily produce and maintain twenty more.

Empires create a culture of pride and pomp, and foster a rhetoric of superiority. Pericles, Virgil, and Kipling all talked and wrote of the grandeur of imperial domain. How odd, then, that what America's literary pantheon—Norman Mailer, Gore Vidal, Susan Sontag, and Alice Walker—said about 9/11 would either nauseate or bewilder most Americans.

Pericles could showcase his Parthenon from the tribute of empire; Rome wanted the prestige of *Pax Romana* and *Mare Nostrum;* the Sultan thought Europe should submit to Allah; and the Queen could boast that the sun never set on British shores. Our imperial aims? We are happy enough if the Japanese can get their oil from Libya safely and their Toyotas to Los Angeles without fear; or if China can be coaxed into sending us more cheap Reeboks and fewer pirated CDs.

Our bases dot the globe to keep the sea-lanes open, thugs and murderers under wraps, and terrorists away from European, Japanese, and American globalists who profit mightily by blanketing the world with everything from antibiotics and contact lenses to BMWs and Jennifer Lopez—in other words, to keep the world safe and prosperous enough for Michael Moore to rant on spec, for Noam Chomsky to garner a lot of money and tenure from a defense-contracting MIT, for Barbra Streisand to make millions, for Edward Said's endowed chair to withstand Wall Street downturns, for Jesse Jackson to take off safely on his jet-powered junkets.

Why, then, does the world hate a country that uses its power to keep the peace rather than rule? Resentment, jealousy, and envy of the proud and powerful are often cited as the very human and age-old motives that prompt states irrationally to slur and libel— just as people do against their betters. No doubt Thucydides would agree. But there are other more subtle factors involved that explain the peculiar present resentment toward America—and why the French or Germans say worse things about free Americans who saved them than they did about Soviets who wanted to kill them.

Observers like to see an empire suffer and pay a price for its influence. That way they think imperial sway is at least earned. Athenians died all over the Mediterranean, from Egypt to Sicily; their annual burial ceremony was the occasion for the best of Hellenic panegyric. The list of British disasters from the Crimea and Afghanistan to Zululand and Khartoum was the stuff of Victorian poetry. But since Vietnam, Americans have done pretty much what they wanted to in the Gulf, Panama, Haiti, Grenada, Serbia, and Afghanistan, with less than an aggregate of 200 lost to enemy fire—a combat imbalance never seen in the annals of warfare. So not only can Americans defeat their adversaries, but they don't even die doing it. Shouldn't—our critics insist—we at least have some body bags?

Intervention is supposed to be synonymous with exploitation; thus the Athenians killed, enslaved, exacted, and robbed on Samos and Melos. No one thought Rome was going into Numidia or Gaul—one million killed, another million enslaved—to implant local democracy. Nor did the British decide that at last seventeenth-century India needed indigenous elections. But Americans have overthrown Noriega, Milosevic, and Mullah Omar and are about to rid Iraq of Saddam Hussein, to put in their places elected leaders, not legates or local client kings. Instead of the much-rumored "pipeline" that we supposedly coveted in Afghanistan, we are paying tens of millions to build a road and bridges so that Afghan truckers and traders won't break their axles.

In that regard, America is also a revolutionary, rather than a stuffy imperial society. Its crass culture abroad—rap music, Big Macs, Star Wars, Pepsi, and *The Beverly Hillbillies* reruns—does not reflect the tastes and values of either an Oxbridge elite or a landed Roman aristocracy. That explains why *Le Monde* or a Spanish deputy minister may libel us, even as millions of semiliterate Mexicans, unfree Arabs, and oppressed southeast Asians are dying to get here. It is one thing to mobilize against grasping, wealthy white people who want your copper, bananas, or rubber, quite another when your own youth want what black, brown, yellow, and white middle-class Americans alike have to offer. We so-called imperialists don't wear pith helmets, but, rather, baggy jeans and backward baseball caps. Thus far the rest of the globe—whether Islamic fundamentalists, European Socialists, or Chinese Communists—has not yet formulated an ideology antithetical to the kinetic American strain of Western culture.

Much, then, of what we read about the evil of American imperialism is written by post-heroic and bored elites, intellectuals, and coffeehouse hacks, whose freedom and security are a given but whose rarified tastes are apparently unshared and endangered. By contrast, the poorer want freedom and material things first— and cynicism, skepticism, irony, and nihilism second. So we should not listen to what a few say, but rather look at what many do.

Critiques of the United States based on class, race, nationality, or taste have all failed to explicate, much less stop, the American cultural juggernaut. Forecasts of bankrupting defense expenditures and imperial overstretch are the stuff of the faculty lounge. Neither Freud nor Marx is of much help. And real knowledge of past empires that might allow judicious analogies is beyond the grasp of popular pundits.

Add that all up, and our exasperated critics are left with the same old empty jargon of legions and gunboats.

Written on November 25 and published in
National Review Online *on November 27, 2002.*

34

Korea Is Not Quite Iraq

HYPOCRISY IN SERVICE TO VICTORY IS NO VICE

Hypocrisy is not always a bad thing when it is a matter of dealing with nuts with nuclear weapons. Although it is not surprising that both principled critics and cynics should call for sterner action right now against nuclear North Korea than they do against a non-nuclear Iraq, it is hard, after a sorry decade of appeasement, to move precipitously against a rogue nation that could ruin Tokyo or Seoul in a few minutes. The sad truth is that once an outlaw regime possesses nuclear weapons, it wins special consideration as the range of our own countermeasures diminishes—hence the mad scramble of utterly failed regimes in the post–Cold War era to acquire such expensive weapons in the first place, and, in turn, the importance not to appease them. Imagine the idea of a Kosovo war had Milosevic had one or two nukes.

Apples and Oranges

There are a number of reasons why we should move right now on Iraq but try to avoid a sudden use of military force against Korea. The first, of course, is the wisdom of hindsight: we wish Iraq not to become the problem of another North Korea. Precisely the fact that we have so few real choices against Pyongyang is good cause to ensure that we not repeat our mistake by allowing similar nuclear proliferation in Iraq. With a dozen or so Iraqi nukes, much of the world's oil supply would be subject to atomic blackmail, and twenty or so countries in the region would be bullied by Saddam Hussein even as rational and opulent Japan and South Korea are now being intimidated by a lunatic North Korea.

Second, we are already at war with Iraq and have been since 1991, when it broke all of the armistice agreements that had ended the first Gulf War. Those who question that glum assessment should ask what would happen if American ships and planes took a brief vacation from patrolling the no-fly zones and the Persian Gulf. I fear that thousands of dead Kurds and Shiites, coupled with the arrival of tons of new destructive weapons at Iraqi ports, would be the immediate answer. True, we have thousands of troops at the trip wire in both the Middle East and North Korea, and so far they are already in daily combat in the former, but not yet in the latter.

Third, the geopolitical situation of the two regions is both similar and yet different. Sustained containment offers greater hope of regime collapse in North Korea than in Iraq. Whereas there is not a democracy or a successful balanced economy anywhere near Baghdad, Japan and South Korea now loom large right by Pyongyang. Iraqis see little freedom and affluence in a Jordan or Saudi Arabia, while North Koreans are surrounded by radically different, democratic, rich—and strong—states just a few miles away. Iraq has oil that can sustain even its mismanaged and brutal lunocracy; North Korea has no natural resources to fuel its state criminality and is at the point of collapse, in desperate need of basic energy.

Baghdad also has no patrons left; a neighboring nuclear China is uneasy over North Korea and could eventually play India to its

Pakistan. And even if China remains deeply anti-American and rabidly Communist, its own radical economic reforms have convinced its leadership of the cynical advantages of peace, capitalism, and open trade—if for no other reason than to beat the West at its own game by acquiring high-tech weaponry. Thus Beijing has some incentive to corral the North Koreans, as does a neighborly Russia. Both care little anymore about Saddam Hussein and have even less influence on him, but are within the radioactive winds of the Korean peninsula. By the same token, taking out Saddam won't draw in a hostile Russia or China, but we cannot quite be sure of our backs in that region should American jets bomb Korea off either of their coasts.

Fourth, there is a direct connection between Iraq and our current war on terror in ways that go beyond our historic conflict with Korea. Whether or not one believes Iraq was involved at the planning level in 9/11, there is proof that it had something to do with the first World Trade Center bombing, had intelligence meetings with members of al Qaeda, tried to assassinate a former president of the United States, and offered sanctuary to Middle Eastern terrorists, from Abu Nidal to Abu Abbas. North Korea is not sending money to suicide bombers and proclaiming itself the center of Middle Eastern resistance to the United States. And through Saddam Hussein's demise, a reconstituted Iraq will have a positive effect on the war against terror—both by removing a historic supporter of terrorist cabals and by the creation of a postbellum consensual government that can offer millions some hope of a more stable region. To Islamic fundamentalists, the destruction of Saddam Hussein—who is now the self-proclaimed keeper of the faith—will be far more worrisome than the liberation of North Korea.

Fifth, strategically it makes more sense to confront the less-formidable power first, much as we invaded Italy before Germany. If it eventually comes to a shooting war with Korea, it would be better for U.S. troops to have come off a victory against Iraq, rather than to know that after a brutal war against Pyongyang, more fighting looms in the Middle East. And, psychologically, we might also gain some deterrence by previous success in Iraq, which the Americans at least associate with Middle Eastern terrorism in a way they do not with North Korea. Saddam Hussein accepts that we will attack him, and in the desperation of his eleventh hour will not be all that intimidated by prior proof of American willpower. By contrast, the North Koreans are still not sure of our resolve—especially considering the ease with which they have tricked past American diplomats—but can learn of it from our defeat of a similar despot who had sought weapons of mass destruction.

Ripples to Follow

There are lessons to be learned from all this that go all the way back to the Korean War and should teach us the bitter wages of not achieving victory—whether in 1951 or 1991—when it was within our grasp. Let us hope that our third glaring mistake, Vietnam, chooses to follow the Chinese, rather than the North Korean, model. We have at least learned that only one thing is worse than not confronting a bully at all—letting him slink off when he is beaten.

Sometime in the late 1980s or early nineties, someone in some administration was asleep at the wheel in allowing North Korea to achieve nuclear status, a blunder that rivals the disaster of Pakistani nuclear acquisition. Now part of the enhanced Bush doctrine must be to stop absolutely the further proliferation of such weaponry. If we don't, two very bad things will follow.

First, crazy, failed states will seek to use their atomic status to blackmail the West and its allies for either economic gain or political advantage. Unfortunately the age-old burdens of the West—its freedom and affluence create a reasoned and circumspect, though often naïve, citizenry within an unreasoned and reckless world—leave it particularly vulnerable to illogical demands from outlaw nations. People sipping latté in La Jolla or West Hollywood find the entire notion of nuclear saber-rattling in the Pacific unthinkable; not so those who are starving or often routinely murdered in Iraq, Pakistan, or North Korea. Being crazy with nothing left to lose can create a powerful psychological advantage in brinkman-ship. Any veteran of tough schools can attest that thugs paraded their own nihilism as central to their intimidation: "Why stand up to a loser like me, when even if you beat me, you—not I—have everything to forfeit?"

Second, European or Westernized sane nations like Germany, Italy, Spain, Japan, South Korea, and Australia at some point will chafe at being held hostage by two-bit thugocracies and thus themselves decide to go nuclear. Japan may shudder still at Hiroshima, but no great nation of its caliber will sit idly by while an upstart failed society sticks nuclear missiles in its face.

In reaction, at that point the United States will confront a real dilemma, being forced either to agree with its allies' new remedies—and thereby perhaps elevating future multilateral rivalries and spats to confrontations between nuclear powers—or to ensure absolute American guarantees that we will retaliate in kind to threats against our friends, and so extend the American nuclear shield to half the globe. That may be the case right now, but the American people will not sleep well once they realize that they may be nuked for pledging San Francisco to protect an antsy Seoul.

Is the Horse Out of the Barn?

What should we do, then, with this Korea mess? First, the banal remedy: work with our allies (Europe, Japan, Russia, and China) to contain North Korea through diplomatic means—the stick of sanctions, boycotts, embargoes, and encircling hostile alliances, with the carrot of unspoken assurances not to attack. Both China and Russia may see an opportunity of gaining international pres-tige by banding together against a bankrupt North Korea—espe-cially in fear that its nukes could either be used against them or handed over to South Korea after reunification.

Second, intercept all North Korean weaponry in transit to the Middle East on the high seas—and place an embargo on its exports of missiles and nuclear technology to other rogue regimes.

Third, have some tough discussions about the "German disease" with the South Koreans, and point out that their recent anti-Americanism and inane talk of a third way have only emboldened their enemies. We must remonstrate—given South Korea's far larger population and gross national product—that there is not necessarily a need for American troops to defend a wealthy nation when they are not wanted. South Koreans can be resolute allies or erstwhile friends, but not something in between when it may be a matter of facing down a truly evil and crazy nuclear rogue state. If they really wish to pay bribe money and accede to blackmail, then they can leave nearly 40,000 Americans out of their calculus of appeasement.

There is something reprehensible about South Korea's current sneers about American brinkmanship, when almost 50,000 Americans once died in their snows—and millions more for fifty years have watched their borders—to ensure the freedom they now apparently take for granted. Indeed, a cynic might believe that some South Koreans feel they can amalgamate their enemy without a war—and through such unification at some future date inherit nuclear status by default.

Fourth, we must accelerate our current ABM programs, with special attention to mobile seaborne missiles that can be stationed at sea off the coast of likely aggressors to serve as first-chance, low-trajectory interceptors of hostile weapons as they take off. Such deterrent antiballistic missiles should be discussed publicly once they near deployment, precisely to apprise the North Koreans and others of our own protection against their nuclear extortion.

Lately, following resolute victories in Kosovo and Afghanistan, we have just begun to regain a sense of deterrence after a decade of appeasement. But it is a long, slow process and we cannot stop now, when for the foreseeable future the dangers of complacency will continue to dwarf those of action.

Written on January 8 and published in
NATIONAL REVIEW ONLINE *on January 10, 2003.*

35

So Long to All That

Why the Old World of Bases, Alliances, and NATO Is Now Coming to an End

John le Carré and Harold Pinter tell us that we are the enemy. Gerhard Schroeder wins an election only through anti-Americanism. French diplomats warn us not to consider a conniving Saddam Hussein out of compliance—and are seconded by Communist China. The demonstrations in European capitals did not arise with Iraq but started—remember October 2001?—with our "amoral" war against the fascist Taliban in Afghanistan. And European polls reveal widespread anti-Americanism, suggesting that hostile politicians and intellectuals there are *not* out of step with public opinion.

In response, even our own New York–Washington old guard and Euro-functionaries are finally rustling from their comfortable slumber, even if to raise only the *wrong* questions about the inevitable drift: "Are we too unilateral?" "Is Bush too brusque?" "What did we do wrong?"

They should note instead that in the aftermath of major wars, the world is rarely put back together quite the same. When

Rome entered the Punic Wars it was an agrarian republic; it finished as an imperial Mediterranean power. Waterloo reordered Europe for a century, and the defeat of Germany and Japan ushered in the fifty-year-long protocols of the Cold War, in which enemies became friends and friends then enemies. Who could sort out the shifting Sparta-Athens-Thebes relationships following the Peloponnesian War?

It is not just that winners dictate and losers comply, but that even among allies, war and its aftermath often tear away the thin scabs of unity and expose long-festering wounds of real cultural, political, historical, and geographical difference. So it is with this present war against the terrorists and their sponsors, which when it is finally over will leave our world a very different place.

In this present crisis, Americans have few choices but to follow the accepted way of doing business until the darkness passes. But pass it will. And when it does we—liberals and conservatives alike—will have to take a long, hard look at the sixty-year-old way in which we have conducted our foreign policy.

The stuff of diplomacy is, of course, reason, circumspection—and stasis. But a nation's alliances must also take into consideration a strong element of emotion and spirit—and no accord can endure that ignores popular opinion entirely in favor of strategic Realpolitik. A few days of French denunciations, weeks of lectures about "the German Way," or months of anti-Semitic attacks are one thing, but a year and a half of such sustained hostility following upon the greatest attack on American soil in our history finally has had a sobering effect on the American people. Our citizens in their disgust with Continental Europeans are far ahead of the diplomats—who seem shackled by a Cold War world of bases, expeditionary troops, and grand old alliances. Far from being inflammatory or reflecting the angst of the "neocons," Mr. Rumsfeld, in his matter-of-fact use of "Old Europe," was astutely reflecting grassroots public opinion.

Much of the harshest criticism of the United States comes from our friends in Western Europe—not those in Poland, the

Czech Republic, or Bulgaria. It is not just specific disagreements over particular actions, but rather a deductive anger that seeks out, or indeed creates, issues over which to vent. Forget questions of ingratitude—that France was the 1940s version of a surrendered Kuwait likewise reborn as a result of American courage and resolve, or that the now grand city of Berlin arises only because the old one was saved from Russian tanks.

Much of the problem, as so many have observed, is the dividend of a postmodern and ultimately antidemocratic European Union— one now seemingly free from foreign invasion—whose nature became clearer only in the months following September 11. In addition, spite arises over the global reach of the United States coupled with the diminished, though cynical, world roles of countries like France, Germany, and Russia—which have a sorry collective track record of unilateral action in Africa, selling contraband to Saddam, and flattening Muslim cities such as Grozny.

The EU is realizing that its psychic investment in international organizations can be no substitute for moral confidence coupled with military power. Each time the United States derides the election of Libya as a player on the UN Commission on Human Rights, it undermines the legitimacy of an organization to which a militarily weak but culturally influential Old Europe is deeply wedded— even if a murderous Syria does sit on the Security Council.

Indeed, there is a great fear among many Europeans that unless something is done now to check the United States, the sheer dynamism (or crassness) of American popular culture and its radical cultural egalitarianism could come to define Westernism itself. We may have already sunk to the point where many Europeans would not be all that happy with a quick, American-led victory in Iraq—one *without* a sufficient number of U.S. body bags (the absence of which is a favorite lament abroad), shrill "I told you so" lectures about our "imperialism," and plenty of humiliation for "cowboy" George Bush's "arrogant" and "reckless" America.

Forget the tales that will come from postbellum Iraq of the liberation of thousands, of decades of mass murder, of Hussein's destruction of the environment, of the caches of terrible weapons, and of the stability a reformed Iraq will bring for Europe; instead, for Europeans the only story will be bad American hyper-puissance. Indeed, such is the sad state of affairs, that we are surprised less that our so-called friends are no longer allies than that they are not yet overt enemies.

We should accept that, taken as a whole, the current anti-Americanism is beginning either to trump—or to reveal old differences in—our deeper common heritage. Indeed, the only thing that may yet salvage a strategic partnership is a radical change in our political relationship, beginning with the withdrawal of American troops from Germany—quietly, professionally, permanently—and from any other European state that seems uneasy with our presence. *Only such action—steady and studied—will bring back an air of reality to our relations.*

Our diplomats, of course, advise us to ignore our pique and as mature adults to focus on the critical strategic advantages that accrue from forward deployment in Old Europe—vestiges of self-interest and the archaic NATO slogan, "Russia out, America in, Germany down." But, unfortunately for our policy experts, ultimately leagues and alliances need some basis of mutual admiration and support if they are not to become utterly ossified as circumstances change. Yet many Americans are beginning to question our formal *military* affiliation with European nations and would perhaps prefer some sort of vague friendship of the type we now enjoy with Sweden, Brazil, and Switzerland. Why?

First, there is "teenager disease"—the notion that through our predominant military strength and omnipresence in Europe we have become resented and parental. The young rant and rave at their stronger benefactors as expressions of angst over their dependence, both psychic and material. Allowing the Europeans to chart their own course in matters of security would be healthy for both parties—as overprotective mothers and fathers are quick to learn when their twenty-something offspring finally moves out.

Second, our bases are creating a weird sort of "hostage syndrome," in which the host country exercises inordinate clout over the guest beyond considerations of mutual defense, rent, and the practical problems of putting thousands of adolescent men and women in a foreign culture. Germany finds it can turn on its traditional patron precisely because we have so many Americans within its borders and seem so intent on keeping them there at all costs. We claim we are there to create stability; they counter that we merely use their bases as transit centers to facilitate mischief abroad.

And, sometimes, even our enemies seem to wish our continued presence abroad. True, South Koreans can seem lax and complacent thanks to 37,000 GIs, while on other occasions claiming that Americans are an obstacle to their reunification with their kin to the north. But even North Korea seems as cynical, almost welcoming our continued deployment—taking a certain satisfaction in the prospect of being able to kill and wound thousands of nearby Americans in hours, an unattainable task if our presence is restricted to an assortment of cruisers, subs, and carriers at sea.

Do bases in the post–Cold War era really offer strategic flexibility and serve as trip wires to cement alliances—or do they multiply political and military liabilities, as both hosts and adversaries use their presence to dictate and curb American military options? Military theorists once deprecated aircraft carriers as obsolete sitting ducks; in fact, they amount to quick-moving runways of American sovereignty, not subject to worries over rent, blackmail, compromise, or terrorism.

True, carrier war is dangerous and expensive—but then so is bunking overnight in Saudi Arabia, basing thousands on the DMZ, being told by the Germans that we are "allowed" to use airspace actually already guaranteed under NATO protocols, and forgiving billions in debt to the likes of Pakistan. Personally, I'd rather spend $20 billion to have American workers build an additional ten to fifteen acres of aggregate floating American runways than pour billions annually into countries that either do not like us, resent both the protection and the rent, or are themselves inherently unstable.

Third, in the post–Cold War world it is not all that clear that such bases are crucial for meeting our defense responsibilities—as we learned from our withdrawal from so many facilities in Greece and the Philippines. We surely protect no one in Europe from conventional enemies but rather use the bases to project power abroad. In lieu of these resources, we could cache supplies and weapons in relatively uninhabited depots and rely more on airborne and naval-based troops. And, if we do need conventional bases for larger traditional contingents, we should seek ports and stations in Eastern European countries who wish close ties with us and who do not quite believe that they are at the end of history with Germany or Russia.

Such a posture would be not isolationist but rather an expression of muscular independence—as we continue to fulfill our commitments abroad, but in very different ways. We should accentuate areas where we can act in concert precisely because we are no longer allies in lockstep, and thus are not so vulnerable through blackmail, by the basing of American troops, to protect those who do not always profess they want such protection.

If many NATO allies oppose the United States as it removes a fascist dictatorship, if France expresses daily a visceral dislike of America, and if a continental intelligentsia sees America—not the Taliban, Saddam Hussein, the Iranians, or the North Koreans—as the world's real problem, then surely America already has enough enemies without allies and dependents such as these.

Without rancor or anger, it really is time sadly and quietly to move on and sigh, "So long to all that."

Written on January 29 and published in
NATIONAL REVIEW ONLINE *on January 31, 2003.*

36

---◦※◦---

Muscular Independence

No More Buying, Bullying,
and Begging Abroad?

The events of the last six months in crafting an alliance—
mostly for political rather than military advantage—to remove a murderous Saddam Hussein are prompting contradictory
emotions in many Americans. Our hearts wish to disengage somewhat from "allies" like the French, Germans, Turks, South Koreans, Pakistanis, Saudis, and a host of others. These guys are costly,
either to our pocketbook or psyche—without offering in exchange much military or political support for any operation outside their immediate borders. If such allies are neutral rather than
hostile we are satisfied.

We all recall the unilateralism of the sheriff in *High Noon,* but
such an illusion also involves, in the end, tossing away the badge,
leaving such parsimonious and fickle folks to themselves, and taking
the buckboard out of their town. After Iraq and North Korea, I
think, the worry will be not endless American interventions but a
consensus that we have done enough to mete out justice to outlaws.

We wonder why we give billions of dollars to Egypt when 100,000 fanatics in Cairo scream hatred for the United States, or base ships in Chania, Crete, when tens of thousands of Greeks demonstrate against almost anything America does? When even Canadian politicians call our president a "moron" and us Americans "bastards," isn't it time politely to let all these people be and let them do as they please without us?

By contrast, our heads tell us: Hold on! The world is not so simple. An authoritarian Musharraf helps us round up terrorists; the duplicitous Saudis at times cut off al Qaeda funding; and bribe money to Jordan, Egypt, and Palestine supposedly curbs aggression toward Israel, while European obstructionists still jail fundamentalist terrorists. The South Koreans aggravate us—but not to the extent that we can so easily pull out of the DMZ and allow the battle of Armageddon with the North in which millions of innocents would perish.

Yet the American people are growing tired of this notion of "it makes sense in the long run." And perhaps they are right, since this entire old way of doing business—treaties, alliances, bases, deployments, arms credits, special aid packages—and indeed our very mentality of coalition building are all part of a world gone by, one predicated on the old bipolar rivalry with the Soviet Union and finally blown to bits by 9/11.

Building coalitions, crafting containment, surrounding enemies—all that Dullesesque globe-trotting presupposes the need to corral a monstrous nuclear Soviet Union when our present foes are in fact more diverse, weaker, and insidious, our allies no longer allies by any classical definition, and our friends opportunistic rather than benevolent. The only drama left in the looming Iraqi War is whether France & Co. will smile or remain mute on news of American losses.

The presence of over 80,000 American troops in Germany makes no sense when Eastern Europe is a democratic buffer between Russia, which itself is no longer a Communist empire. Maintaining the myth that France is really an ally and a NATO member is silly when its nuclear forces are not needed to provide wild-card deterrence against the Soviet Union and Frenchmen are nakedly trying to create a European axis in opposition to the United States, willing in the process to break with America over the safety of a psychopath.

With the world awash in airbuses it makes no sense for any European military to rely on American airlift capacity. Mediterranean bases in Spain, Italy, Greece, and Turkey may have been necessary to monitor the Soviet fleet, but in the present world, ports and runways in two rather than all four could provide us enough forward deployment. A hundred thousand troops—plus planes, ships, and bases—in South Korea and Japan once posed a strong deterrent to the Soviet Union and are useful in reminding China to think twice about storming Taiwan. But ultimately powerful countries like Japan, South Korea, and Taiwan, after sixty years of an American presence, will have to provide for their own defense, with or without us.

What the United States should seek is a sort of military autonomy, a muscular disengagement that lessens dependence on other mercurial and conniving countries and yet allows us strategic flexibility—and, yes, the freedom to move in the interest of freedom-loving peoples abroad *who wish to act in concert with us.* We should prefer a series of bilateral arrangements and a new tactical doctrine that does privilege "exit strategy" but simply states that the purpose of all (rare) U.S. interventions is military victory and the political will to define and then ensure such an outcome. Removal of a fascist like Saddam Hussein from Kuwait or stripping him of weapons of mass destruction both have exit strategies, but will never solve the problem of Iraqi state support for terrorism—him!—until the regime is defeated, humiliated, and ended.

We need to find a new approach that seeks alternate basing in Eastern Europe, greater reliance on lightly manned military depots and caches, a multifaceted sea- and land-based antiballistic missile system, renewed commitment to carrier forces, and novel technologies that might provide floating, mobile airfields, rapid ship transport, and increased airlift capacity.

If we believe that North Korea means to blackmail the United States by holding Los Angeles hostage, the way out of that dilemma is not to bully an appeasing Seoul, or rally a confused Tokyo, but rather to be prepared stealthily to encircle the peninsula with naval ABM systems that can hit Pyongyang's nukes in their nascent trajectory, sit still, and then let the concerned powers ask us for advice and support rather than vice versa.

The key is to avoid the deplorable spectacle of begging and buying off a democratic Turkey, offering either threats or concessions for a corrupt Mexico's UN vote, or thanking the Germans for protecting our bases from their own demonstrators. If it were not for a few courageous British, Spanish, and Italian statesmen, public opinion in all those countries would make their governments as anti-American as those in France and Germany. American power, and the willingness to use it successfully for moral aims and in our national interest, alone will win far more allies than sitting through yet another sanctimonious UN debate and an open-air auction for support.

It is time quietly to accept that the UN and the EU are inimical mechanisms that seek to oppose, isolate, and weaken the United States, for both natural and less-than-honorable reasons. The obstructionism of Germany and France and the fickleness of Turkey are no longer mere irritants but may well result in strengthening the resistance of our enemy Saddam Hussein and thus lead to unnecessary American deaths.

We are well beyond the nuances of debate and chic sophistry; the drama now hinges on to what degree a NATO ally's behavior will increase the number of Americans killed in action. France, remember, did not reluctantly vote against the United States but actively sent its diplomats throughout Africa and Asia to lobby countries to oppose America, a visceral hostility not matched by either Russia or China—or even any of the Arab League. NATO, in other words, as we knew it, is almost dead and buried.

Bases in this baffling new world are a polite mechanism for blackmail and concessions—and are, increasingly, as much trouble as they are worth. Whether we think we protect them or they think they are exploited by us, it matters little: we are held hostage by our very professed desire to want something they have. Every time we beg for votes in the General Assembly, try to buy a Turkish vote, bully a pacifistic South Korea, or beseech the Saudi kleptocrats for help, we only weaken America. And we end up looking hypocritical in the bargain—as recently as when we thanked the dictator Musharraf while castigating a republican Turkey.

Nothing is worse for a great power than to ask others far less moral for permission to use its power; and nothing weakens a great power more than intervening and intruding frequently but rarely decisively. Had we simply ignored the UN—as Mr. Clinton did in Kosovo—and moved unilaterally last fall (like Russia and France do all the time), Saddam Hussein would be gone, and we now would have more impressed friends than we do disdainful enemies. Instead, we await China's moral condemnation of our unilateral action—this from a regime that in the last fifty years butchered more of its own citizens than any government in the history of civilization, annexed Tibet, invaded Korea and Vietnam, and threatened to annihilate Taiwan. France hysterically alleges that we will harm the city of Baghdad in its liberation, but is silent about the Russian destruction of Grozny in its subjugation. And so on.

The American people are not naïfs who yearn for isolationism, but they are starting to ask some hard questions about the way we have been doing business for fifty years, and it may well be time to grant the French, Canadians, Germans, Turks, South Koreans, and a host of others their wishes for independence from us: polite friendship—but no alliances, no bases, no money, no trade concessions, and no more begging for the privilege of protecting them.

Written on March 12 and published in
National Review Online *on March 14, 2003.*

37

⋆═◉═⋆

Gone but Not Forgotten

MAKING WAR AND PEACE IN THE
NEW POST-SOVIET WORLD

It has been well over a decade since the fall of the Berlin Wall. Yet many, still caught up in past institutions and protocols of that bygone age, forget the degree to which the collapse of the Soviet Union is with us today and helps to frame almost all of our struggles since 9/11.

Our troubles with Europe are said to arise from differing views of the world order and an imbalance in military power. Yet these new tensions cannot truly be understood without the appreciation that there are no longer 300 Soviet divisions poised to plow through West Germany. With such a common threat, natural differences between Europe and the United States—from the positioning of Pershing tactical missiles on German soil to prevent Soviet nuclear intimidation, to Continental criticism of the American role in Vietnam and Central America—always were aired within certain understood and relatively polite parameters of common history and interests.

America, after all, was appreciated for ending Hitler's rule—and immediately after for pledging its youth and national security in an effort at keeping a murderous totalitarianism out of a recovering Europe. With a common and deadly enemy nearby, Western Europeans had no utopian illusions that the United Nations, rather than NATO and America, could stop an aggressive Soviet premier should he choose to fire up his tanks. The idea that a German president would bark out anti-American invective at a mass rally would have been inconceivable twenty years ago. But now Herr Schroeder does so routinely—not because his people hate us or because we deserve his antipathy, but simply because he can.

In the shadow of the Soviet threat, Western European statesmen dared not disarm, but rather accepted the tragic reality that the world was a dangerous place and that deterrence—and not the bureaucrats of the Common Market—kept pretty awful people at a safe distance. With a Stalinist regime bloodied by the murder of thirty million of its own, and with World War II criminals of every stripe still lurking in its shadows, even hack lawyers in Brussels had no time to go after an American diplomat or general on bogus charges of genocide.

Outnumbered three to one on the ground, a beleaguered Western Europe grudgingly invested in its own defense. Residents then accepted the bitter truth that the welfare state had gone about as far as it could—without its social expenditures taking away resources from the tanks, planes, and troops that alone could ensure its national survival.

Poor France. So long as the old bipolar world was engaged in high-stakes nuclear poker, its independent *force de frappe* gave it leverage with both East and West. Though without much conventional strength, the French nevertheless could warrant respect from the Soviet Union since, in theory, they had the power to take out Moscow. Despite having a pitiful conventional deterrent, France was nevertheless courted by the United States as a strategic bulwark against the rising nuclear arsenals of China and Russia.

No longer. In today's world, except along the Pakistani-Indian border and in North Korea, there are no real reasons for the club of nuclear powers to go to war with one another. Instead, deterrence against rogue regimes and terrorist enclaves—which cannot be nuked, or threatened with nukes—means deploying special operatives and costly conventional forces of which France is pitifully short. It can blow up the planet with its few hundred aging missiles, but it wouldn't have been able to deal with the menace of a ragtag Taliban in Afghanistan even if al Qaeda had smoked the Louvre.

The demise of the Soviet Union also created this strange thing called "Old" and "New" Europe, as all of a sudden half a continent was transmogrified not merely from enemies to neutrals, but in fact to rather close friends. All those American characteristics that so bothered sophisticated Western Europeans—our deep distrust of socialism, our embrace of religion, our emphasis on free will and individualism, our very brashness—in fact endeared us to the newly liberated Eastern Europeans, who faulted us not from the left, for our knee-jerk anti-communism, but rather from the right, on the grounds that we did not use force earlier to fight Stalinism in 1947, 1956, and 1968.

But nowhere is the ghost of the Soviet Union more evident than in the Middle East. And the changed circumstances involve much more than the end of tolerance for conniving right-wing despots looking to prevent commissars from controlling the world's oil supply. We have gained some flexibility—with perhaps more to come—from the idea that Russia is now itself a vast oil exporter and in some ways serves our interests in lessening the world's dependence on Persian Gulf oil. Today's Russians want to sell more of their own petroleum, not take over that of others.

The Arabs fought four major wars against Israel—in 1948, 1956, 1967, and 1973—but none since. Why? Have the leaders of Syria, Jordan, Egypt, and Iraq come to their senses, and thus entertained kinder and gentler notions about the Jewish state? Or was it, instead, that there was no longer a nuclear Russia around to threaten the United States on about day four or five of such conflicts, warning us to call off the Israelis lest they park their own tanks in Cairo or Damascus?

Surely the absence of such a nuclear patron explains the present reluctance of conventional states to attack Israel. Tel Aviv's neighbors accept that there is nothing between their own aggression and a humiliating defeat except their own degree of military prowess—or, rather, lack of it. Mr. Arafat and his clique can deal with Mr. Sharon or Mr. Bush—or nobody. Quite literally, in the post–Cold War tumult, there is no one else left in the region with whom to barter and banter.

We forget that there is an entire generation of Arab dictators and terrorists—from Arafat to Saddam Hussein—who were trained or welcomed in Moscow, and who predicated their policies on the idea that Soviet intelligence, Soviet weapons, Soviet money, and Soviet opposition to America could provide them a degree of security otherwise unwarranted by their own resources or ability. The first Gulf War would never have occurred had Saddam Hussein convinced his tottering patron Mr. Gorbachev to do the usual Russian thing of threatening us with nuclear-tipped missiles—or had the Iraqis waited until 1995 or so, to acquire through an indigenous nuclear program what they had lost with the collapse of the Soviet Union.

In that context alone should we understand the race by Middle Eastern tyrants and despots to acquire weapons of mass destruction. WMD is a polite name for some sort of surrogate Soviet nuclear deterrent, used to coerce or blackmail the United States from acting freely to promote the establishment of democratic government and freedom and the removal of terrorist enclaves.

A liar like "Baghdad Bob"—Mohammed Saeed al-Sahaf, the Baathist so-called "information" minister—did not learn his craft reading the *Arabian Nights,* or from the braggadocio and tribal mythmaking of the Arab coffeehouse. No, he was a product of the Baathist police apparatus—and thus, indirectly, of Soviet-style disinformation protocols, according to which lies in service of a criminal state were not really lies at all. If the West shudders at the state-controlled untruth in the Arab world, it should remember that the closer a state's former ties with the Soviet Union—whether it be Syria, Iraq, Egypt, Palestine Authority, or Libya—the greater propensity it displays for censorship, fabrication, and an intrusive Big Brother.

Perhaps the biggest change is in the nature of terrorism itself. Gone are most Russian and Eastern European money and training for hijackers and assassins. The Czech or Bulgarian police are more likely to round up killers than to subsidize them as they did in the past. Polish commandos help Americans fight terrorists rather than helping terrorists to fight Americans. Berlin is not a haven for spies with Middle Eastern operations, but is rather undergoing massive construction to return it to its former status as Europe's premier capital. In short, the playing field of the terrorist has shrunk considerably, as a fourth of the planet has suddenly done an about-face and joined in to stop rather than foster killers.

Our own defense capability reflects these new opportunities. That we may soon move 80,000 military personnel out of Germany would have been impossible in the Cold War. With such new flexibility, should Turkey or Saudi Arabia forbid use of their bases, why should we be paying material and political capital for runways and hangars in the first place when we cannot use them? Suddenly the old paradigm—that we had to scheme with rightists to gain their soil to corner the Soviet Union—no longer matters; instead, the renter, not the landlord, now holds the greater hand, as we craft our armed forces to be more mobile, flexible, and independent from blackmail or coercion, from "friends" and neutrals alike.

That we are refitting some of our nuclear submarines with conventional cruise missiles to take out terrorists, rather than to strike Soviet cities, is also the kind of new thinking that has in it an ominous message for rogue states once protected under the old Soviet nuclear umbrella. If the free world has now doubled or tripled in size, so have American military resources, to focus on a diminishing terrorist stronghold. We fought so well in Afghanistan and Iraq in part precisely because we now have the freedom to devote our efforts to unconventional warfare without worrying that we are shorting our heavy armor and tactical aircraft—once so critical to stopping a Soviet assault in Europe. Ten thousand Special Forces may not have kept the Russians from blasting into Germany, but they were invaluable in Afghanistan and Kurdistan. Lumbering B-52s might have been blown out of the skies by Soviet Migs, but they rained fire and ruin on the Taliban with impunity.

With the demise of the Soviet Union perished also the idea of spreading Marxism by force across the globe. Our enemies could always bring in the Russians if we proved too demanding of reform; cynical neutrals could play us off against them to gain aid or attention. In the world's impoverished and desolate expanses, naïve dreamers and psychopathic killers alike could always justify their quasi-allegiance to Stalinism on the grounds that a coercive socialism was closer to brotherhood than wide-open American capitalism.

Islamist fascism entertains neither these utopian pretenses nor the air of shared struggle that trumps racial, religious, or geographical boundaries. If you are female or gay, your correct politics don't really matter. If you are Christian or non–Middle Eastern, too bad. If you are addicted to Western freedom or consumerism, you might as well save the trouble and go straight to Hell now. So Khomeinism or al Qaedism is not Soviet-enhanced Marxism: it lacks not merely the resources of a vast continent at its call but also an ideology that misleads and confuses with false promises of social justice. With the Islamo-fascists you get what you see—a return to the thirteenth century and all its darkness.

What do such new realities portend in our current struggle? We must remember that much of our frustration with our European allies can be attributed to the absence of a global rogue nation that could destroy Europe with a flip of a switch, and that their pique with us is not predicated on what we do or say but, rather, on the changing global realities.

And if we are exasperated with Cold War institutions like the UN and NATO, it is precisely because they are paradigms of a bygone age that have remained fossilized rather than evolving to meet the challenges of a new era. So, in most cases, the United States is at last in a singular position to promote freedom and democracy without either cynicism or the Realpolitik that today's elected Socialist will be tomorrow's Soviet puppet. It is becoming quite a different world—and one, thank God, that at least a few in our government have sized up pretty well.

In short, for the first time in a half-century, Ronald Reagan's threat to terrorists and their supporters that "you can run but not hide" is at last true. The world of al Qaeda is shrinking as we speak—and there is no person or force left that can bail any of them out from the doom that awaits them all.

Written on May 28 and published in National Review Online *on May 30, 2003.*

VIII

POSTSCRIPT

38

History or Hysteria?

OUR VULTURE PUNDITS
REGURGITATE RUMOR AND BUZZ

Instantly televised images are broadcast with no in-depth analysis. A national television audience sighs and cheers second to second—not unlike the mercurial Athenians lined up on the shore of the Great Harbor at Syracuse who, in dejection and euphoria, watched their fleet lose, win, and lose in the sea battle against the Sicilians.

But rather than trying to digest and analyze the tempo of battle, our vulture pundits instead regurgitate rumor and buzz—which are usually refuted by the next minute's events. The subtext throughout seems to be disappointment that the war so far has lasted seven rather than two days.

Reporters at the beginning of the week were hysterically railing that Basra, cut off and surrounded, was not yet taken. A voice on NPR told us that after three days there would be "no food or water"—as if we had not cut off the power, water, and bridges at Baghdad in 1991 for forty-four days, as if Marines getting shot at had electricity in the field. Things happen in war. Surely a temporary interruption in service is not so high a price to pay for lasting freedom.

I flipped the channel. Another pundit was lamenting that we were outnumbered by the Republican Guard; 1,000 planes with the best pilots in the world apparently don't compute in his strategic calculus. Yet another philosopher worried that we "were angering the Arab street"—as if anger does not naturally rise in war. He should have asked why a German public that hated us in 1941 did not do so in 1945. Not to be outdone, another expert— wrong in the past on everything in Afghanistan—smugly announced that in five days of war "everything has gone wrong!"

Have these people any intelligence or shame?

Casualties, POWs, and skyrocketing costs blanket the airwaves; rarely mentioned is the simple military fact that in a single week a resolute American pincer column has driven across Iraq and is now systematically surrounding Baghdad—and with far fewer killed than were lost in a single day in Lebanon. When American soldiers move decisively against terrorists and killers in the Middle East, they have a far greater chance of surviving than they do sitting in their barracks as living targets under "rules of engagement."

In disgust at the hysteria, I took a drive to Washington to the National Cathedral on Sunday. Big mistake. All except one of the entrances were closed due to security concerns. I walked in under the wonderful sculptures of Frederick Hart, an authentic American genius who almost single-handedly restored classical realism to American sculpture. A small statue of a kneeling Lincoln, who sent thousands into battle to eradicate slavery, was in the corner. A plaque of quotations from Churchill, about the need for sacrifice in war, was on the wall. So I was feeling somewhat good again— until I heard the pious sermon on "shock and awe." In pompous tones the minister was deprecating the war effort, calling down calumnies upon the administration, and alleging the immoral nature of our nation at war.

Such a strange man at such a strange time, I thought. His entire congregation, by its own admission, is in danger from foreign terrorists (why else bar the gates?). His church is itself a monument to the utility of force for moral purposes. His own existence as a free-speaking, freely worshiping man of God is possible only thanks to the United States military—whose present mission he was openly deriding at the country's national shrine.

All these people need to calm down, take a deep breath, and read their history—computing the logistics of fighting 7,000 miles away and considering the hurdles of vast space, unpredictable weather, and enemies without uniforms. And? In just a week, the United States military has surrounded one of history's most sadistic and nasty regimes. It has overrun 80 percent of the countryside and has daily pulverized the Republican Guard, achieving more in five days than the Iranians did in eight years.

Twenty-four hours a day, thousands of tankers and supply trucks barrel down long, vulnerable supply lines, quickly and efficiently. There is no bridge too far for these long columns. One hundred percent air superiority is ours. *There is not a single Iraqi airplane in the sky.* Enemy tanks either stay put or are bombed. Kurds and Shiites really will soon start to be heard. Seven oil wells are on fire (with firefighters on the scene)—no oil slicks, no attacks on Israel. Kuwait City is not aflame. "Millions" of refugees fleeing into Syria and Jordan have not materialized. Even Peter Arnett is no longer parroting the Iraqi government claims of ten million starving and has moved on to explain why the Iraqis were equipped with chemical suits—to protect Saddam's killers from our WMDs!

Few, if any, major bridges in Iraq have been blown; there are no mass uprisings in Saddam's favor. The Tikrit mafia fights as the SS did in the craters of Berlin, facing as it does—and within weeks—either a mob's noose, a firing squad, or a dungeon. Through 20,000 air sorties, no jets have been shot down; there is nothing to stop them from flying another 100,000. They fly in sand, in lightning, high, low, day, night, anywhere, anytime. Supplies are pouring in. Saddam's regime is cut off and its weapons will not be replenished. This is not North Vietnam, with Chinese and Russian ships with daily resupply in the harbor of Haiphong. British and

Americans, with courageous Australians as well, are fighting as a team without even the petty rivalry of a Montgomery and Bradley.

Our media talks of Saddam's thugs and terrorists as if they were some sort of Iraqi SAS. Meanwhile, the real thing—scary American, British, and Australian Special Forces—is causing havoc to Saddam's rear guard. In short, for all the tragedy of a fragging, Iraqi atrocities, misdirected cruise missiles, and the usual cowardly antics inherent to our enemy's way of war, the real story is not being reported: a phenomenal march against overwhelming logistical, material, and geographical odds in under seven days has reached and surrounded Saddam Hussein's capital.

At home there have been none of the promised terrorist attacks. A supportive public—stunned by initial losses, now angered by atrocities—is growing more, not less, fervent, determined not merely to defeat but to destroy utterly the Baathists. The Arab world snickers that we cannot take casualties; the American public is instead growing impatient to inflict more of them—and is probably already well to the right of the Bush administration. We are a calm and forgiving people, but executing prisoners, fighting in civilian clothes, and using human shields will soon draw a response too terrible to contemplate.

Just as unusual has been American ad hoc logistical flexibility. Saudi Arabia caved early on—and we moved to other Gulf states. Turkey caved late—and we went ahead with a single thrust. France connived both early and late—and they are quiet. Russia, as the Soviets of old, proved duplicitous in ways that we are just learning—and it made no difference. Indeed, their night-vision equipment and GPS jammers will help Saddam no more than did the German-built bunker he was bombed in.

We should recall that in the first Gulf War we bombed for *over forty-four days*. Critics in 1991 by day ten were complaining because after the first few nights' pyrotechnics, Saddam's army had not crumbled. In turn, earlier swaggering air advocates had promised victory in three weeks—only to be unjustly slandered that they had failed to end the war in six. Gulf War I is considered a great victory; it required forty-eight days of air and ground attacks by an enormous coalition to expel the Iraqi army from Kuwait. Our present attempt, with half the force, seeks to end Saddam Hussein altogether—and on day seven already had him cut off, trapped, and besieged.

In the campaign against Belgrade, the ebullience was gone by day ten when Milosevic remained defiant. By the fifth week, criticism was fierce and calls for an end to the bombing widespread. On day seventy-seven, Milosevic capitulated—and no critics stepped forward to confess that their gloom and doom had been misplaced. Does anyone recall the term "quagmire," used of Afghanistan after the third week—and how prophets of doom promised enervating stasis, only days later to see a chain of Afghan cities fall? Yet no armchair doom-and-gloom generals were to be found when the Taliban ran and utterly confounded their pessimism. Our talking heads remind me of the volatility of the Athenian assembly, ready to laud or execute at a moment's notice.

The commentators need to *listen to history.* By any fair standard of even the most dazzling charges in military history—the German blast through the Ardennes in spring 1940, or Patton's romp in July—the present race to Baghdad is unprecedented in its speed and daring, and in the lightness of its casualties. We can nitpick about the need for another armored division, pockets of irregulars, a need to mop up here and there, plenty of hard fighting ahead, this and that. But the fact remains that, so far, the campaign has been historically unprecedented in getting so many tens of thousands of soldiers so quickly to Baghdad without losses—and its logistics will be studied for decades.

Indeed, the only wrinkle is that our present military faces cultural obstacles never envisioned by an Epaminondas, Caesar, Marlborough, Sherman—or *any* of the other great marchers. A globally televised and therapeutic culture puts an onus on American soldiers that could never have been envisioned by any of the early captains. We treat prisoners justly; our enemy executes them. We protect Iraqi bridges, oil, and dams—from Iraqi saboteurs. We must treat Iraqi civilians better than do their own men, who are trying to kill them. Our generals and leaders take questions; theirs give taped propaganda speeches. Shock and awe—designed not to kill but to stun, and therefore to save civilians—are slurred as Hamburg and Dresden. The force needed to crush Saddam's killers is deemed too much for the fragile surrounding human landscape. Marines who raise the Stars and Stripes are reprimanded for being too chauvinistic. And on, and on, and on.

When this is all over—and I expect it will be soon—in addition to a great moral accounting, I hope that there will be deep introspection and sober public discussion about the peculiar ignorance and deductive pessimism on the part of our elites. In the meantime, all we can insist on is absolute and unconditional surrender—no peace process, no exit strategy, no UN votes, no Arab League parley, no EU expressions of concern, no French, no anything but our absolute victory and Saddam's utter ruin. Unlike in 1991, commanders in the field must be given explicit instructions from the White House about negotiations: there are to be absolutely none—other than the acceptance of unconditional surrender.

Written on March 26 and published in
NATIONAL REVIEW ONLINE *on March 28, 2003.*

39

---◈═◎═◈---

The Surreal World of Iraq

LET US THANK OUR SOLDIERS
ON THIS INDEPENDENCE DAY

What are we to make of the last four months? In twenty-one days at a cost of less than 200 fatalities, the United States military ended the twenty-four-year reign of one of the most odious dictators in recent memory and freed his subject people. In response, here at home there were no mass victory parades in appreciation for our soldiers' proven bravery or public braggadocio about their own singular prowess. Some of our fighters, who in a moment of martial zeal had raised the flag of their country above the toppling statue of a horrific tyrant, were more likely chastised as undisciplined chauvinists rather than praised as enthusiastic patriots.

Indeed, intense media scrutiny of Iraqi, not American, suffering and discomfort was the new gospel—despite the clear evidence that at some danger to our soldiers we had sought to avoid hurting civilians and their infrastructure. A soldier or terrorist who had shot at Americans, been wounded, and then tossed away either his uniform or weapons was more likely to be tallied by the world's press as an unfortunate civilian casualty than as an injured combatant hurt in the hammer and tongs of battle. Under the new war, using enough force to beat soundly the enemy and convince him in the aftermath to accept defeat—or else—was seen as excessive, while the effort to mitigate the violence of fighting may have suggested to the Baathists that they had not really been beaten after all.

Not to be outdone, domestic critics of our military who had forecast "millions of refugees" and "thousands of casualties"—and who in week one of the war, during a sandstorm, had continued on with a chorus of "stalemate," "quagmire," and "Vietnam"— now post facto paradoxically reversed course. They suddenly played down our own soldiers' competency by concluding (in their infinite wisdom from the rear) that the Iraqi army was a paper tiger—hardly capable of waging modern war after all! In a blink of an eye their horrific quagmire became a bullying cakewalk.

In the first postbellum one hundred days, the Americans lost about sixty additional lives in trying to pacify a Muslim and Arab country of some twenty-six million, wracked by factions, foreign agents, and plagued by thousands of former Baathist fascists who had transmogrified into drive-by shooters and assassins—all in a post-9/11 world where it has been often difficult to distinguish "moderates" in the Middle East from complacent onlookers who were not especially sad to see two towers filled with three thousand Americans disintegrate.

In such a climate, Marines and Army units were asked to evolve from combatants to peacekeepers to reconstructionists in literally a matter of hours—as enemy soldiers who ran from battle, now on occasion shot at them for American felonies like directing traffic, seeking to restore electricity, and other unmentionables like treating the sick and organizing local councils. The protocol was for American soldiers in Kevlar and body armor to help 99 percent of the Iraqi population achieve a stable society while less than one percent sought to kill them—to more or less indifference from the beneficiaries who demanded the help (but not to the degree that they would quite yet thank or help protect the helper). "Smile while you shoot back" was perhaps the unspoken mandate for twenty-year-olds from New Mexico or New Jersey.

After risking American lives during the war to preserve Iraqi assets, our soldiers were then blamed for not anticipating that the Iraqis—unlike any liberated or occupied populace in history— would then themselves, as natives, destroy what we as foreigners had sought to save. Indeed, stung by charges of "occupation" and "imperialism," the American military erred for the first time, and for about thirty days sought an unrealistically low profile, worried that their presence would be deemed intrusive and thus aggravating to the sensitivities of the Iraqi public—only to be immediately condemned by the same citizenry as either naïve or deliberately lax for not applying the iron hand to protect them from themselves.

Along the way, wild charges circulated that our generals had allowed 170,000 priceless artifacts to be looted in order to protect "corporate oil." When such calumnies were subsequently refuted, unchecked demonstrations—impossible under any current Arab regime in the Middle East—were then adduced as proof that our military had nearly lost control of the country.

Here and there reporters interviewed an irate Iraqi screaming, "Americans, leave us to ourselves!" as cars in the background whizzed around a supposedly traumatized Baghdad. Here at home the poor television viewer's only solace, I suppose, was his hunch that should we have indeed abandoned our responsibilities, that same reporter in a few months would interview that same irate Iraqi, who would then rail, on cue, "The cowards left us to ourselves."

Anecdotal stories flooded our airways, about an Army doctor who had refused to treat an Iraqi civilian, or about a soldier who had mistakenly shot a fiery demonstrator—while accounts of public councils, progress in restoring order and power, and private thanks from the aggrieved were relegated to sound bites or omitted altogether. Indeed, the world seemed far more worried that a populace that for the first time in three decades was not in fear of a knock on their door at night was without air-conditioning in their homes—as their rank-and-file liberators slept outside in ad hoc miserable tents without most of the amenities that they were so damned for failing instantaneously to provide for others.

A few Iraqis in plush, walled estates seemed especially eager to complain of lawlessness to CNN reporters, now freed from paying bribe money to Baathist handlers, who ventured a few blocks from their hotels—secure that such ignorant sensationalists would never ask them, "What did you actually do under Saddam Hussein to deserve such plush digs?"

While our soldiers continued their work at policing and re-construction, back home their achievement and sacrifice were almost immediately put into question by the same tired critics, now citing the temporary absence of stockpiles of chemical and biological weapons and a supposed lack of manifest al Qaeda links. Stories linking al Qaedists to the Hussein regime or documents attesting to WMD were on the back pages; headlines, by contrast, blared FRAUD and LIES about the preconditions for war. Somehow soldiers on the front lines were supposed to ignore all this and remember that their sacrifice and toil were, after all, for both a noble cause and vital to the security of the United States. And in fact they did just that.

The earlier conundrum put to rest by the rapidity of our vic-tory insidiously resurfaced as it became clear that it was not a cost-free task for 140,000 Americans to institute democracy among twenty-six million Iraqis tyrannized for three decades. Newspaper pundits, NPR commentators, and Democratic aspirants, knowing nothing of the challenges of postwar Okinawa, the dilemma of ex-Nazis in occupied Germany, or the mess in 1946 Korea, implied that sixty American dead meant failure and a Chechnya-style inferno. Our soldiers' job, of course, was made no easier by the usual Arab mendacious fare broadcast freely into the country—Jews were now buying Iraqi land; Jewish troops were capitalizing on the occupation; Jews, Jews, Jews. . . . Worse still, it was not only that our enemies wished us to fail, but our so-called friends in the region were equally apprehensive that the virus of democracy might well be contagious.

Meanwhile, the assassins of American soldiers in Iraq were lionized on the West Bank—itself nursing the fresh wound of losing the murder subsidies from Saddam Hussein, whose mug still adorned the coffeehouses of Gaza and Ramallah. We, the American public, were asked for forbearance—to ignore that some Palestinian militants were canonizing the murderers of American soldiers—as we went forward to save the same Palestinians from the righteous anger of Israel. "Stop the Apaches and the F-16s so we can cheer in peace those Saddamites who shot your soldiers," they must think. What a weird group, who hate Israel so much that they are infuriated that the "Zionist entity" is walling itself off from the likes of them.

As the Americans patrolled the streets of Iraq, and sought to avoid RPG attacks, machine-gun sprays, and kidnaping murderers, the left at home, the European parlors, and the Arab street all seemed oblivious to (inadvertent) images on their television screens that belied the accompanying biased analysis: only in Iraq were Arabs demonstrating for any cause they wished; only in Iraq were local councils voting democratically; and only in Iraq were men in helmets and guns prohibited from brutalizing the population. American occupying soldiers were, in fact, more careful to respect the lives of a defeated enemy than were Arab constabularies with their own people elsewhere.

At this point, I must ask: How do our men in arms do what they do? We so often forget that their dilemma is not just age-old material challenges of time and space—Iraq, remember, is 7,000 miles away, hot, dry, and surrounded by overt enemies and canny neutrals—but the exasperating conditions of both postmodern warfare and fighting in the Middle East in general. Both combine to diminish, if not apologize for, the idea of victory, military prowess being defined not as proof of heroism, discipline, and élan but almost a shameful admission of outdated bellicosity and abject imperialism or colonialism. Indeed, the restraint on the enormous firepower at our military's disposal has almost earned contempt for hesitancy rather than ensured appreciation of magnanimity.

Various explanations come to mind for the unshakable nature of our soldiers put into such impossible circumstances. Of course, there are the age-old motivators: unit morale, group loyalty, ingrained training, chain of command, democratic idealism, patriotism, and simple self-preservation all play their roles—and an understandable desire to return as quickly as possible to the United States. But there is also transcendence at work; such soldiers believe in their role of doing something good for millions in dire need. It seems just as true that the military has somehow distilled from the rest of us Americans an elite cohort with the most direct ties to the old breed of the sort who fought at Okinawa, rolled with Patton, and reconstituted Japan. Such soldiers somehow remain oblivious to unfounded criticism, confident in their own prowess and convinced that their nation and its military are clear forces for good.

Because of such men and women, and despite so many other forces beyond their control, Iraq will not be lost to gangs and criminals, much less to Baathists, pan-Arabists, and Islamicists, who are not so much fueled by ideology as the desire for power and its accompanying material benefits for a tiny few.

We are reaching a great tipping point in Iraq, where the American soldier seeks to impose security and implant freedom faster than former Baathists try to erode it. The Iraqi street we see so often on the sidelines is watching the struggle, unsure whether to rehang their pictures of Saddam Hussein, now ensconced beneath their sofas, or to come forward and join the great experiment with freedom and consensual government.

And through it all the American soldier is asked to do what no others could do—and yet does so with grace under fire. On July 4th we should remember all this and the rare breed who, thank God, are on our side.

Written on June 27 and published in
National Review Online *on July 2, 2003.*